Old Maids

OLD MAIDS TO RADICAL SPINSTERS

Unmarried Women in the Twentieth-Century Novel

EDITED BY

Laura L. Doan

WITH A FOREWORD BY

Nina Auerbach

UNIVERSITY OF ILLINOIS PRESS
Urbana and Chicago

Manufactured in the United States of America
1 2 3 4 5 C P 5 4 3 2 1

This book is printed on acid-free paper.

Library of Congress Cataloging-in-Publication Data

Old maids to radical spinsters : unmarried women in the twentieth-century novel / edited by Laura L. Doan.
p. cm.
Includes bibliographical references.
ISBN 0-252-01731-5 (cloth : alk. paper). — ISBN 0-252-06134-9 (paper : alk. paper)
1. English fiction—20th century—History and criticism. 2. Women and literature—Great Britain—History—20th century. 3. Women and literature—United States—History—20th century. 4. American fiction—20th century—History and criticism. 5. Single women in literature. I. Doan, Laura L., 1951–
PR888.W6044 1991
823′.9109352042—dc20 90–10859
CIP

For MJM

Contents

NINA AUERBACH

Foreword

One question recurs unexpectedly in this collection: with all the supposed freedoms the twentieth century has given women, does the old maid continue to exist? If she doesn't, and we are glad to see her go, why write about old maids in the twentieth century?

A decade ago, I would probably have answered, "There are no more old maids, thank God." At that time I was outlining what may have been my most personal work of scholarship, the chapter "Old Maids and the Wish for Wings" in *Woman and the Demon,* my account of female subversion in Victorian England. I loved writing "Old Maids and the Wish for Wings" because it redeemed the humiliations of the past; it seemed, however, only metaphorically related to the lives of twentieth-century women. After all, women like me no longer had to be maids.

Victorian spinsters were defined by what they could not have. Work and love, those two engrossing components of adult life, were forbidden or allowed only second hand. For the respectable middle-class women who lived out the stereotype of the old maid, allowable work was limited to ill-paid dithering around the fringes of the service professions, while love meant meeting uncomplainingly the demands of aging parents or siblings' children; attachments outside family and, of course, any assertion of sexuality were tabooed. The conservative essayist W. R. Greg, who was given to rhetorical cries of horror at the very existence of spinsters, wrote of their lives as "wretched and deteriorating, their minds narrowing and their hearts withering, because they have nothing to do, and none to love, cherish, and obey."[1]

But Victorian taboos, not the unmarried condition, guaranteed that spinsters would have "nothing to do, and none to love." Inflexible prohibitions defused the Victorian spinster's acute challenge to the family and to the ideology of womanhood which rigidly defined life in terms of family relationships. I wrote in *Woman and the Demon* about the threat of women who were mobile, self-defined, free to establish their own boundaries; beneath the social straitjacketing, the spinster was regarded, even by respectable Victorians, as a disturbingly commanding figure precisely because she evaded family definition. Potentially at least she was an authentic hero.

In revenge against her power, the appellation "old maid" forced on her the most horrible attributes of youth and age: "maid" turns her into a perpetual virgin and humble servant, while "old" mocks the grotesquerie of her preadult status. An old maid is not merely a servile creature out of nature; the long middle of life, the phase in which most of us *make* our lives, is amputated so that there is only a beginning yoked to an end.

Most of us believe gratefully that the twentieth century allows even unconforming women to grow into the shape we choose. In a seemingly flexible age of many available communities as alternatives to families, of commuting couples, of first, second, and third marriages, of unofficial but intensely monogamous live-in love affairs, and of rights to privacy and emotional fluidity we take for granted, most adult women are, in an essential sense, old maids for some of their lives. We no longer need to be absorbed into a marriage to authorize us. Marriage does not own women in the twentieth century. It does not give us love and work; these, we assume, are our birthrights.

Moreover, technology has saved us from what must have been the terrible silence of the Victorian spinster's life. When I was writing "Old Maids and the Wish for Wings," I tried to imagine not only the sexual and professional prohibitions that forced dependency, boredom, and loneliness on obedient old maids but also what it would be like to live alone without telephones, radios, televisions, and VCRs. I could envision it only in dreadful flashes. I always write alone in my apartment, with music playing in the background and my answering machine turned on. At times, I hear the phone ring faintly over the clicking keys and the string quartet; a friend's voice wafts into my study leaving an elaborate, urgent message. After writing my quota, I regain connectedness by returning whatever calls have come in; then I wind down by inviting a group of actors into my home on the VCR. I cannot imagine settling into solitude without those accompanying, comforting noises. Writing "Old Maids and the Wish for Wings," though, I realized that for a Victorian woman living alone, there were no voices, much less voices that could be turned on and off at will. In that perpetual silence, I wondered, how could she write? But of course she could not, under any conditions, write *Woman and the Demon*. No university would support such a book, no archive would let her in, and, most important, no publisher would consider a book called *Woman and the Demon* unless a man had written it.

There were, I was sure, no old maids in the twentieth century; I was convinced then (and I am still) that we shape ourselves to whatever lives social mores permit us to live. Our lives were, or could be, animated by voices, challenging work, and chosen relationships that didn't need to adapt to set formulas. There was no longer, it seemed, a monolithic society that feared unmarried women and thus tried to stunt them. The Victorian old maid, after all, was forced into deprivation so that her life would not be attractive enough to tempt young women and threaten the family. In his phobic essay, "Why Are Women Redundant?," W. R. Greg prophetically defines the reforms he is trying to prevent:

> To endeavor to make women independent of men; to multiply and facilitate their employments; to enable them to earn a separate and ample subsistence by competing with the hardier sex in those careers and occupations hitherto set apart for that sex alone; to induct them generally into avocations, not only as interesting and beneficent, and therefore *appropriate,* but specially and definitely as *lucrative;* to surround single life for them with so smooth an entrance, and such a pleasant, ornamented, comfortable path, that marriage shall almost come to be regarded, not as their most honorable function and especial calling, but merely as one of many ways open to them, competing on equal terms with other ways for their cold and philosophic choice. . . . [2]

These reforms, he goes on to say, are a dreadful mistake, for they legitimize inherently unnatural lives. But Greg's fears have come true, while his supposedly "natural" solution to the "problem" of old maids—enforced colonial emigration—has become a Victorian bogey we laugh at. Ten years ago, essayists like Greg seemed too benighted to worry about. When I first wrote about old maids, I was sure that unmarried women were now normalized despite ourselves. We were no longer burned as witches. We were allowed to fit in.

Times have changed, and I suppose I have too. Living through a decade feminists are optimistically calling a backlash, hearing politicians (and even some of my friends) trumpet in quite W. R. Gregish fashion the sanctity and exclusive right to happiness of married life, and reading this collection of invigorating essays, I realize that while the pinched life of the Victorian old maid can never return, the old maid herself is a social construction (and frequent scapegoat) we will need for at least as long as there are families. She may still, like her Victorian progenitors, gain approval by sighing plaintively on cue at her deprivations, but underneath her trappings of servitude and sacrifice, she evokes, as she did in the nineteenth century, an open, Odyssean destiny that family life cannot give and an identity that is self-created and self-possessed. The old maids of Muriel Spark, Virginia Woolf, Sylvia Townsend Warner, Barbara Pym, and the other authors covered in this collection are by no means isolates, but they *are* self-defined. They can and do love, but they do not use other people to tell themselves and the world who they are.

One movie on my VCR this month was the amazingly popular *Fatal Attraction* (1988). I hated it, but it did remind me that the old maid is not yet obsolete; perhaps she never was and should never be. I prefer to *Fatal Attraction* the more robust masochism of Bette Davis playing old maids in the 1940s, but we have supposedly put behind us those smoldering women who have nothing to do but suffer. Glenn Close is the old maid ferociously modernized, and like all the greedy children of the 1980s she apparently has it all.

She is, to begin with, neither old nor a maid. She is an improbably gorgeous thirty-six, evilly seductive but fretting forlornly about her biological clock. Unlike the Victorian old maid, she is aggressively sexual, but the movie assures us that sex for her is no more than unnatural lust; she has a lovely big bed she scarcely uses, preferring to seduce the movie's feebly married hero in a cage-like elevator or a sink full of dirty dishes.

Her work is what we usually call "interesting"—she is an editor in a publishing house—and her job must be lucrative enough to have horrified W. R. Greg, because she wears good clothes, buys good furniture, and looks enviably expensive. As we see her, though, she never goes to work (she is too busy hovering wretchedly around the hero's family), and her nicely furnished apartment is set in Hell (no one else lives on her street; we see only diabolical workmen who pack animal carcasses while smoke and flames belch out from a mysterious source). Moreover, she has all the appliances designed to connect her to the outside world, but these only feed her mad isolation. She listens to nothing on her stereo except *Madame Butterfly,* so that she can identify with a betrayed heroine who was quaintly retrograde even in her time. Her phone never rings, so she doesn't need an answering machine; the phone has no communicative value, existing only to feed her obsession with a hero she telephones over and over while he tries to escape from her into his family.

In fact nothing in her life does what it is designed to do. All her apparent advantages—glamour, career, money, sex, technology—are discredited as soon as they appear. Her life has only one objective, the same one any nineteenth-century patriarch would assign to the old maid: prowling miserably around the fringes of a family as sanctified and as boring as any Victorian would endorse. Because this apparently modern woman is so evocative of the spectral old maid of the last century, the movie clothes her in virginal white. She puts on a black coat only when she is doing something especially evil to the holy family. Gorgeous, successful, sophisticated, steamingly sexy, Glenn Close in *Fatal Attraction* wears clothes that say she is still waiting at the altar and still, in some sense, a virgin. Sex only "counts," it seems, within the pastoral family, not in a city where there are dirty dishes under you and meatpackers outside.

Fatal Attraction forces feminists who came of age in the 1970s to recognize the changes in popular culture that signal ominously changing times, but it may represent something more hopeful than simply a new conservatism about women and sexual relationships. The movie's terrified belief in its old maid as a maelstrom of sexuality who is able to destroy a cozy but torpid family—a family valued mainly as a sanctuary against the passions of the world outside—may revive our own belief in the old maid's power. Many of us may have become too sanguine about our ability to blend in; perhaps we were too complacently eager to do so. *Fatal Attraction* and its ilk should remind even women who hate it that we *have* set ourselves outside conventional norms and that our most vibrant role is that of the outsider.

Feminist criticism itself has been feeling its age lately, preening itself on token victories. The old maid in *Fatal Attraction,* a witch-like destroyer of the snug family that excludes her, may be more galvanizing than the nurturing angel of some recent feminist work. Carol Gilligan's influential *In a Different Voice* is, in its own way, as symptomatic of the conservatism of the 1980s as the spinster/monster of *Fatal Attraction* is. Gilligan maintains that women are by nature more concerned than men with relationships, with "taking care." She relies on such authorities as eleven-year-old "Amy" and "Jake," who chatter on predictably. Here is "Amy": "Well, like some people put themselves and things for themselves before they put other people, and some people really care about other people. Like, I don't think your job is as important as somebody that you really love, like your husband or your parents or a very close friend."[3] In an adjacent column, "Jake" holds forth conveniently about sports and fairness and atom bombs and success in school and all those other things women are too busy relating to care about.

Some female readers may fear that the "different voice" Gilligan assigns them is the only voice available; like good Victorian women, they are learning who they are only through their relationship to others, and like Victorian women too, they are told that selfless relating is natural to women. Belief in the paradigm of the old maid as a self-determined woman is a salutary check to Gilligan's altruistic paragon, who evolves too easily from a liberating to an enforced identity. The old maid in *Fatal Attraction* is a cautionary monster of solitude, but her solitude may be a galvanizing if extreme antidote to too much acceptability. *Old Maids to Radical Spinsters* reminds us that acceptability is only a partial virtue; it may be time to exercise our resistance. Moreover, this anthology reminds us that twentieth-century writers have seen the old maid as a far friendlier, more welcoming, figure than recent conservative works allow us to believe is possible.

The great strength of these essays lies in their diversity. They differ as dramatically, in their methods and subjects, as women do from each other. What unifies them is their belief in the fundamentally deviant figure of the old maid and in the power—and satisfactions—of deviance itself. These rich essays do more than present a series of positive role models, though they do remind us of a fact most women know, but few admit: living alone is fun and often a great nourisher of relationships. These essays do more than hold up individual old maids, in and out of novels, for our admiration. They show a salutary belief in the old maid as a durable (if mutable) and healthy human type. She has made fundamental refusals, but negations and refusals do not define her. Because she lives in opposition to accepted norms, she does not have to make herself acceptable to live. Her opposition is at best flexible and friendly. The figure who emerges from this collection is somewhere between the exemplar of acceptability many of us once thought we were and the witch-like destroyer with which *Fatal Attraction* tries to frighten us. The old maid of Doan's anthology lives in a tolerant, sometimes tender truce with the society that wants to stigmatize her.

The great strength of these essays collectively is their awareness that individuals change as society does. There might always be old maids, but the old maid today is not the impoverished figure of the nineteenth century or the overanalyzed, complex-ridden figure she was turned into in the 1950s. Perennial as a type, she is, as a literary figure, intensely fluid. Judy Little's wonderful essay on Muriel

Spark shows how Spark's spinsters evolve over time. Jean Brodie, probably a frightening model for many of us who teach, is, in Little's brilliant analysis, a monster-martyr of the 1930s who, in another decade, might be neither betrayed nor self-betrayed. Little shows how Muriel Spark's acceptance of the spinsters who had always haunted her imagination changed as her times did; Sybil Oldfield shows the same evolution in Virginia Woolf's spinsters, and Joan Kirkby finds a similar development in Elizabeth Jolley. These sensitive readings reveal three woman writers for whom the old maid is a demonic muse they can begin to embrace when society begins to relax its taboos.

Old maids will continue to be dynamic presences in our literature and our culture, but there has never been one essential old maid, and there never will be. Just as she becomes a warmer, stronger figure in the later novels of Muriel Spark, Virginia Woolf, and Elizabeth Jolley, so she will, I hope, show her many sorts of warmth and strength as social mores warm toward her. Probably she will never join the ranks of the respectable, but as she is more freely understood, she will be freer to share the wisdom of her refusals. *Old Maids to Radical Spinsters* is an inspiring act of understanding that should free readers of all sorts to embrace an often-forbidden muse.

NOTES

1. W. R. Greg, "Why are Women Redundant?" 1862; rpt. in *Literary and Social Judgments* (Boston: James R. Osgood, 1873) 277.
2. Greg 300.
3. Carol Gilligan, *In a Different Voice: Psychological Theory and Women's Development* (Cambridge: Harvard University Press, 1982) 36.

Laura L. Doan

Introduction

> It may be time for feminists to circle back to those "images" of angels and demons, nuns and whores, whom it seemed so easy and so liberating to kill, in order to retrieve a less tangible, but also less restricting, facet of woman's history.
>
> —Nina Auerbach, *Woman and the Demon*

The spinster is so enmeshed in cultural stereotyping that it is difficult to extricate her from negative connotations. Yet the label is as ambiguous as it is ambivalent. Society has deliberately deemed her pathetic to mask its fear of the unmarried woman. The image of the old-fashioned, genteel schoolmarm or the prying town gossip effectively cloaks the more dangerous threat of an autonomous woman and provokes a number of questions. How many readers can be certain, for instance, that spinsterhood implies virginity or celibacy or asexuality? Are all women without men (lesbians, widows, divorcees, nuns) to be considered spinsters? Are there racial or class (in other words, white, middle-class) boundaries involved in this category? Is the designation "spinster" essentially socioeconomic or psychosexual? Finally, can we still speak of the "old maid" or "spinster" after the second wave of feminism in the 1960s and 1970s? These questions, and others like them, are further complicated because, as we shall see, our cultural understanding of the spinster shifts to correspond to sociocultural change in the late nineteenth and early twentieth centuries.

Mary Daly, the radical feminist philosopher, in her scrutiny of the Merriam-Webster dictionary entries under "spinster" and "old maid," notes the implicit negative attributes such superficial definitions promote. Her critique is worth repeating in its entirety, for within her etymological review she challenges and ridicules the way the voice of authority confirms "the common contemptuous and pitying attitude toward 'spinsters'":

> The first meaning given for *spinster* . . . is "a woman whose occupation is to spin." Another definition is . . . "a woman past the common age for marrying or one who seems unlikely to marry—called also *old maid*." Next comes the term *spinsterhood*, whose definition

> comes right to the point: "the state or condition of being a spinster: OLD MAIDHOOD." Following this comes the term *spinsterish,* which is churlishly defined as "having the habits, appearance, or traits of a spinster: OLD-MAIDISH." In case anything should be left to the imagination, it is possible to look up *old maid.* We are informed that it means "a prim nervous person of either sex who frets over inconsequential details: FUSSBUDGET." The mendacious use of the expression "of either sex" is obvious, especially if one looks up *bachelor* and finds, of course, no reference to *old maid, old-maidishness,* or anything of the kind. (392–93)

Condemning what she terms the "double-double think" designed to control women's minds, Daly asserts that underneath the traditional definition lurks a "whirling dervish, spinning in a new time/space," who, like a witch, possesses tremendous and dangerous abilities to disrupt the so-called natural order (3–4). Yet in spite of Daly's rescue attempt of the words "spinster" and "old maid" to signify a positive, self-affirming image of the single woman, some readers, feminists in particular, may continue to find these terms irredeemably derogatory and insulting and hence object to their use here. Both terms have been deliberately retained—and used extensively—throughout this anthology because they are essential in delineating the transformational process that informs the larger argument. Our aim is to illustrate the transition from old maid to excellent woman, from excellent woman to a new, radical spinster.

How does this transformational process in the literary representation of the spinster intersect with historical, political, economic, and sociocultural change in the status of single women in the twentieth century? Our concern is with the spinster—a category of women not always easily subsumed by the phrase "single woman." By specifying spinster per se, as opposed to the single woman in general, we wish to denote a highly particularized entity, emerging from a complex set of historical circumstances, with a defined relationship to a particular class, race, and so forth. We do not in any way claim to examine the experience of all single, independent women in this period, pretending that their experience is monolithic for all decades and for all countries. The specific interest in the way certain writers work and rework the spinster stereotype—rather than the more general fictional treatment of the single woman—defines and confines the context.

Three important studies by contemporary feminist historians carefully document the political and social changes affecting independent women in Britain and America: Martha Vicinus's *Indepen-*

dent Women: Work and Community for Single Women, 1850–1920 (1985), Sheila Jeffreys's *The Spinster and Her Enemies: Feminism and Sexuality, 1880–1930* (1985), and Carroll Smith-Rosenberg's *Disorderly Conduct: Visions of Gender in Victorian America* (1985) (though not dealing primarily with the single woman, one chapter is devoted entirely to the subject of the New Woman, "The New Woman as Androgyne: Social Disorder and Gender Crisis, 1870–1936"). A clearer definition of what constitutes "spinsterliness" emerges in these writings, and a brief review of their conclusions offers the sociohistorical contextualization necessary to understand whether or not the spinster's appearance in fiction heralds or responds to change.

Vicinus, Jeffreys, and Smith-Rosenberg all limit their discussion of single women to members of the middle class. Such middle-class women were normally prohibited by "Victorian notions of respectability from leaving home, or engaging in the trades open to working-class women" (Jeffreys 87). Yet spinsters without an allowance or an inheritance had, by choice or necessity, to pursue a vocation, unlike many working-class women who had to work outside the home whether married or not. The social strictures against certain types of employment limited the options available to spinsters, yet, at the same time, according to Vicinus, their education and "personal confidence [enabled them] to take advantage of larger social changes" (6). Smith-Rosenberg likewise distinguishes between the social classes in her discussion of the New Woman in American Victorian culture and describes her not only as "economically autonomous" but also with a "social standing" that "permitted her to defy proprieties, pioneer new roles, and still insist upon a rightful place within the genteel world" (245). Of course, not all spinsters, as we understand the term, are as economically advantaged, highly educated, politically committed, radical, and aggressive as the New Women. Not all spinsters were New Women, but all New Women were spinsters (i.e., unmarried, middle class). Most single women of this period, Vicinus explains, "believed passionately that in order to help others, unmarried women of the middle class had a right and duty to train for and seek out paid work" (1). This commitment to paid work in middle-class occupations sharply delineates single women of the nineteenth century from single women in earlier historical periods, as Vicinus points out:

> Single women had held key positions in preindustrial society, including the management of large convents in the Middle Ages, the administration of vast estates during the Renaissance, and the running

> of countless shops, small businesses, and inns throughout the early modern period in English history. But increased wealth and consolidation of bourgeois social values in the early nineteenth century condemned spinsters to unremitting idleness and to marginal positions in the home, church, and workplace. The genteel poor woman had a choice of three underpaid and overcrowded occupations—governess, companion, or seamstress. (3)

The designation spinster, then, is most certainly socioeconomic *and* historical.

But is it also psychosexual? Vicinus credits Victorian England with the creation of a symbolic triad, powerful cultural forces to control women by delineating extremes: the ideal mother/wife, the celibate spinster, and the promiscuous prostitute (5). Consequently, Vicinus continues, "the spinster had thrust upon her absolute purity and goodness. She was supposed to remain virginal and utterly self-sacrificing. . . . Celibacy . . . became a vital and empowering ideal" (5). But by the 1920s, Jeffreys explains, the "definition of spinsters was changing. . . . Whilst previously the word spinster had simply meant unmarried woman, it was coming to mean, specifically, women who had not done sexual intercourse with men" (175). The ideal state of celibacy promoted in Victorian culture began to read as "abnormality" at the hands of sexologists in the early twentieth century (even as they perpetuated the presumption of celibacy), and the spinster's apparent lack of sexual experience left her vulnerable to attack. Jeffreys further speculates that "this new meaning [of the word 'spinster'] is much closer [to] the present-day meaning of the word" (175). Yet, even as the term "spinster" gradually shifted in the 1920s to refer to single women uninterested or inexperienced in sexual intercourse, some novelists depicted spinsters as sexually active, either with men outside of the prescribed norm of marriage or with women.

The spinster's erotic involvement with women not only removes her from the realms of the celibate, where the sexologists tried to confine her, but also raises the issue of what distinguishes spinsterhood from lesbianism. When the single woman's erotic desire is directed toward women, the line between the spinster and lesbian is blurred: some spinsters claim to be lesbians—or have been called lesbian by others—and vice versa. The similarities between the spinster and the lesbian are striking: both reject the primacy of heterosexual marriage and choose a life-style that, in threatening patriarchy, signals some measure of social deviancy. Yet the spinster and the lesbian—appellations at once problematic and elusive—exist on two parallel tracks which, although conflated by patriarchy in its attempt both to devalue and marginalize their unique experience, remain separate. Whether the definition of such a socially complex figure as the lesbian is narrow and restrictive (such as Catharine Stimpson's: "a woman who finds other women erotically attractive and gratifying" [97]) or expansive (such as Adrienne Rich's well-known definition that conceivably embraces all women whose "primary intensity [is] between and among women, including the sharing of a rich inner life, the bonding against male tyranny, the giving and receiving of practical and political support" [648–49]), the essential common denominator excludes what we might call a traditional spinster. By definition, the lesbian—even the celibate lesbian—relates, in a special way (whether erotically or emotionally), to another woman or women. Therefore, in the context of this study, it makes little difference whether a spinster is homosexual or heterosexual since what distinguishes a spinster—even if sexually active with women or men—is her deliberate, positive choice *not* to define herself in relation to a significant other. The spinster's primary commitment in life is not to partnership but to independence and autonomy, and, as a result, she relies on her own resources to meet emotional, psychological, and, whenever possible, material needs. (For this reason, widows and divorcees should also be excluded, since they have at one time had traditional attachments to men, and nuns, with solemn vows, are thought to be "married" to God and are not confronted with the problem of choosing an occupation for social survival.)

The spinster, as a historical subject and as a literary representation, thus stands outside of possible relational schemas and resists any comfortable assignment to binary thinking. Within the symbolic order, the spinster is defined by absence; she lacks a primary relationship with a man to fulfill her role as wife and mother. Other available kinship roles (aunt, daughter, or sister, for instance) achieve only marginal importance and cannot compensate for the inadequacy of her single status. Feminist literary critics have questioned this dominant ideology that defines women primarily through their sexuality. Joanne S. Frye argues that such a restricted "femininity text" means that it is impossible to "simultaneously perceive femaleness and autonomy . . . [the] self [exists] *only* in relationship, with marriage and/or motherhood as the appropriate denouement, or the demise of the self" (3). Yet when feminist critics shift their focus from the restrictive binary opposition of male/female to relationships between women (mother/daughter, sisters, and female friends/lovers), they in effect perpetuate the delimitations of the relational schema set by the femininity text. Since, as I have argued, relationships between women are largely meaningless in defining the spinster, the spinster resists this schema. And since the spinster does not easily fit into a network of female relations, feminist critics have tended to place her on the margins of the social order and on the margins of their critical discourse. This neglect is curious because inasmuch as the spinster is paradigmatic of unrelatedness to a significant other, her depiction in the modern novel suggests the ideal starting point for the resolution of femaleness and autonomy.

As early as 1877, Susan B. Anthony positioned the single woman outside of any relational schema and, further, elevated her as a model for all women to emulate: "'[Single women] are not halves, needing complements, as are the masses of women; but evenly balanced well rounded characters; therefore are they models to be reached by the average women we everyday meet'" (quoted in Simon 29). Daly clearly realizes this in *Gyn/Ecology* where she describes a spinster as "she who has chosen her Self, who defines her Self, by choice, neither in relation to children nor to men, who is Self-identified" (3). By defining the spinster as "Self-identified," Daly shows just how radical the spinster can be. The spinster's challenge to domestic hegemony impels the creation of a stereotype to deny the embodied threat and to disguise the political motivations underlying societal censure. Thus, definitions such as "past the common age of marrying" or "one who seems unlikely to marry," which automatically define the spinster by her lack of a man, must be rejected as politically loaded. What the spinster lacks is an "other" to be defined against or in relation to, and if, as Elizabeth Meese argues, "the future of feminist criticism rests on defying oppositional logic currently sustaining the concept of privilege," the spinster's defiance—as refuser of oppositional definition—invites us to "stay clear of a hegemonic role reversal that results in an infinite series of upended oppositions such as male/female, insider/outsider and center/margin, where the second term simply replaces the first in an unending regression within an oppressive economy of Sameness" (17). By turning our attention to this potentially radical, transgressive figure, this present study promises to move beyond the dichotomous thinking of male/female opposition, even female/female relationships, to examine a new area of feminist literary criticism, one in concert with Ellen Messer-Davidow's call for an investigation into the ways "complex sex/gender ideologies circulat[e] through cultural systems" (84).

The final question left to consider—whether or not we can still speak of the spinster after the second wave of feminism in the 1960s and 1970s—will be taken up in several of the essays. Repeatedly, society grapples with the "problem" of the spinster in an attempt to bridle her once again to the conventional, old-fashioned sphere of limited domesticity. Victorians labeled her "surplus"; 1920s sexologists diagnosed her as sexually deviant; in the aftermath of both World War I and World War II women were hurriedly scuttled back into domesticity; the familial ideology of 1950s America and of Britain's welfare state excluded the single woman; and the 1960s and 1970s style of feminism found her uncomfortable and anachronistic, out of step with the so-called sexual revolution. Most recently, the call for the return to "family values" cloaks an unconscious desire to retie all of these women who have elected singleness or life outside of marriage.

Studies of the spinster in Victorian literature and culture, such as Nina Auerbach's incisive dismantling of the "grand myth of spinsterhood" in *Woman and the Demon* (1982) and Susan Katz's *"Singleness of Heart": Spinsterhood in Victorian Culture* (forthcoming), complement the work of feminist historians. Literary studies engaging with the spinster in the modern novel, however, have lagged somewhat behind. Inasmuch as the modern novel coincides with the historical moment when the spinster herself is disappearing and the spinster as a significant concept is challenged as problematic, it seems all the more imperative that we extend our attention to the twentieth century. The only book-length study of the spinster in twentieth-century literature remains Dorothy Yost Deegan's *The Stereotype of the Single Woman in American Novels,* published in 1951. Deegan locates the source of what she terms the "spinster formula" far earlier than the Victorian period and contends that "much of the disapprobation associated with the 'old maid' in England was carried to America through fiction. The word 'spinster' . . . appears in its most disparaging form in the English novels of the eighteenth century" (7). Her speculation that American writers appropriated the spinster stereotype from English prototypes accounts for the tenacity of the stereotype in the English novel to this day. No evidence appears to dispute Deegan's claim that eighteenth-century British novelists created the first stereotype of the spinster—a model that later British writers enhance and develop, and a model

American writers inherit, faithfully emulate, or slightly modify. The spinster stereotype is a peculiarly British invention. Of the thirteen writers covered in this anthology, the majority are British (eight, including Elizabeth Jolley who, though born in England, moved to Australia in her mid-thirties) and the rest are American. Since this British legacy was adopted into American fiction (and culture), the fictional representation of the old maid has remained remarkably homogeneous within the narrow range of the Anglo-American tradition.

In her meticulous, at times statistical, survey of attitudes toward the spinster in novels from 1800 to 1945, Deegan offers the first systematic analysis of the stereotype only to conclude that single women were usually objects of pity or ridicule. Deegan writes that "almost without exception [spinsters] are old and drab and unattractive . . . there is little or no adventure in their lives. They have achieved nothing beyond their mere existence and show no ambition to improve or escape their lot in life" (119). Spinsters cannot find satisfaction, respect, or influence within the few available jobs, even in the so-called spinsterish occupations (governess, schoolteacher, librarian, dressmaker, postmistress, and the like). In Deegan's enumeration of professions available to single women, we find further evidence to associate the spinster with the bourgeois gentlewoman: virtually every line of work is middle class, with the possible exception of domestic and charwoman, and even these women were often poor relations serving in the home of a wealthier relative. According to Deegan, the deleterious effects of this unnatural life-style are evident in the sort of personality spinsters develop; thrown upon their own resources to find happiness in life, spinsters rarely speak about themselves personally or articulate their needs and desires. Deegan's findings, which stem more from the absence of a feminist sensibility than the unavailability of textual evidence, are irredeemably negative: "It is almost impossible to find among all the single-women characters women who are wholly admirable. If their overt activities are above reproach, if they are decorous and conventional, they are sad or bitter or dull or queer or utterly resigned to a life of pettiness. Where is there one a young girl would want to emulate?" (185). For Deegan, the improved social position of women in the twentieth century should have culminated in a more positive image of the single woman, but, paradoxically, the old stereotype persists.

Deegan's bleak assessment of the spinster is not shared by Susan R. Gorsky, Barbara A. Johns, Annis Pratt, and others whose brief studies of the spinster in literature range over a large number of novels from the nineteenth century to the present. (Although Susan Koppelman's important compilation *Old Maids: Short Stories by Nineteenth Century U.S. Women Writers* focuses on a genre other than the novel, it should nevertheless receive mention here. Koppelman is among the first to recognize that women writers "defend unmarried women from cruel, demeaning and limiting stereotypes that are still used to frighten and coerce women" [1].) Unlike Deegan, Gorsky, writing in 1973, notes that some degree of progress can be detected in the distinction between an old maid and a New Woman. Although the stereotype persists at the end of World War I, new roles for the single woman could be contemplated. In the style of "images of women" criticism, popular in the early 1970s, Barbara Johns presents a typology of the New England spinster based on what she terms "patterns of spinsterhood": "The patterns include an appearance that is plain and somber but that does not necessarily reflect a repression of sexuality; a social role that is linked to New England 'duty' and that is rewarded by the approval of society; and a solitude and freedom of thought that can contemplate the radical reordering of traditional sex roles" (33). Like Johns, Pratt's section on old maids in *Archetypal Patterns in Women's Fiction* (1981), exploiting the rich advances in feminist criticism during the 1970s, underscores the importance of those women who deliberately choose singleness: "In a society that associates feminine sexuality with subordination to a male, both women who refuse permanent heterosexual relationships and women who choose celibacy are outcasts" (119). Pratt is more sensitive to the potential for subversion than Deegan and Johns, pointing out, for example, that May Sarton "stands the stereotype [of the spinster] on its head" (121). Ultimately, those critics who answered Annette Kolodny's call for an exploration of how "stereotyped formulations of women's roles in society become codified in literary texts" were limited by the survey approach (75). Their brief reading of a wide number of novels suggests the value of a more extended, careful reading of individual novels together in one volume.

Our method, then, is to break new ground by returning to the familiar stereotype to see what earlier feminist critics missed. This strategy—closely focusing on an established literary stereotype—possesses both possibilities and limitations. As we have seen, by historical definition, the spinster resides in a narrow, particular social milieu. The traditional spinster is defined as a woman who never married (or is self-identified, to use Daly's more useful term), who may or may not be sexually active with women or men, who is from a white, middle-class background, and who is genteel and professional and though she may work is not of the working class. Although we examine the transformation of the spinster stereotype to a new, more radical spinster, our subject is essentially and necessarily exclusive; this approach necessitates that we leave a wider range of other issues (the intersection, for instance, of ethnicity or other social classes) aside and invite others to pursue these closely related, yet distinct, trajectories.

What has yet to be explored is the manifold ways twentieth-century novelists have appropriated the stereotype of the spinster for their own ends and how that stereotype, in turn, controls and restructures narrative strategies: some writers cooperate with the controlling myth and offer only a tentative critique; some adapt it to their own purposes; still others stretch it nearly beyond recognition. By organizing the anthology around these three central strategies, we will see how the literary spinster—a figure who cannot be accommodated by the ideology of the traditional romance plot—breaks out of the confines of conventional narrative strategies and demands that both the writer and reader invent new, alternative literary forms.

The answers to the questions posed in the opening of this introduction are complicated because of the diverse range of fictional spinsters: some writers retain a more conservative, traditional type; other writers usurp the stereotype, collectively dismissing it because of its inadequacy, and create new definitions and possibilities. When the rigidity of the stereotype is broken down, the rules of the patriarchal order become the stuff of protest. Implicit in the title *Old Maids to Radical Spinsters* then is the notion that there has been a gradual rupturing of the negative image of the spinster in the modern novel: from a lonely, powerless victim to a newly independent woman who discovers her own authentic voice and becomes what Barbara Pym calls an "excellent woman." Pym invents the phrase to accommodate her redefined spinster, a self-reliant and autonomous single woman. However, there is still some distance between an excellent woman and the sort of "whirling dervish" Daly envisions, a profoundly radical spinster who bears some resemblance to the sort of woman Nina Auerbach discovers within the Victorian old maid. In *Woman and the Demon,* Auerbach asserts that the old maid "tolerated most easily as society's piteous victim, is in her fullest incarnation its leader, endowed with ambiguously awesome powers that intimate the destined future of the race" (145). This anthology takes its lead from the powerful subversion of convention that Auerbach's book suggests. By examining the Victorian old maid's afterlife, or progress, through the twentieth century, we project those "ambiguously awesome powers" into the future of feminist studies.

Exploring a diverse range of representations, the anthology includes essays on Jane Bowles, Ivy Compton-Burnett, E. M. Forster, Gail Godwin, Elizabeth Jolley, Toni Morrison, Barbara Pym, May Sarton, Dorothy L. Sayers, Muriel Spark, Sylvia Townsend Warner, Virginia Woolf, and the unusual collaborative novel *The Whole Family.* The order of the essays does not present a historical progression because there is no correspondence between chronology and the sort of spinster represented; for instance, Townsend Warner's more liberating treatment of the spinster was published before Pym's more conservative work. Nor is it our intention to offer a comprehensive or historical survey of the spinster in the twentieth-century novel; rather, selected texts show the continuum implied by the anthology's larger structure, the movement from the narrowly defined stereotype to a radical re-visioning of the independent woman. The novels under consideration represent almost equally each of the decades of the twentieth century, with fewer works published during each of the world wars. According to the works covered here, the old maid appears from the beginning of the century until the late 1950s; the excellent woman from 1908 to the 1980s; and the radical spinster from 1926 to the 1980s. Finally, the variety of critical methodologies—literary-historical, new historicist, psychoanalytic, Anglo-American and French feminist, Marxist, materialist-feminist literary criticism—demonstrates the compelling nature of a stereotype that requires deconstruction from all angles.

The anthology is divided into four sections. Judy Little's exploration of Muriel Spark's fiction stands on its own as Part 1 ("Defining the Spinster Code") because it provides a condensed overview of the changing status of the spinster from the late nineteenth century to the 1980s. In her "'Endless Different Ways': Muriel Spark's Re-Visions of the Spinster," Little traces the development of a spinster code vis-à-vis four attitudinal categories that remain constant during a period of social change: vocation, sexuality, community and friendship, and power. Using literary history as her base, Little shows how Spark reinterprets and re-visions the spinster and the myths surrounding her over a span of three decades.

The other essays are grouped into three main sections, each corresponding to a major change in the old stereotype and the subsequent transformation of that stereotype. Part 2 ("Old Maids") opens with an essay that explores the limits of choice for the single woman. In "Contented Spinsters: Governessing and the Limits of Discursive Desire in the Fiction of I. Compton-Burnett," Marlon Ross points out that Compton-Burnett acknowledges the restrictions placed on women by a repressive social order but assigns the spinster, especially the educating spinster, a special position in relation to language and the social order. Compton-Burnett's spinsters—who must maneuver within the narrow confines of a system that demands conformity—are survivors rather than rebels, outsiders who work within the system to satisfy their own needs while trying to minimize any sense that they could become a threat to that system. Compton-Burnett explores the stereotype (of the spinster-governess) but does not reclaim the potential subversive power of that stereotype; she allows the spinster a "degree of contentment and a state of disempowerment that ironically grants her both greater power and more vulnerability."

In the next two essays, Susan Katz and Sybil Oldfield argue that Forster and Woolf use the novel to resolve their conflicting feelings about the spinster, the most powerful influence in their personal lives. In "Writing for 'Monie': The Legacy of the Spinster to E. M. Forster," Katz contends that while Forster begins by invoking the most superficial qualities of the Victorian old maid, as the narrative unfolds the stereotype deepens into a "psychologically and symbolically complex character." In Forster's reconceptualization of the unmarried woman, the spinster-as-cliché disintegrates to emerge as an exalted transcendent figure, a vehicle to facilitate positive values. In "From Rachel's Aunts to Miss La Trobe: Spinsters in the Fiction of Virginia Woolf," Oldfield discovers a similar tension between Woolf's important, "life-enabling" friendships with individual single women and her inclination to "collude" with the stereotype. Oldfield suggests that Woolf's spinster characters undergo a gradual metamorphosis: from the stereotypically bitter and unsympathetic Miss Kilman to the honest and intelligent artist, Lily Briscoe, to Miss La Trobe, "the perpetual Outsider/Outcast/Witch/Artist/Observer." At this point, we are able to identify with the spinster rather than accept the ironic treatment of her in Spark's fiction, for instance.

Part 3 ("Excellent Women") presents writers who do not abandon an awareness of the stereotype but nevertheless signal a tentative move forward in supplanting or reclaiming the stereotype. Mary Wilkins Freeman and Dorothy Sayers co-opt the old stereotype by redefining the spinster role. In "The Politics of Collaboration in *The Whole Family,*" Dale Bauer unravels the repercussions of Freeman's decision to introduce "a sexually vibrant and transgressive spinster" (i.e., a nonstereotypical construction of the old maid) into the collaborative novel *The Whole Family.* By interposing a spinster into the narrative—and onto the ten authors who write the following chapters—we see that "who controls representation controls social power." Freeman forces the other collaborators to deal with the spinster, who becomes a force to be reckoned with rather than simply a figure of ridicule, albeit within the traditional confines of the family. In "Detecting a Novel Use for Spinsters in Sayers's Fiction," Catherine Kenney argues that Sayers exploits the spinster stereotype in a humorous, though not spiteful, way by carefully revising the myth of the spinster busybody. Sayers reclaims certain skills attributed to spinsters (such as close attention to detail and curiosity) as logical and necessary for a sleuth. Like Compton-Burnett's governesses, Sayers's spinster heroines turn their status into an advantage through the proper employment of their skills. Sayers's spinster-sleuth works as a positive role model—rather than as a warning for those exploring the nonmarriage option—because her occupation provides her with a new image of herself as well as the means to independence.

In "Pym's Singular Interest: The Self as Spinster," I argue that Barbara Pym's novels become an opportunity to undermine traditional notions of the spinster and to create a positive self-identity. Pym transforms a socially problematic status to facilitate her own personal reconciliation with the unmarried state so that the novel is a text of persuasion, compelling an identification with the heroine and convincing readers of the validity of her life-choice. Ultimately, Pym's spinsters are content with their lot in life, but they do not celebrate this distinction. In "Spinning Friends: May Sarton's Literary Spinsters," Valerie Miner shows how Sarton also reclaims a positive spinster in a cautious and limited way. Since Sarton's spinsters are "role models" for others to emulate (though in the style of an excellent woman rather than as a radical new spinster), spinsterhood represents a vocation of social responsibility. Sarton, who never abandons a strong sense of transgression, recognizes that spinsters and lesbians are defined by what they are not. The final essay in this section, "An 'Old Story': Gail Godwin's *The Odd Woman,*" explores the traditional literary depiction of the spinster in light of the options available to the single woman in the twentieth century. Gayle Greene explains that Godwin addresses a problem familiar to women writers: "how to adapt essentially conservative narrative conventions to a new and unconventional view of woman." Like Pym, Godwin reaffirms the importance of choice: the single woman must find a place for herself, since the single life is no longer to be feared or escaped.

Part 4, ("Radical Spinsters") brings together novelists who push the stereotype to the limits by defying social categories, (re)claiming the margins, and subverting traditional narrative strategies. Some radical spinster heroines willingly and wildly risk danger, others playfully celebrate the label "weird," still others pay a high price for their transgressions. These spinsters correspond to Daly's "whirling dervish" and to her proclamation that "in essence, the Spinster is a witch. She is derided because she is free and therefore feared" (394). In "Flying the Nets at Forty: *Lolly Willowes* as Female Bildungsroman," Barbara Brothers demonstrates how, for Sylvia Townsend Warner, the spinster disrupts literary conventions by creating new plot configurations. In fusing psychological realism and satiric fantasy, Townsend Warner's narrative breaks the conventions of the realistic novel, and her spinster heroine in turn breaks out of the spinsterish role of maiden aunt. Townsend Warner demands more than writers like Pym who require only acceptance; her spinster establishes a new set of rules. In "Jane Bowles's Other World," Andrew Lakritz reveals that Bowles shatters generic expectations and presents a radical spinster who refuses to accept the "evaluative freight" of the term—she resists the name society reserves for its deviants and refuses normalcy by identifying it with mediocrity. Like Bowles's, Elizabeth Jolley's spinsters are both sexual and radical, marking a departure from the expected, the conservative, the traditional. Her spinsters pose a threat to the social order by refusing to remain outsiders. Drawing on psychoanalytic theory in "The Spinster and the Missing Mother in the Fiction of Elizabeth Jolley," Joan Kirkby shows how Jolley experiments "with the limits of identity in a playful language that overturns, violates, and pluralizes the symbolic order." All three writers here play with the notion of reconceptualization. What Kirkby says of Jolley's characters could apply equally to Townsend Warner's and Bowles's: "[Jolley's spinsters] are all visionary spinsters attempting to effect innovative life-styles outside the dominant gender system."

Finally, in "A Ghost of An/Other Chance: The Spinster-Mother in Toni Morrison's *Beloved*," Susan Jaret McKinstry argues that in the system of slavery we discover the most definitive—and radical—spinster of all: "women who are, like white spinsters, kept on the margins of the social system, defined by (failed) relationships." Like Bowles's Christina Goering and Townsend Warner's Lolly, Morrison's heroine Sethe demonstrates how radical spinsters "must reject the cultural ideology that defines them as objects, possessions, spiritless bodies with economic value" and must refuse those categorizations and dichotomies that seek to control women's lives.

The persistence of the spinster stereotype, when the sociocultural order has changed so significantly and the notion of the spinster appears so hopelessly unfashionable, irrelevant, and anachronistic, is a testament to its pervasiveness and strength. The self-identified woman has posed—and continues to pose—an immense threat to patriarchy, a threat culminating in the emergence of a controlling myth in the guise of the spinster stereotype. From within the superficial appearances of a reliable stereotype, feminists can recover and document an important form of resistance in the woman considered so frightening she is labeled unnatural. By retracing the history of the spinster from powerless other to self-empowering subject, we can answer Auerbach's call to "retrieve a less tangible, but also less restricting facet of woman's history" (3). While some might mourn the spinster's passing (her obituary has appeared in an article by Molly Haskell in the *New York Times Magazine)*, her survival (at least in British fiction) seems secure. We call on the reader to reconceptualize the spinster and to welcome a fully realized and radicalized woman as envisioned by twentieth-century writers.

WORKS CITED

Auerbach, Nina. *Woman and the Demon: The Life of a Victorian Myth.* Cambridge: Harvard University Press, 1982.

Daly, Mary. *Gyn/Ecology: The Metaethics of Radical Feminism.* Boston: Beacon, 1978.

Deegan, Dorothy Yost. *The Stereotype of the Single Woman in American Novels.* 1951. New York: Octagon Books, 1969.

Frye, Joanne S. *Living Stories, Telling Lives: Women and the Novel in Contemporary Experience.* Ann Arbor: University of Michigan Press, 1986.

Gorsky, Susan R. "Old Maids and New Women: Alternatives to Marriage in Englishwomen's Novels, 1847–1915." *Journal of Popular Culture* 7 (1973): 68–85.

Haskell, Molly. "Paying Homage to the Spinster." *New York Times Magazine,* May 8, 1988.

Jeffreys, Sheila. *The Spinster and Her Enemies: Feminism and Sexuality, 1880–1930.* London: Pandora, 1985.

Johns, Barbara A. "Some Reflections on the Spinster in New England Literature." *Regionalism and the Female Imagination.* Ed. Emily Toth. New York: Human Sciences Press, 1985.

Kolodny, Annette. "Some Notes on Defining a 'Feminist Criticism.'" *Critical Inquiry* 2 (1975): 75-92.

Koppelman, Susan, comp. *Old Maids: Short Stories by Nineteenth Century U.S. Women Writers.* Boston: Pandora, 1984.

Meese, Elizabeth A. *Crossing the Double-Cross: The Practice of Feminist Criticism.* Chapel Hill: University of North Carolina Press, 1986.

Messer-Davidow, Ellen. "The Philosophical Bases of Feminist Literary Criticisms." *New Literary History* 19 (1987): 65–103.

Pratt, Annis. *Archetypal Patterns in Women's Fiction.* Bloomington: Indiana University Press, 1981.

Rich, Adrienne. "Compulsory Heterosexuality and Lesbian Existence." *Signs* 5 (1980): 631–60.

Simon, Barbara Levy. *Never Married Women.* Philadelphia: Temple University Press, 1987.

Smith-Rosenberg, Carroll. *Disorderly Conduct: Visions of Gender in Victorian America.* New York: Knopf, 1985.

Stimpson, Catharine R. *Where the Meanings Are: Feminism and Cultural Spaces.* New York: Methuen, 1988.

Vicinus, Martha. *Independent Women: Work and Community for Single Women, 1850–1920.* Chicago: University of Chicago Press, 1985.

PART ONE

Defining the Spinster Code

JUDY LITTLE

"Endless Different Ways": Muriel Spark's Re-visions of the Spinster

Fleur Talbot, the young unmarried novelist in Muriel Spark's *Loitering with Intent* (1981), speaks of the writer as a "mythmaker"; she asserts that "the wonder of the art resides in the endless different ways of telling a story, and the methods are mythological by nature" (139). These myths are also by nature not true, though they may point toward, or evoke, a truth. Spark herself has said in an interview with Frank Kermode that fiction consists of "lies" and that her own work is "a collection of lies from which emerges a kind of truth" ("House of Fiction" 79–80). If there is a truth that emerges from Spark's changing portrayals of the spinster over the course of decades, it is that anything can be reinterpreted and remythologized; the myth can be dismantled and re-visioned.[1] In particular the spinster character, transformed several times, seems to have a special attraction for Spark, herself single most of her life, although once briefly married and the mother of a son.

Like her autobiographical character Fleur, Spark knows that a story can be told in "endless different ways," and she has given readers a generous variety of spinsters in her fiction. In *The Bachelors* (1960), Spark dealt in particular with the social and spiritual predicament of unmarried men and women, the divorced, and the widowed. She felt at the time that everyone was in a sense "a bachelor" ("House of Fiction" 80). The ideology or myth of that novel is conservative, perhaps reflecting Spark's conversion to Catholicism in 1954. As one of the novel's unmarried males says, "It's everyone's duty to be fruitful and multiply," whether in marriage or in a religious calling (71). There is no hint in such a remark that a never-married woman who is not a nun could have a morally legitimate or fruitful life.

The unmarried women in this novel, like those in Spark's other novels of the 1950s and 1960s, usually wish to marry. They are not, so to speak "called" to be spinsters, except for the remarkable Jean Brodie. Most of the young career women in *The Girls of Slender Means* (1963) are looking for marriage, although Joanna Childe seems content to be a spinster; she is a rather religious person, perhaps still a "child" sexually and socially, and she dies in the fire that destroys the boardinghouse. Similarly in *The Mandelbaum Gate* (1965) Barbara Vaughan, having fallen in love in her thirties, still refers to herself as a "spinster" but is glad to let go of that identity for marriage to Harry Clegg. It is significant that Barbara, a Jewish convert to Catholicism, is more detached from the specifically Catholic ideology of marriage than were the characters of *The Bachelors*. Barbara and Harry have been lovers, and even if Harry can't get an annulment of an earlier marriage, Barbara plans to marry him (which would put her in a state of "sin") and forget about practicing her new faith.

This detachment, or process of detaching, from a strictly Roman Catholic (and pre-Vatican II) myth of vocation as either marriage or religious life continues in Spark's novels. Her later work, novels written in the 1970s especially, generally dispense with any overt exploration of Catholic issues, though Spark's distinctly moral perspective continues to examine characteristic themes of good and evil, power and manipulation, vocation and identity—including the identity and myth of the spinster.

Although Spark's work contains many spinsters as secondary characters, three novels feature the spinster as the central figure: *The Prime of Miss Jean Brodie* (1961), *The Driver's Seat* (1970), and *Loitering with Intent* (1981). Published at approximately ten-year intervals, these novels show both the author's and society's changing view of the spinster. Several studies have examined the changing image, or myth, of the unmarried woman in Britain, particularly in the crucial period from the mid-nineteenth century through the 1930s. During this time, the spinster rises from the status of being perceived as an unhappy, deprived, "surplus" person, to being a major agent in the social reform and suffrage movements, to once again being seen as an unhappy and even suspect person by the 1930s—the period of Jean Brodie's "prime." As the twentieth century moves into its second wave of feminism during the 1970s, the cultural myth of the unmarried woman seems to be changing again, perhaps toward a more positive image.

To describe this changing image of the spinster in history and in Spark's three novels, it will be useful to focus on four attitudinal categories throughout the period of change: vocation, sexuality, community, and power. These categories are present in the characterization of each spinster in the three novels under consideration, but the woman's definition of vocation, sexuality, community, and power varies considerably, as does the culture's own myth about these aspects of the spinster's life. The ways in which these four elements are expressed amount to a kind of code by which one can read the authorial and cultural revisions of the Sparkian spinster over several decades.

Before turning to the novels themselves, I want briefly to sketch the development of the spinster code during the past one hundred years in relation to the woman's vocation, her sexuality, the availability of community and friendship, and her access to power. A crucial period for any consideration of the spinster in Spark's work is the 1930s, the era of Miss Jean Brodie. Winifred Holtby, writing during this decade (*Women,* 1934), noted with alarm and amazement the massive shift of public opinion *away* from the spinster. More recent studies by Martha Vicinus (*Independent Women,* 1985) and Sheila Jeffreys (*The Spinster and Her Enemies,* 1985) have exposed the roots of this violent, postsuffrage change of attitude. These scholars have traced the rise and fall of respect for the spinster. With the pioneering example of Florence Nightingale behind them, unmarried women were by the 1880s actively defining a positive image of themselves in occupations outside the family and outside the traditional work of governess and companion. These spinsters did not perceive themselves as burdens on family or society; they saw their new roles as nurses, settlement administrators and workers, or college teachers as vocational choices which allowed them independence and yet gave them an opportunity to serve others (and hence permitted them to retain a certain "feminine" identity). Teaching was a "vocation," and one's work in the school, hospital, or the suffrage movement was a "mission" (Vicinus 15–16, 37–42, 174). The spinster of the late nineteenth and early twentieth century could choose the unmarried state and know that this implied a positive vocation.

This sense of vocation was reinforced by a positive ideology of sexuality, by the strong support of the community in which the spinster worked, and by an emerging acceptance of power as a legitimate, necessary aspect of the single woman's responsibilities. Sheila Jeffreys emphasizes the important point that the turn-of-the-century feminists, most of whom were spinsters, developed a distinctive philosophy of sexuality. Advocates of this sexuality believed that men could control their supposedly strong passions and that such control, reinforced by legislation, was the best route for ridding society of prostitution and eliminating the sexual abuse of wives and children. Along with such control, a "spiritual" love between men and women was to be encouraged (27–85). Although this sexual ideology received a lot of ridicule, especially after the demise of the feminist movement, it provided a positive rationale for the celibate life of the spinster. It defined her, though childless and never married, as a complete human being. Her celibate sexuality, like her vocation of service, was part of a positive code.

This positive code also included a strong community life, reinforced by close friendships among women (friendships that were sometimes virtually love affairs), and new opportunities for women to exercise power. Living together, as administrators of colleges or hospitals, spinsters could express their emotions as well as their skills; evidence from letters and diaries, as Vicinus argues, indicates that many spinsters found their lives quite satisfying (85–162).

Yet a reaction was in progress even while single women were enjoying a new sense of vocation, power, community, and philosophy of sexuality that allowed the spinster a certain legitimacy and respect. By the 1890s the notion of separate spheres had redefined a woman's vocation as childbearing and being the passive partner in marriage. Her true "liberation," as even some feminists began to advocate, came with being sexually responsive to men. Exercising power in an independent life outside the family indicated, according to the new code developed by sexologists, that the woman was "frustrated," "frigid," or perhaps "lesbian." These were fighting words, words used in attack, argues Sheila Jeffreys as she documents the changing climate of opinion. One of the attack words was "spinster," which had formerly simply indicated an unmarried woman but by the 1920s and 1930s was used derisively for women who had not had sexual intercourse (Jeffreys 93–99, 129–45, 166–96).

Among others, Winifred Holtby wrote in protest of the new ideology. Pointing to the suspicion, prevalent in the 1930s, that girls' schools were sinister places, Holtby very perceptively describes the problem: "the legend of the Frustrated Spinster is one of the most formidable social influences of the modern world" (125). Before Michel Foucault had described the power of discourse and ideology as a force for social control and Roland Barthes had examined the way a myth determines how we perceive a given issue, Holtby precisely described the nature and effect of the new ideology of the spinster. In the "modern" world of the 1930s, Holtby perceived that a very limiting new legend or code defined the spinster as unfulfilled, sexually and in every other way. By the 1930s the prevailing code of society, a code reflected in its fiction, denied the spinster a vocation, gave her a very limited ideology of sexuality, denied her the support of friends and community, and perceived her attempts to exercise power as suspect.

Into this era of changing sexual ideology comes Miss Jean Brodie, a spinster in her prime. Spark has described her best-known character as a woman of "completely unrealized potentialities" ("Keeping It Short" 411). Why are these potentialities not realized? And especially why is the energy that Jean Brodie does express used so destructively? These are the kinds of questions this novel encourages a reader to ask. As critics have emphasized, the form of *The Prime of Miss Jean Brodie* turns our attention away from suspense. The many flash-forwards tell us how the story turns out; Jean Brodie is dismissed from her job because she was "betrayed" by a member of her own chosen "set." The flash-forwards show us this betrayer, Sandy Stranger, many years later a nun nervously clutching the grillwork of the cloister's parlor and still obsessed with the memories of her favorite teacher. The nonchronological structure of the novel forces the moral issue to the center of attention, and most readers diagnose the aura of moral sickness in the novel as Jean Brodie's attempt to gain intimate control of her students' lives. Indeed, it is the teenage Sandy herself, obsessively enthusiastic about psychology and religion, who sees the extent of Jean Brodie's presumption: "She thinks she is Providence, thought Sandy, she thinks she is the God of Calvin" (176). If the focus of the novel is the sinister misuse of power, why is this particular misuser a spinster, a teacher ambivalently loved and hated by her students?

The role of the ludicrous yet poignant overreacher fits Jean Brodie quite precisely, because she responds to the ambiguous code of the spinster in her generation. A spinster of the 1930s is a perfect choice to play this role in fiction. She is caught between a rapidly vanishing era of respect for the independent unmarried woman and the new cultural regime in which "the legend" of the unfulfilled spinster is beginning to prevail. We are told, for instance, that there were "legions" of Jean Brodie's kind in this period, "progressive spinsters" and feminists, who were keenly interested in social welfare, education, and religion and who promoted music, the theater, and birth control (62–64). In other words, there were still many who filled their "war-bereaved spinsterhood" (62) with exactly those activities that had defined the vocation or mission of the much earlier, turn-of-the-century spinsters. Jean Brodie, like many other spinsters, retained a strong sense of social responsibility well into the twentieth century.

Yet Jean Brodie manifests this sense of mission in an exceptional, strained way. Instead of teaching in the more experimental schools, the narrator notes, she chose the traditional Marcia Blaine School. Her reasons for doing this imply a heroism that would have better suited the stature and era of Florence Nightingale who rode (and created) the first wave of female independence in the nineteenth century. Nearly a century later, when the last ripples of respect for independent women were rapidly collapsing, Jean Brodie still assumes the hero's stance; she teaches in a traditional school to be, along with her students, "a leaven in the lump" (15–16). She claims for herself, in an era that denied it to her, a spinster's vocation, a dedication to heroic independence.

Also like the early feminists, Jean Brodie has formulated a philosophy of sexuality that reinforces her sense of vocation. She has developed a point of view, a sexuality that supplies a rationale for her sacrificing the woman's usual role of wife and mother to serve her students. The early spinster feminists developed a language to explain and foster their celibate vocations, a language that spoke of "spiritual" love and the capacity of males to control themselves. Likewise, Jean Brodie has developed a language of sexuality, and the key word is "prime," a word suggesting the fertile peak of sexual readiness as well as the vocational dedication of "the moment one was born for" (19).

With amused awe, Jenny and Sandy grope for an understanding of their teacher's sexual code. During Sandy's birthday party, they laugh and sputter their way toward an important distinction: unlike Miss Brodie, their parents "don't have primes"; instead "they have sexual intercourse" (25–26). Although the girls are somewhat misreading Jean Brodie's sexual code, they have grasped a point that the turn-of-the-century spinsters made and one that Jean Brodie is reasserting: the unmarried have a special, distinctive ideology of sexuality, an ideology that the married lack.

Jean Brodie's philosophy, however, differs from that of the earlier spinsters in two important ways. First, she is building the notion of her mysterious and vital prime entirely on her own. Unlike the women of a generation or two before her, she is not part of a supportive community with a developed language about what sex and vocation mean to the spinster. Yet a fundamental insight of sociological studies is that the individual's self-understanding relies heavily on the attitudes and myths that the culture encourages him or her to have. Sociologist Peter Berger emphasizes that one's personal quest depends on the quest that society allows (149). In developing her myth of spinsterhood, Jean Brodie is trying to do on her own something that usually requires the support of a large community or an entire culture. In an era when the idea that a spinster could have a publicly valued vocation was in rapid decline, Jean Brodie alone, and very eccentrically, still spins her theory about how to perceive and fulfill one's prime.

In addition to lacking a group of kindred thinkers, Jean Brodie differs from the earlier spinsters in that she is influenced by the advanced notion that a spinster may and should have an active sex life. Winifred Holtby argued in the 1930s that the popularization of Freud led to an ideology of sexuality which declared heterosexual activity to be an absolute requirement of good mental health. Holtby affirmed that the popular understanding of Freud's ideas and the notoriety of D. H. Lawrence's novels propagated "the current superstition that madness or bitterness lie in wait for virgins" (133). For Holtby this attitude is only a "superstition," just part of the legend of the "frustrated" spinster. Jean Brodie, by contrast, demonstrates her acceptance of this view that was popular in her time (indeed, in her prime), a view that affirmed the medicinal importance of heterosexual experience for all, including spinsters. As Holtby notes, contraception was available, and "in some still limited circles" the spinster was not perceived as immoral if she was sexually active outside marriage (128–29). Jean Brodie indicates by her matter-of-fact weekend affair with Gordon Lowther that she considers herself to be above censure. She also declares that her student Rose Stanley, like a heroine of D. H. Lawrence, has "instinct" and is thus destined to be a great lover; Rose is "above the common moral code" (160–61).

Jean Brodie clearly perceives herself as a thoroughly modern spinster. Unwilling to be involved in an adulterous relationship with the married art master, Teddie Lloyd, whom she loves, she spends weekends with the bachelor music teacher. She is, as her chosen students perceive, "working it off on Mr. Lowther" (87). The phrase reflects the sexual ideology of the 1930s: the hormonal tension must be relieved or the person will be frustrated. When Velma Richmond claims that Jean Brodie substitutes fantasies of a lost love for a "recognition of her own sexuality" (23), Richmond is misreading Jean Brodie's sexual code. This spinster teacher does in fact show a recognition of her sexuality. It is a recognition based on the prevailing sexual ideology of the 1930s; following the expectations and assumptions of her era, she sleeps with Lowther and thus works it off so she will not be frustrated.

Yet she is frustrated or thwarted, if not sexually then in every other way. Sexual expression is the least of her difficulties. Of the four elements I have identified in the code of spinsterhood, sexual activity is the only one for which a moderately positive, though simplistic, ideology still existed in the 1930s. Spinsters could partake of sex, and Jean Brodie does. They could no longer, however, expect their culture to perceive their independent work as a valuable calling; they no longer worked in supportive communities that shared an ideology of mission and dedication. Further, spinsters were no longer encouraged to wield power, exercise administrative skills, or organize reform movements as the early feminist spinsters had done. Jean Brodie's distortions of moral issues and her destructiveness are most severe in just those areas of the spinster's life that her culture denied her or defined in negative terms.

I have already noted the implications of strain and difficulty in her effort to develop, a decade or so too late, a philosophy and practice of the spinster's mission. As I have indicated, she can somewhat more easily fit the pattern of what was expected sexually of spinsters. But with regard to community and power, Jean Brodie sails dangerously into hazardous seas, in an era that sought to deny spinsters (and any other women) access to both. By way of community, she organizes her fiercely controlled set. She becomes a sort of Christ, the "head," as Sandy perceives, of the obedient "body" of disciples (45–46). Jean Brodie, lacking any social or political power as a single woman, admires fascists and sets herself up as Providence. In a society that was reacting to feminist gains and whose cultural ideology was pressuring women to accept marriage as their only vocation, Jean Brodie arbitrarily assigns vocations to her girls, telling them who will be famous for sex, insight, and so forth. Her grotesque attempt at community is also her attempt at power. In neither attempt does she differ essentially from the period's clichés about spinsters, as expressed in popular fiction and journal articles that warned of the emotionally manipulative teacher.[2]

What is unique about *The Prime of Miss Jean Brodie* is the subtlety of Spark's treatment of the spinster of the era. By using the ambivalent perspective of the girls, the narrator manages to avoid passing harsh judgment on Jean Brodie. Sandy in her cloistered parlor and Eunice visiting Jean Brodie's grave comment on Jean Brodie from the wise perspective of many years. In the late 1950s Eunice tells her husband that Jean Brodie was "just a spinster" but "full of culture," "an Edinburgh Festival all on her own" (40–41). Eunice respects and appreciates Jean Brodie's efforts to provide her special girls with a broad, exceptional education. Sandy's mother had entertained a similar respect for Miss Brodie's interest in the girls' "general knowledge" (38). Sandy herself, having recovered years later from "a creeping vision of disorder" over Jean Brodie's relationship with Lowther, at last "could look back and recognise that Miss Brodie's defective sense of self-criticism had not been without its beneficent and enlarging effects; by which time Sandy had already betrayed Miss Brodie and Miss Brodie was laid in her grave" (126). With some care Spark protects her spinster hero from the worst ravages of the 1930s code of spinsterhood. That is, she prevents her character from turning into the cliché of her kind by portraying Jean Brodie's efforts to resist the cliché and her efforts to maintain certain enlarging expectations in an era that severely restricted the spinster's life.

That the student Sandy, whose supposedly insightful eyes are quite small, could see very few positive features in her eccentric teacher shows Sandy is very much a child of her time. Unlike Jean Brodie's generation of outdated spinsters, Sandy's generation had no acquaintance at all with the militant suffrage movements or the peak period of the unmarried woman's political and social activism. Sandy's vision of Jean Brodie reflects all the contemporary clichés about spinsters. A student in the new field of psychology, Sandy knows that "many theories from the books of psychology categorised Miss Brodie," and Sandy categorizes her teacher as "an unconscious lesbian" (176), a label frequently used for spinsters at the time.

Although Sandy is fascinated by Jean Brodie's sex life, she rightly sees her teacher's sense of mission and her efforts to impose a vocation on her students as the more dangerous problem. She realizes that Jean Brodie perceives herself as the God of Calvin, assigning destinies to her subjects (176). Sandy discerns that Jean Brodie has "elected herself to grace in so particular a way and with more exotic suicidal enchantment than if she had simply taken to drink like other spinsters who couldn't stand it any more" (160). The language in this passage shows (perhaps "betrays") both Sandy's fascinated awe about her teacher's complex behavior and Sandy's readiness to employ stereotypes about spinsters to explain that behavior. The position of "suicidal," between "exotic" and "enchantment," gives an air of mystery, dash, and wonder to Jean Brodie's hubristic self-election to grace. Rather than seeing this Promethean folly as evidence of unrealized potentialities, however, Sandy applies the new psychology about the "frustrated spinster." Her insight is merely the simplistic "legend" that Holtby describes; Sandy thinks all spinsters are frustrated and "can't stand it any more." By the end, the discourse has moved from poetry to cliché, traveling the same route as Sandy's mind.

Sandy betrays Jean Brodie; that is, Sandy hints that the teacher brought fascist politics into the classroom, and this accusation leads the headmistress to dismiss her. Yet Jean Brodie had been betrayed in a more general and thorough sense by the subtle historical change in what it meant to be a spinster. By the time she met and cultivated her girls, spinsters were beginning to be perceived as valueless, sexually warped, dangerous, and ridiculous. Jean Brodie's efforts to preserve a former code of positive, radically active spinsterhood in an unfriendly climate make her a somewhat sympathetic character, and her massive failure to preserve this code gives the novel its satiric edge.

Spark's other two novels in which a spinster occupies center stage are not as well known, but a brief look at each will indicate how this author's vision of the spinster has changed. Almost ten years after *The Prime of Miss Jean Brodie,* Spark sketched an updated version of the alienated spinster in *The Driver's Seat* (1970). With blithe malice, the author draws the characterless character of Lise, a nearly anonymous spinster in her middle thirties who makes a holiday trip from an unnamed northern country to a similarly general Mediterranean one to seek her death at the hands of her "type" of man. Hers is a successful quest, for this tragedy in cartoon form puts Lise in "the driver's seat," where she can control her destiny; she manipulates her chosen man, a "sex-maniac," into killing her. As in *The Prime of Miss Jean Brodie,* there are flash-forwards which let us know long before the end that Lise will be successful in her endeavor. Further, the narrator's detached descriptions and questions prevent us from reading this story as "realistic" fiction in which suspense and character development might be expected. The style and form, as in so many of Spark's novels, force the reader to consider the moral issues rather than suspense and characters.

Perhaps it is the shocking cruelty of the satire that leads some critics to identify the moral issues quite simplistically and then dismiss the work. Although many readers have emphasized that Lise's self-destructive quest is closely linked to other destructive movements in society at large (such as the anarchic demonstrations, outlandish diets, and the inverted feminism described in the novel),[3] others indulge in a common misreading. The misreading is exemplified in Rosalind Miles's remark in *The Fiction of Sex,* which contends that Lise's problem and fate amount to "a massive neurosis due to shortage of sex" (21–22). Such a reading is parodied within the text, however, so one needs to be cautious about diagnosing Lise's problem as merely the lack of sexual gratification. The narrator mocks Lise's acquaintance, Bill, who preaches a "macrobiotic" diet and advocates an orgasm a day for good health. Nothing in the novel suggests that the answer to Bill's problem, the social disorder, or Lise's unhappy quest is an orgasm per day for everyone.

Perhaps this misreading arises because Lise herself seems to offer it as the rationale for her behavior. She wants death at the hands of a sex offender as the solution to her problem. Her problem itself, however, she identifies as a "lonely grief"—not lack of sex. Visiting a park's empty pavilion at dusk with Bill, she looks through the windows and sees the chairs piled up in the vacated room. She starts to cry, explaining, "I want to go back home and feel all that lonely grief again. I miss it so much already" (105). Her problem, as she herself identifies it, is grief, especially the grief of loneliness. Indeed, studies of the unmarried in recent years indicate that loneliness (rather than lack of sex) is a very frequently mentioned problem.[4] Certainly, Lise identifies loneliness as her authentic problem; this is the real one.

Further, she has had sexual relationships, and she remarks that sex is "all right at the time, and it's all right before." Afterward, though, it is "pretty sad" (113). Lise's despair is not the result of a shortage of sex; it derives from grief and loneliness. This grief is so much her issue that she misses it, regrets being away from it. Her grief is the issue she would prefer to continue to acknowledge, yet she does not acknowledge it, except on that one occasion.

Instead, she writes a clichéd script for herself, one already prevalent in the popular imagination: a sexually frustrated spinster "asks for it," asks for violence from a sex offender. When her cornered assailant says that women get killed in dark, isolated parks, Lise says, "Yes I know, they look for it" (114). Lise insists she does not want sex, though the man rapes her before he kills her. Shortly afterward there is a flash-forward in which he sees the police questioning him; he sees their defensive clothes, the buttons, "the holsters and epaulets and all those trappings devised to protect them from the indecent exposure of fear and pity, pity and fear" (117). And grief—one could add.

The Aristotelian catharsis of human emotion is denied, this novel suggests, in a mechanized and disordered modern society. Pity, fear, and Lise's grief are indecent; they cannot be acknowledged.

Since Lise's culture does not allow her to name her problem as grief and loneliness, she adjusts to the societal imperative. She reorganizes her destiny around something that her culture does allow a spinster to acknowledge: sex and violent death. Her quest becomes one of the tidy little clichés of popular culture—the sexually distressed woman looking for Mr. Goodbar.

Again it may be useful to recall that sociologists and anthropologists emphasize the connection between the way an individual may want to identify or describe an issue and the limited number of ways a given society allows an individual to identify it. Most people, in labeling a problem and living their lives, use the "channel" that their society provides, as Ruth Benedict noted in her famous study *Patterns of Culture* (113). Denied the acknowledgment of grief and loneliness as the roots of her despair, Lise accepts a socially approved diagnosis: any loneliness must be a sexual lack or sexual denial, so the frustrated spinster goes asking for violence from sex offenders.

Spark's novel cruelly mocks Lise's (and her society's) simplistic interpretation of deeper, more profound losses. We can get some idea of these losses when we notice how stark the code of spinsterhood has become, at least in Muriel Spark's vision, by the 1960s when Lise takes her holiday. Lise has only a parodic vocation, for instance. As she searches for the right dress, one that is not stain-resistant (so that her bloodstains will show), her lips, nostrils, and eyes are open "in one mission, the sensing of the dress that she must get" (7). Her mission is her death. It is not social reform and not even the attempt to provide an education for a chosen set of students. Lise is a much more extraneous, more "surplus" spinster in her own eyes, and in the eyes of society, than Jean Brodie was. She has no set, no community that cares for her, even as ambivalently as Jean Brodie's students did. Lise also manifestly lacks the supportive friendships of the turn-of-the-century spinsters in their settlement houses and hospitals.

As for power, Lise has no socially approved room for creative self-assertion. In her office she is symmetrically sandwiched in a middle position with "five girls under her and two men. Over her are two women and five men" (6). In her one allowable mission of self-destruction, she can assume the driver's seat and powerfully direct the death script for the surplus, unmarried woman: "they look for it." If Jean Brodie is a woman who still vigorously resists the deteriorating code of the spinster in the 1930s, Lise, three decades later, no longer resists. She accepts her socially defined position as a nonperson and cooperatively arranges for her own death.

Lise is not Muriel Spark's latest word on spinsters, however. In *Loitering with Intent* (1981), Spark gives us a completely revised and updated version in the buoyant Fleur Talbot, an established and never-married novelist of the 1980s who is writing a retrospective portrait of herself as a young woman in 1950. The focus of the novel is the "changing-point" in Fleur's life, which occurred in June 1950 as she sat writing poetry in a graveyard in Kensington. The changing-point is Fleur's full acknowledgment of her vocation, her commitment to writing; other interests, attachments, and worries settle into their proper place as a consequence. Fleur resigns as secretary-editor for Sir Quentin's Autobiographical Society, realizing that Sir Quentin is manipulating his society into a phony and discouraging "frankness" about their memoirs that even leads one member to commit suicide. He is also plagiarizing large sections of Fleur's manuscript novel. Fleur recognizes that as an artist she herself is something of a sleuth and a manipulator, although for joyful and creative purposes; she craftily arranges to retrieve a stolen copy of her manuscript which is eventually published. She knows that her lover is interfering with her writing, so she drops him; she acknowledges that it is wonderful to "be an artist and a woman in the twentieth century" (26). Happy in this calling, she frequently repeats to herself a phrase from one of her favorite autobiographers, Benvenuto Cellini: "I am now going on my way rejoicing" (125).

This portrait of the artist as a young spinster is a re-vision in several ways. Not only is it the third major variation on the spinster theme in Spark's work but Fleur is a re-vision of *some* elements in Spark's own early career and of some elements in her first novel, *The Comforters* (1957). These biographical transformations certainly attest to Fleur's statement that there are "endless different ways of telling a story." One of Spark's own ways of telling her life, now as she looks back on it, is to describe her autobiographical artist figure as a spinster, even though Spark herself has been married. The mature artist, though married in her youth, chooses to reimagine her early life as if she had been a cheerful, self-assured, never-married woman.

Perhaps the increasing numbers of women in recent years who are postponing marriage, and the renewed public discussion about those who have chosen not to marry, have placed the spinster once again in a positive light. For instance, Nancy Peterson's sociological study *Our Lives for Ourselves: Women Who Have Never Married* differs from the negative, psychologically prescriptive books of the 1920s and 1930s which predicted frustration and ill health for spinsters. Instead, the data from Peterson's interviews show the single life as a positive choice for many women. Certainly for Spark, the spinster code seems to have changed during the approximately twenty years between her portrayals of Jean Brodie and Fleur Talbot.

With regard to vocation, Fleur approaches her writing in a brisk matter-of-fact way, convinced that this activity is her central mission in life. This assurance reflects that of Muriel Spark, who has indicated that writing is for her "a vocation" ("My Conversion" 61). Fleur's individualistic sense of dedication and her frank ambition to become a published, respected writer mean that her expression of a sense of vocation is different from the way the nineteenth-century spinsters expressed their mission, which was typically social service. But Fleur shares with them an understanding that her life has value and purpose. Unlike the troubled Jean Brodie, defensively carving a purpose for herself in a society that was beginning to withdraw respect from the spinster, Fleur does not have to elect herself to grace. She feels that she has been elected, that she has quite naturally discovered her gift of writing.

She is so sure of her calling that it becomes the touchstone for decisions about other areas of her life. When an acquaintance asks if she will ever marry, Fleur replies, "No, I write poetry. I want to write. Marriage would interfere" (28). Her ideology of sexuality, like that of the early spinster feminists, is thus closely tied to her strong sense of purpose in life. Although Fleur is having an "off-and-on" affair with her friend Dottie's husband, Fleur doesn't want the relationship to conflict with her work, and she tells Dottie this (28). Fleur's perception of the demands of love and art parallel those of her author. Muriel Spark writes in a 1949 letter that a relationship ended because the man wanted complete dedication from her, something she could not give because she had a son to support and a desire to write.[5] Fleur's choices are portrayed as less complex than those of her author, since the spinster Fleur has no child, but the artistic calling operates in both instances as a criterion for measuring the conflict between relationship and work.

Just as the turn-of-the-century spinster and Jean Brodie had a highly developed code on sexual matters, Fleur Talbot has a clear and positive understanding of the place of sex in her life. She assertively corrects the misapprehensions of others when they try to label her; she rejects the word "mistress" because it does not accord with her "independent liaison" with Leslie, Dottie's husband (56). So independent is Fleur that she gives up the relationship once her work on her novel becomes all-absorbing. Besides, as she puts it, writing her novel is "like being in love and better" (60). Her dedication to, and delight in, her work reminds her of Cellini's "long love affair with his art" (124). Unlike Jean Brodie and Lise, whose distorted perceptions of vocation and sex became destructive, Fleur is comfortably creative in both areas. She redefines sexual relationships in a way that respects her independence, and she gives her most serious and joyful passion to her work.

Fleur seems to lack intimate friendships, although her feelings about "Solly, my friend, my friend" (216) imply a trust and enthusiasm she does not often extend to others, and he did send her manuscript to the press that eventually published it. Fleur has friends but few close ones. She is kind to the eccentrically lovable Edwina, Sir Quentin's mother, but Fleur has no confidantes among women. In this respect she is very different from the spinsters of the nineteenth century.

Fleur, like the earlier spinsters, feels strong and uses her strength to shape her life; she is in the driver's seat, but she doesn't use her power destructively. Although Spark consistently satirizes and condemns her other manipulative characters, including Jean Brodie and Lise, she lets the autobiographical Fleur off the hook. She is a "mythmaker"; this belongs to her vocation as a novelist (139). Yet Fleur does not devise myths for the purpose of viciously deceiving or controlling others. Jean Brodie tried to impose a life-myth on each member of her set, but Fleur's storytelling ability is one that frees any single myth from being rigidly imposed, for there are "endless different ways of telling a story" (139). As a novelist, then, Fleur uses power to re-vision life, even her own life, in a creative and freeing way.

So does Muriel Spark, especially in the three portrayals of spinsters discussed here. Her latest myth about the never-married woman, Fleur Talbot the novelist, is distinctly a re-vision of Spark's previous myth of herself as a young writer. In *The Comforters,* the writer Caroline is in a state of mental distress, as was Muriel Spark when she was struggling to publish. Like her character Caroline, Spark heard voices. Like Caroline, she was a recent convert and lived for a while at a retreat house. Unlike Caroline, who is engaged, the divorced Spark already had a son to support. Such was the earlier portrait of Spark as an artist in the early 1950s. In astonishing contrast, almost thirty years later, Spark gives us the confident, never-married, and never-planning-to-be-married Fleur Talbot, who is finishing her novel in 1950.

Society's perception of the spinster has changed over the decades, and perhaps in response Spark's own view of the unmarried woman has also changed. She can find the spinster code so positive in recent years that she enthusiastically appropriates it as the myth of her own younger self. She does this even though she was not a spinster when she was beginning her career as a writer. From the defensive, yet imaginative manipulation of Jean Brodie through the self-destruction of Lise, Spark revises her myth of the spinster. Lately, in an era somewhat more accepting of the independent woman, Spark imagines herself as a young spinster artist in Fleur Talbot.

NOTES

1. I use the word "re-vision" here to indicate the radical critique of an earlier text or image, especially when the image is that of a woman. For this usage, see many feminist critics but especially Rich (18–25).

2. Vicinus examines this literature in *Independent Women* (206–10).

3. See, for instance, Kemp (126–27) and Richmond (112–17).

4. Weiss examines the documentation in "The Study of Loneliness" (152–64).

5. Whittaker paraphrases Spark's unpublished letter (23), and I have followed her paraphrase closely.

WORKS CITED

Benedict, Ruth. *Patterns of Culture*. Boston: Houghton Mifflin, 1934.

Berger, Peter. *Invitation to Sociology*. Garden City, N.Y.: Doubleday, 1963.

Holtby, Winifred. *Women*. London: Bodley Head, 1934.

Jeffreys, Sheila. *The Spinster and Her Enemies: Feminism and Sexuality, 1880–1930*. London: Pandora, 1985.

Kemp, Peter. *Muriel Spark*. London: Paul Elek, 1974.

Miles, Rosalind. *The Fiction of Sex*. London: Vision Press, 1974.

Peterson, Nancy. *Our Lives for Ourselves: Women Who Have Never Married*. New York: G. P. Putnam's Sons, 1981.

Rich, Adrienne. "When We Dead Awaken: Writing as Re-Vision." *College English* 34 (1972): 18–25.

Richmond, Velma Bourgeois. *Muriel Spark*. New York: Frederick Ungar, 1984.

Spark, Muriel. *The Bachelors*. London: Macmillan, 1960.

———. *The Comforters*. Philadelphia: Lippincott, 1957.

———. *The Driver's Seat*. New York: Knopf, 1970.

———. *The Girls of Slender Means*. New York: Knopf, 1963.
———. "The House of Fiction." An interview with Frank Kermode. *Partisan Review* 30 (1963): 79–81.
———. "Keeping It Short." An interview with Ian Gillham. *The Listener* 84 (September 24, 1970): 411–13.
———. *Loitering with Intent*. New York: Coward, McCann, and Geoghegan, 1981.
———. *The Mandelbaum Gate*. New York: Knopf, 1965.
———. "My Conversion." *Twentieth Century* 170 (1961): 58–63.
———. *The Prime of Miss Jean Brodie*. Philadelphia: Lippincott, 1962.
Vicinus, Martha. *Independent Women: Work and Community for Single Women, 1850–1920*. Chicago: University of Chicago Press, 1985.
Weiss, Robert S. "The Study of Loneliness." *Single Life: Unmarried Adults in Social Context*. Ed. Peter J. Stein. New York: St. Martin's, 1981.
Whittaker, Ruth. *The Faith and Fiction of Muriel Spark*. London: Macmillan, 1982.

PART TWO

Old Maids

Marlon B. Ross

Contented Spinsters: Governessing and the Limits of Discursive Desire in the Fiction of I. Compton-Burnett

In the first chapter of *A Father and His Fate,* amidst one of those convivially competitive family debates so common in the novels of Ivy Compton-Burnett, Miles Mowbray is compelled to defend the sheltered lives he has arranged for his three daughters against the mordant jesting of his nephew Malcolm, who claims that the young women have not "'known many instances of anything'" in the life they have led. "'What life?' said Miles, looking up. 'Would you have them go out as governesses, may I ask? Would you have them earn their bread? I despise a father who allows his daughters to do such things. I hold him unworthy of the name of a man.'" After one of his daughters reminds him that the governess, Miss Gibbon, is present, Miles responds: "'Is she? Well, of course she is, when we are here ourselves, and she is one of us. She does not take my words to herself, or fancy they bear upon her. It does not need saying'" (5–6). This conversation places Miss Gibbon in an impossible situation. On one hand, if she agrees with Miles, she effectively dissolves her own identity, her capacity to desire any object other than that provided by the father's own desire. On the other hand, if she disagrees, she brings even more attention to the awkwardness of her predicament, for regardless of what she desires, she is obligated to rein in that desire—to deny it—for the sake of fulfilling the father's will. The hard reality is that she must earn her bread; Miles has already pointed out how distasteful this must be for a lady. To disagree would be to imply that she does not need the work Miles provides, or, even worse, it would imply that a governess can *afford* (pun intended) to ignore the desires of the family she is hired to serve.

The educating spinster—especially the governess—is a crucial figure (as a character and a figure of speech) in Compton-Burnett's fiction, for she best embodies and represents that problematic intersection of discursive structure and social structure, the point at which the will to speak and the power to will limit each other, the point at which silence and desire bind each other. Because the educating spinster lives between the words that others speak and in the margins of others' worlds, she holds a special place in Compton-Burnett's fiction; she is able to achieve a degree of contentment and a state of disempowerment that ironically grant her both greater power and more vulnerability to the vicissitudes of discourse and social reality. Moreover, her special relation to language and to social behavior best represents the condition of women (as actual beings) in society and best presents the process in which woman (as concept) becomes caught in the inescapable net of discourse, in which the manless woman becomes a negative concept needed to define the positive conception of man. We need to go in both directions at once: to think of governesses as a socioeconomic group of actual women who were most prevalent during the mid-Victorian period, while also thinking of governessing as a concept of womanhood needed within patriarchal discourse as a result of rapid socioeconomic change during the period. With this double movement, we may come to see the relation, even if it is a conflictual one, between spinsterhood as a dependent condition of social behavior and spinsterliness as a discursive activity that enables psychic contentment.

The paradoxical position of the spinster who is an educator is capsulized in the word "governess." She is one who steers, directs, and commands, but her "government," unlike a governor's, is conducted within private space. She is directed to steer her course within a limited, domestic environment rather than within the larger sociopolitical sphere, and what she must learn to govern most of all is herself, her own private desire. Because the capacity to speak what one desires is a sign of actual power over one's own life, the governess must deny her own will to speak. She must learn to keep silent, even when she is the object of attention, to confirm that she has no will to power, no desire to assert her own desire either within the domestic sphere or in the larger sociopolitical arena. Effectively, she learns to deny that she has any desire at all, even when she speaks, though speaking itself is unavoidably an expression of desire.

Readers often note how in Compton-Burnett's novels all the components of fiction seem to become excuses for incessant dialogue. Action, scene, characterization, narration are all reduced to dialogue that could begin at any point and go on interminably, one speaker motivating the next in a continuous chain of playful banter. We don't care much about what happens, even as it is happening to the characters; we instead care about what is being said—or not said—in these novels where the word seems soulless. It is words that get people into trouble and as easily can get them out. Fate is wholly determined by the word, and morality always threatens to become merely a word without any point of reference outside itself. We never move inside the characters' minds, so we begin to feel that if we could, we would find not motivations but more words, an internal discourse fueling external dialogue. Whether we travel outward toward the world or inward into the soul, we end within discourse itself.[1] Perhaps it is Miles himself who puts it best: "'A few words can make or mar a human life. Whether they are spoken or written, they have the power'" (128). For Compton-Burnett, discourse seems to have a will of its own, defining the characters, their relations to one another, and their potential influence over others and at every point delimiting their desire. As their speaking expresses their desire, their will to prove the power of the individual self in relation to others and to the world, it also always reveals the failure of desire and self-will. Discourse gives power solely to itself, even as it empowers others to speak through it. Speech in the Compton-Burnett novel becomes a contest of power, not only among the wills of individuated, desiring characters but also between the human will and the will of discourse itself.

Although the range of choices within discourse is necessarily limited for all speakers, it is most limiting for the governess, whose peculiar status demands that her speech always present itself as a form of consent. There are various ways of signifying compliancy: through silence whenever possible, through cryptic assent when necessary, through more elaborate verbal means only when absolutely constrained. At any decibel of vocalization, however, there is duplicity, even to an extent the governess herself may not recognize. Silence can veil resistance as much as surrender; assent can hide dubious (dis)agreement; acknowledged complicity can suppress a heightened sense of exactly who deserves blame. Even though she does not even have the full range of discursive possibilities, the governess still retains the pregnant and impregnable uncertainties that make discourse itself possible. In fact, because she exists in the margins of discourse where dialogue is more the rhetoric of assent than the competitive arena of battling voices, she develops an intimate relation with both voiced and voiceless silences intrinsic to language, both the silences intended and those unwilled. Like the reader, who obtains a slightly privileged position on the edge of the novel's discourse, the governess is an eavesdropper, and though she cannot totally absent herself from the dialogue—for no one, not even the reader, can—she can maneuver a surprising amount of safety on the outer edge of the dialogue. In Compton-Burnett's eyes, to be an eavesdropper within the silences of discourse is, in some ways, the safest place to be. The governess who knows how to maneuver those silences and to maneuver within them has the opportunity to be more content than the most powerful patriarch.

Miles's precariously potent position within his own family indicates how discontentment necessarily accompanies patriarchal power. Believing that his desire should be absolute, he must constantly try to prove that it can be, and he constantly feels his desire tested (when demanding whatever he wants despite its effect on others) and contested (when others speak even to acknowledge the primacy of his desire). Whereas Malcolm's comment becomes a direct insult to Miles, it becomes an indirect insult by extension to his wife, Ellen, whose "name" is woman, an extension of Miles's own name. "'I wonder you can sit and say such a thing before your aunt,'" Miles says to his nephew, as Miles implies that for Ellen to be the mother of girls who must make their own way in life bears directly on Ellen's failure or success as mistress of the house. "'It did make me remember that I was in the room,' said Ellen, smiling." Because Ellen as woman, as wife and mother and aunt, is the articulated supplement of Miles's name, Miles feels comfortable bringing attention to her presence and is aware of how Malcolm's words bear upon her. However, the bearing of his own words upon Miss Gibbon must be brought to his attention, for the governess is the unarticulated supplement of his name. She is securely under his rule and fulfills his desire, but indirectly through her relation to his wife and daughters rather than through a direct sociosexual relation to him; even as she seeks shelter in his home and through the honor of his name, she retains her own name. Just as his wife represents the potential for fully fulfilled sexual desire and the perpetuation of his name, so the governess, his kept spinster, represents the extension of his rule even beyond the immediate terrain of his estate. The governess is the virgin territority that he wants bound to his desire even without the need to penetrate it. If Ellen as wife and mother must be violated and must express reciprocal, though not equal, desire, in being taken as the object of Miles's desire and in taking her husband as the primary subject of her desire, then Miss Gibbon as maiden governess, as virgin mother, must remain unviolated, neither a subject of desire nor possessing objects of desire herself.

Do Miles's words bear upon Miss Gibbon? In the strictest sense, his words do not refer to her, for he is talking about himself through the concept of governessing. He is engaging in combat with his heir designate, his nephew, and because Miss Gibbon, a governess, just happens to be there, his words apply to her only arbitrarily, in retrospect. Anxious to assert his own self-will, to prove that he is worthy "of the name of man," Miles also inadvertently proves that the spinster who must earn her bread by educating others' daughters is not worthy of any name, cannot be granted her own desire. Miles's insult, first direct and then indirect, becomes mere self-referring discourse because that which is named (the governess) is merely a negative concept for referring to the power of his own self-will, for reaffirming his own manliness, his own value as the source and gauge of everyone else's position. A governess is what no one within his rule must become, and yet he must hire (possess) a governess to name the rule of his desire.

While Miles tests his mettle in the fired caldron of discourse, Miss Gibbon contentedly inhabits the spinsterly zone of silence. Miles's insulting reference to governesses forces Miss Gibbon, otherwise invisible, to appear. How does Miss Gibbon respond to her dilemma of being all of a sudden the subject of discourse while being denied the subjectivity of her own desire? First, she mimics her master's words. When Miles says, "'She does not take my words to herself,'" Miss Gibbon responds, "'No, I did not refer anything to myself'" (6). Mimicry, of course, can signify any number of things, from the thoughtless acceptance of and obedience to another's will (like the child mimicking the parent's words in the recital of a bedtime prayer) to the considered acceptance of and obedience to a higher authority (like the bride and groom who mimic the marriage vows first spoken by the priest), from furtive parodic rebellion (like the testy student who mimics the teacher's words for the class behind the teacher's back) to blatant counterattack, however refined or duplicitous (like the critic who uses the opponent's words to attack that opponent). Needless to say, it is difficult to discern the decibel of (dis)agreement veiled within Miss Gibbon's reply, no matter how loudly or clearly the words themselves may be spoken. By overassenting—agreeing with Miles's words more than might be necessary—she returns herself to absence and silence but in a duplicitous way, for she brings attention to the limits of Miles's discourse, and therefore to the limits of his desire, and to the silent disturbances lurking within Miles's own discourse, within his head. His thoughtless insult cannot disturb her psychic contentment, even though he has total power over her capacity to earn her bread. Miss Gibbon turns their potentially insulting talk about governesses into an abstraction. She then takes this abstraction further and deflects attention away from her peculiar situation by stating what is obvious and therefore what cannot be the catalyst for further dissent. "'We all have different lives, of course,'" she says. "'It is only natural.'" Her strategy works, as Miles returns to the original subject of his daughters' lives and his own authority for determining their lives: "'And my girls have the one they ought to have. A life in the family home, with the protection and provision that is fit for them. What more could they want?'" (6). It is only natural that they should want no more than what his own desire commands, and it is no coincidence that the governess *apparently* reaffirms his capacity to protect and provide for his daughters.

"It does not need saying" that Miss Gibbon has no claim even to "fancy" that the words are directed at her. Even if Miles's words do not bear upon Miss Gibbon in the sense that they refer only to a concept, to someone who is not anyone, they do bear upon Miss Gibbon. They demand first her silence (and invisibility), then her verbal consent and even her complicity in his insult of her. Miss Gibbon, abstaining for as long as possible, enters the discourse by not entering it. She agrees that she can be no point of reference, though of course she is the primary point of reference. Her presence gives all the other characters their meaningful positions in the discourse. Her self-dissolution, her capacity to serve as the ultimate negative concept and the ultimate instrument of others' desire, allows Miles to stake out his own name and to attribute others' existence to it. She is the blank space on which the others mark themselves as discrete willing beings.

The fate of Miss Gibbon represents the status of the spinster in Victorian society, and her discursive manner reveals the ideological maneuvers of a social system that subordinates the unattached female, even when—or especially when—she possesses considerable knowledge and talent. Compton-Burnett novels resonate with the paradoxes and complexities of the institutional game that must be played to earn bread, to survive in the context of both the upper-class Victorian family and the patriarchal society at large. It is a game whose ostensible object is to harmonize different lives into a natural and orderly state in which the welfare of each individual is achieved through the cooperation of all. The genuine object of the institutional game, however, as revealed consistently and convincingly in Compton-Burnett's novels, is more sinister; it is the will to power, the will to triumph by fulfilling one's own desires by manipulating the needs and vulnerabilities of others.

Although the title states—no doubt ironically—that the father's fate is at stake here, his institutional fate (his position, his power, his authority within the social structure) is actually least threatened by the traumatic events of the novel. It is all of the other members of the family whose fate is threatened by Miles's whim to remarry, when his first wife is supposedly lost at sea. Malcolm stands to lose the inheritance if Verena, the new wife, bears Miles a son. The oldest daughter stands to lose her newly inherited place as head of the household. The younger daughters can easily become even more disempowered as Verena's desire and her children begin to hold first place in Miles's heart. Since only he and Miss Gibbon know that Ellen is actually still alive, Miss Gibbon could use her knowledge of his secret bigamy against him, but significantly she chooses not to do so. Even though Miss Gibbon's position is the most vulnerable (she does not even have the advantage of a blood tie), it is also the most open-ended. How she is perceived in the new order, under the new mistress of the house, depends primarily on how she conducts herself, on how she manages the rhetoric of assent. What is at stake for Miles is his noninstitutional will to power, his desire, and it is ironically Miss Gibbon, unable to influence the institutional power of her master, who determines the fate of the father's desire. Like discourse itself, desire cannot be fully institutionalized. It has a will of its own that carries the father along its course and subjects him to the kind of vulnerability that Miss Gibbon knows so well. Desire, like discourse, binds the father to the governess—mocking and muting his institutional power, if not making it insignificant.

As Miss Gibbon, at the most opportune time, restores Ellen to her rightful place in the social order, she disables Miles from obtaining the true object of his desire, Verena. Miles is unable to refocus his desire to accord with the dictates of social reality. The father's power is useless to him, and he is brought (by the governess) unwillingly into the governess's zone, where discourse and desire are impermeable to the arrangements of social power. The father, however, does not have the governess's resources for existing contentedly within the realm of thwarted desire. He considers himself a courageously tragic figure for enduring what he has suffered. How ironic that he interprets his rare moments of vulnerability as tragic, whereas Miss Gibbon, whose whole life is like those rare moments, views her life as neither tragic nor courageous. Toward the very end of the novel when Miles's nephews and Miss Gibbon mistakenly discover that Miles has slept with Verena, Miles rather foolishly praises himself in an attempt to diminish the awkwardness of the moment: "'I have borne what no other man has borne, what cannot be fathomed by you who have borne nothing. I have suffered long miseries of every kind. And I will suffer no further'" (201).

It is once again Miss Gibbon who nonchalantly settles the matter and saves the father from further embarrassment. "'Everything is in order now,'" she says (201), as she discharges the telling evidence of Verena's nightclothes, which had been thoughtlessly left in the drawers of the master bedroom. But the nephews' trenchant sense of humor compels them to note the ironic situation. "'Uncle admires you, Miss Gibbon,' said Rudolf. 'But he does not admire you enough. He directs his appreciation towards himself'" (202). Miles has no choice but to admire Miss Gibbon, who has repeatedly controlled his fate without the slightest hint of ridiculing him or demanding something for herself. The easy and contented manner in which she conducts her life, however, implicitly mocks the father's self-proclaimed heroics, regardless of her own assent—her silent complicity in his sins.

Miles, the good soldier, is no doubt in awe of Miss Gibbon, who seems so content with so little, and he is quick to naturalize her potential for self-dissolution explicitly as an attribute of gender and implicitly as an attribute of spinsterhood. When the family is debating whether it is better to be a man or a woman, Miles directs the question at Miss Gibbon, who responds, "'Well, I have not the choice, Mr. Mowbray. And I am content with my life and what I have done in it'" (20). Everyone else, except Ellen, has chosen sides, but Miss Gibbon does not even presume the desire of such fanciful wishing. Miles points out that a woman, unlike a man, "'is supposed almost to like'" self-sacrifice. And then he uses Miss Gibbon as the example: "'You will be tossed about from pillar to post, and asked to do this and go thither, and never know whether you have an object in life or not. We are grateful to you for accepting the position. And we ought to be'" (21). Because the governess must live as though her desire has no object (sexual or otherwise), she must live as though she has no desire. Nevertheless, Miss Gibbon is content, or, more precisely, she is content as a result of this pretense of nondesire. She, unlike the father, who is buffeted by his own self-will and used to having the objects of his desire, comprehends the limits of her desire and moves within the immovable boundaries of desire's own course. There is a point in the novel where the daughters become distressed because Miss Gibbon seems to have acquired an object of desire, a purpose beyond her service to them. They mistakenly think that Miss Gibbon gives Ellen's clothes to a friend without consulting the family. The daughters feel compelled to inform their father, who knows that Miss Gibbon's mysterious new friend is actually Ellen. Anxious to keep Ellen's return a secret, Miles is put in the paradoxical position of having to defend Miss Gibbon's right to her own desire. "'She may do as she pleases and thinks fit. After all her years with us, it is her right to do so. You need not have asked my consent. And she need not have asked yours'" (126). The tyrannical patriarch, whose every whim is his family's command, finds himself constrained to acknowledge the force of his governess's desire.

In the first chapter, Miles defends the lives his daughters are forced to live by marking them as nongovernesses; in the second chapter, he forces his daughters to defend their lives by testing their willingness to become governesses within their own home. In both cases, of course, what is at issue is his own power, his will over their existence, and in both cases it is the concept of governessing that determines his capacity to will and defend and also the daughters' capacity to counterwill and counterfend. Miles confronts the family with a financial crisis, telling them that "'great retrenchment must be made'" (14). Then he waits "with a half-smile" for suggestions. By feigning a crisis, Miles forces his family to verbalize the relation between utility and status, between utility and gender. The issue immediately becomes Miss Gibbon's contribution to the family rather than the family's sustenance of itself. "'I do not want any more teaching,' said Audrey. 'That need hardly be said. Miss Gibbon could perhaps do things that would save expense'" (14). Miss Gibbon's expendability becomes the subject of Miles's crisis, as each of the daughters claims to be able to take over some aspect of her responsibilities. Having no "natural" work themselves, they defend the natural value and utility of their lives by taking work from Miss Gibbon, whose life is ironically of least value, according to the family hierarchy. Just as Miles attempts to mark his authority in the first chapter by measuring the immeasurable distance between his daughters and the ultimate negative concept of governessing, the daughters try to defend their status in the second chapter by marking the superfluity of the governess. She is the overflow with which they can measure their own value and need. She becomes the more "superfluous" vehicle who can be used to measure their greater productivity.[2]

"'Can you suggest nothing that does not displace our good friend, Miss Gibbon?'" Miles asks his daughters. "'I was thinking of things that depended really on yourselves'" (15). If there really were a financial crisis, Miss Gibbon's presence would become a burden. Upper- and middle-class girls are not educated for work; they are educated to make the work of their male relatives rewarding. The governess is hired, then, not as a source of utility and productivity but as a sign of wealth and prestige. In "The Victorian Governess: Status Incongruence in Family and Society," M. Jeanne Peterson discusses how "the employment of a gentlewoman as a governess in a middle-class family served to reinforce and perpetuate certain Victorian values. But inherent in the employment of a lady was a contradiction of the very values she was hired to fulfill. The result was a situation of conflict and incongruity for both the governess and the family" (4–5). Peterson goes on to explain the sources of this conflict more specifically:

> The structure of the household, too, pointed to the governess's anomalous position. She was a lady, and therefore not a servant, but she was an employee, and therefore not of equal status with the wife and daughters of the house. The purposes of her employment contributed further to the incongruence of her position. She was hired to provide the children, and particularly the young women of the family, with an education to prepare them for leisured gentility. But she had been educated in the same way, and for the same purpose, and her employment became a prostitution of her education, of the values underlying it, and of her family's intentions in providing it. Her function as a status symbol of middle-class gentility also perverted her own upbringing. She was educated to be a "nosegay" to adorn her "papa's drawing room," and as a governess she had sold herself as an ornament to display her employer's prestige. (11)

Miles has his girls educated as a sign of his "name," a man of means who can afford to have his daughters educated. The woman who educates girls is needed only when there is a class of men who want to mark their superior status by possessing girls who have the extraneous luxury of possessing a teacher. Miss Gibbon is doubly parasitic because she is hired to teach decorative knowledge to girls who have no useful function in the first place. Without this double parasitism, the father could measure neither his utility within his own family nor the status of his family within society.[3] In a purely pragmatic patriarchal order, the governess, as an actual being, would be unnecessary. As a sign or concept, however, she is indispensable. She is the silenced excess in patriarchal discourse, an excess that ironically articulates masculine fitness, for she serves to define the absolute value and relative status of the father, who is then able to claim that he does not need her.

Like Jane Austen, Compton-Burnett reveals the complex relation between money and gender in the premodern patriarchal family. In the social and discursive system, the governess is an excess, but ironically an excess needed for the system to function. Likewise, in the economic system, the governess reveals a contradiction even more fundamental than the social incongruence that Peterson explains so well. To guarantee the dependence of the educating spinster, she was notoriously underpaid. Martha Vicinus states that "jobs offering as little as £5 and £10 per year with room and board would be flooded with applicants" (23). Peterson points out how, in some ways, the governess's financial situation, like her social position, was more precarious than that of common servants, because it was much more ambiguous:

> A governess always faced the danger of unemployment, either because her work with the children was finished or because her employers were dissatisfied with her. The aristocratic practice of continuing to support domestic servants who had outlived their usefulness after long service was not often extended to aged governesses in middle-class families. . . . In the event of illness or old age and inability to work, the governess faced the prospect of charity, such as that provided by the Governesses' Benevolent Institution in the form of small annuities for retired governesses. The number was limited, however, and reports of governesses in workhouses or asylums were not uncommon. (9)

Required to present the image of gentility without the means and to educate the children of the higher classes without herself being adequately educated, the governess is put in the position of needing to produce her own earnings but without being economically productive. She represents the function of capital itself, which marks increase of wealth but itself has no productive use outside the operative economic system. To keep her dependent and to remind her of her unproductive value in culture, she must be paid as little as possible. Nonetheless, that she is paid at all unravels the tidy system that would shackle her to the father's desire, for her earnings, however minimal, inadvertently must remind the father that she has needs, if not desires, that must be met. Her earnings also indicate the potential professionalization of the unattached female. As she marks the leisure of others, she becomes a professional wage earner who eventually marks her own entrance into and advancement in the sphere of productive economic exchange. As Virginia Woolf suggests in *A Room of One's Own*, the ability to possess property and earn money might have been more crucial to women's independence than the franchise itself (37–41, 112). By playing a crucial role in legal changes that eventually enable women to possess property and work for pay outside the home, the governess, simply through the anomalous position she holds within the social structure, contributes to the growing independence women experience during the nineteenth century.

Within the structure of patriarchal discourse, then, the concept of governessing signifies pure instrumentality and pure excess. The governess exists to serve others' desires while pretending to have no desire of her own; she is not needed but is fully desired. Within the economic structure of the Victorian family, the governess literally embodies capital, or more specifically surplus value. In the economy of production, she is the value superadded to the family as a result of alienated labor (her own) that produces the capacity for others' leisure. The paradox of the governess's situation is thus the grounding contradiction of industrial capitalism: the worker works merely to earn her bread rather than for her own enrichment; the worker works to provide her master's leisure rather than to produce her own welfare. The governess epitomizes this paradox further because what she produces literally is leisured girls, girls who are educated to understand their roles as markers and bearers of the patriarch's rule through their abstinence from actual productivity within society. This is why when Miles asks his daughters what they would do to diminish a supposed financial crisis, they have no choice but to rob Miss Gibbon of her labor; in fact, their very existence robs her of actual productive labor by giving her a labor that functions to produce social value (prestige and status) without also producing socioeconomic wealth (the material well-being of a society).

Compton-Burnett focuses on that particular historical juncture when the patriarchal family of the old order is being displaced by the modern family of industrial capitalism. Her novels concentrate on the psychopolitics of the provincial upper-class family living on the inherited income of a landed estate (usually entailed) at the very historical juncture when this social arrangement has become obviously problematic. In the late Victorian period, the landed family of leisure has become an economic anachronism, not because such families no longer exist but because this familial arrangement is in fundamental conflict with the triumph of industrial capitalism. As an economic anachronism, the myth of the landed family serves nostalgically as a sign of the continuity between the old and new economic structures. A family aspiring to social prominence needs to present the image of the landed family, with the secure hierarchical order it implies, while in actuality its wealth has been gleaned from commerce, industry, and the commodification of land itself. Or, as in so many of Compton-Burnett's novels, the inherited wealth is actually decreasing to the point of bankruptcy because an already prominent ancient family refuses to participate in the new economic order. In the old system of propertied leisure, there was no such thing as surplus value per se, for the land itself was the reservoir of absolute value, and the family patriarch, as the guardian of the land, transferred this absolute value to himself. As the ultimate preserver of the sacred order of things, he was responsible for distributing value and work as he saw fit at his own leisure—maintaining that sacred order by serving as the upper limit of desire.

With the triumph of industrial capitalism, this social arrangement becomes threatened. The father is still the head of the house, as so many Compton-Burnett novels attest, but his value within the social economy is no longer absolute. Under the new economy, the land is no longer a constant value that determines all other monetary exchange and social ranking within a stable predetermined social order, but instead it becomes a form of currency or a commodity itself, whose value fluctuates according to its fertility, how well it has been improved through modern agricultural techniques, and how well it has been managed as a capital enterprise—in short, according to its exchange value on the agricultural market. Likewise, the father's value in the new social economy is determined not merely by the ancientness of his noble name but by his actual productivity, the utility of his resources (his capital), his tangible contribution to his nation's economic and cultural expansion, and his capacity to hold on to and increase the value of his inherited estate. The father's value becomes relative in economic reality, even though he wants to claim it as absolute in terms of social rank.

This is why so much of the dialogue in Compton-Burnett novels focuses on the question of the relative productivity or value of individual family members and servants. In *A House and Its Head,* for instance, the friends of the family become enmeshed in such a conversation when the long-suffering, self-sacrificing mistress of the household suddenly dies. Dulcia remarks, "'I am prepared to admit I am a much less needed person than Mrs. Edgeworth. . . . And I am sure many people here would tell themselves the same—Oh, what a thing to let slip, unawares.'" Whether Dulcia has let the comment slip "unawares" or not is debatable, but there is no doubt about her intention in choosing to direct her apology toward Rosamund Burtenshaw, one of the two spinsters assembled. Miss Burtenshaw responds, "'I consent to be enrolled in the army of superfluous spinsters'" (101). Dulcia affirms her relative value, beneath that of the fecund Mrs. Edgeworth but at least above that of Miss Burtenshaw and Miss Fellowes. Miss Burtenshaw has no choice but to consent, but at the same time she alters the image of the docile old maiden by enlisting her in an *army* of spinsters. Miss Burtenshaw, having "retired from missionary work owing to the discomfort of the life, a reason which she did not disclose . . . was accustomed to say she found plenty of furrows to plough in the home field" (23). Redirecting her missionary zeal within the comforts of a village home, rather than among the discomforts of a foreign colony, Miss Burtenshaw compulsively attempts to prove her value, as indicated by the fecund image of ploughing the home field. Because she does God's work, she can transfer the value of highest heaven to herself, despite the fact that she is only a superfluous spinster on earth. In this novel and others, Compton-Burnett explores how social value itself is relative and extremely changeable, like currency, and has little relation to rank (even as most of the characters nostalgically strive to raise their rank) and virtually none to actual productivity. When the governess Miss Jekyll marries Mr. Edgeworth (whose name embodies the discomforts of worth examined in the novel), Compton-Burnett demonstrates the unpredictability of an individual's value in a society where the rules are changing faster than the people themselves.

In *A God and His Gifts*, the heir of the house, Hereward Egerton, may see himself as a little god who can violate society's laws, committing adultery and incest, without falling in rank or power, but it is his "gift" as a popular novelist that keeps him afloat financially. When Sir Michael, Hereward's father, announces that "'our home is in danger,'" that "'the old roof'" that "'has sheltered our fathers, may not pass to our son,'" unlike Miles Mowbray's, his financial trouble is real. When the family is forced to sell the most fertile portion of the ancient estate to obtain capital, attention is directed to the meaning of capital itself. Joanna, Sir Michael's wife, asks, "'Is capital exactly money? It is a large amount, that brings in small ones without getting any less. And the small ones are spent; and their being so small leads people into debt. But it seems kind and clever of capital. We should not ask any more. . . . Do I love capital? I suppose I do. It is dreadful to love money'" (13–14). Just as the family name is constantly threatened by bankruptcy despite Hereward's success as a novelist, so Hereward's honor is constantly threatened by his fame as a popular novelist. His income is not assured by his fame, the way a patriarch's should be by his noble name, but instead it is based on the marketing of his books to a fickle public. Further, the family and servants threaten the value of his income and work. Sir Michael suggests that novel writing "'seems an easy thing to do. . . . The mere writing must be a task, even if there isn't much more to it. But I wonder he did not work on a man's line, while he was about it'" (18). The family butler, Galleon, does "'honest'" and "'useful work in the world'" like "'a good many people'" (25), a fact which threatens the value of Hereward's questionable labor and even Sir Michael's genteel leisure. When Galleon says that the family "'circumstances'" are "'unexpected,'" Sir Michael immediately asks whether the butler thinks the family should be "'ashamed'" of his son's labor. "'I see no disgrace in honest work. I need only adduce my own case,'" Galleon says. "'But in some we may look for a difference.'" Sir Michael openly expresses envy of Galleon's productivity and implicitly suggests his own son's labor is neither honest nor manly. Hereward's eldest son, Salomon, "'in a place apart,'" may not have "'to earn [his] bread'" (52), like his younger brothers, Merton and Reuben, but the very fact that his future is taken care of is itself a threat to the value of the father's labor. The second son, Merton, is the biggest threat to his father. When he brings his fiancée, along with her fortune, to the house, his father loses no time in seducing her to reduce the son's threat and diminish his coup in having found such a bargain. Merton also questions the quality of his father's work when he suggests that he, too, wants to write novels but not of his father's "'range and kind.'" "'I should not appeal to the many, and shall be content to write for the few,'" Merton says bluntly. "'But by them, in this country, and beyond it, I hope to be known in the end. And not only known; read'" (52). Even Zillah, Hereward's spinster sister, is actually a threat to him. It is her support that gives him the self-confidence to keep writing. She knows his darkest secrets as well as his temperamental work habits. As she protects him from the family, she functions both as a wife should, engaging in psychic, if not in physical, incest, and as a husband should, making him dependent on her, even as she idolizes him.

In an anachronistic system whose operation is based on the preservation of leisure, how can the father claim the productivity of his own status? Doesn't the father become superfluous? How can the father distinguish between his utility or superfluousness and that of the educating spinster who is supposed to represent the overflow of his own value? Just as the relative productivity of the spinster comes back to haunt the patriarch, so does her knowledge, especially her knowledge of the family itself. Isn't it a contradiction for the patriarchal institution to grant spinsters so much potential influence within the home, considering how power derives so obviously from the handling of knowledge? It is a contradiction that the system cannot rid itself of. In order to disarm the spinster, her access to knowledge—even the knowledge she needs to teach her students—is curtailed.

In *A Father and His Fate*, after Miles's trickery about a financial crisis is over and Miss Gibbon has been given a new role as "'general helpmate,'" the daughters discuss their now former teacher:

> "I am glad Miss Gibbon has something in her life," said Constance.
>
> "Her feeling for Mother makes a thread running through it. It is hard to see what she would have without it."
>
> "I should have thought it was easy," said Audrey. "She would have nothing."
>
> "And you do not feel she deserves much," said Ursula. "That is how we see people who have taught us. They have had to reveal themselves."
>
> "Well, they may think it of people they have taught. They also are not unrevealed. When she wanted an object for her feeling, she did not turn to us."
>
> "I think she sees us with affection," said Constance.
>
> "I think she assumes she does," said Ursula. "Fifteen years must have had some result."
>
> "She is perhaps hardly educated enough for a governess."
>
> "Well, if she was, she would not be one. That is why governesses are not educated." (22–23)

Like Miles, the daughters view Miss Gibbon's objectless desire with wonderment, if not with respect. Ursula errs in thinking Miss Gibbon has revealed herself. Though the limits of the governess's knowledge may be obvious to the students, her secret for surviving successfully within those limits remains unrevealed. Audrey is closer to the truth: the pupils are the ones revealed, and the governess, powerless as she is, can use that personal knowledge as adroitly as she can use any booklearning, exploiting personal knowledge when necessary to compensate for a lack of academic knowledge. Indeed, the governess's knowledge can become a danger, not so much to the family's institutional power as to the individual desire that each family member hopes to fulfill through his or her relative rank and power within the family.

In *A House and Its Head,* Cassandra Jekyll is so clever in handling the secrets of the family that she ends up the mistress of the house, and she has managed her influence on her students so well that they do not resent her taking on the role of their second stepmother—no small feat in a Compton-Burnett novel. The shrewd governess turns her accursed state into a blessed one. She uses her guardianship to gain the admiration of her students, the respect of her mistress, the deference of her master, and the goodwill of everyone. Miss Gibbon manages to do this and to do it as well as anyone could hope. Unlike Miss Jekyll, Miss Gibbon finds full contentment in the margins of others' desire. She will do nothing that would threaten her status as pure instrument of others' power. She does not make her knowing an issue.

Her knowledge is precisely the issue, however. It is her knowledge, ironically, that settles the outcome of the novel; her knowing what no one else knows and her handling of that knowing determine the shape of the novel. Knowledge can be power only when it is not shared by all; Miss Gibbon shares her vast knowledge sparingly. In actuality, what the educating spinster is allowed to teach not only is harmless but also can be seen as contributing to the perpetuation of the institution and her own marginalization. The governess's classroom is not hers but the mother's as an instrument of the father. The governess's language is not hers but the father's. Even when the governess has mastered discourse—as much as it is possible for anyone to do so—she is still mastered by that discourse and must abide by its limits. The potential for subversion within the institution, then, becomes less pragmatic as we consider both the social and discursive limits binding the governess. Since the sphere of the governess is the father's home, he can more apparently have control over his girls' learning than if he were to send them to a boarding school. Unlike the schoolmistress in a boarding school, the governess is always under the eyes of the mistress of the house, who is always under the patriarch's eyes. The probability of a subversive governess, then, a Miss Brodie, is less than slight. In this sense, Miss Gibbon is probably an accurate representation of social reality. Instead of terrorizing the family with her noninstitutional power, she accepts the institution's rule and contributes to its sustenance. She chooses simply to live a life of minimal stress, an option that even the father comes to envy after his distressing fate.

Miss Gibbon dissolves her potential force against the institution to survive happily within it. It could even be argued that she is not a spinster in the most radical sense—a manless woman—because she is symbolically and practically married to Miles. Miles need not commit legal bigamy because he already has at his disposal a more subtle kind of bigamy; he has two wives, two mothers for his children, a personal helpmate in Ellen, and a general helpmate in Miss Gibbon. Since the educating vocation binds the spinster to the father's law and makes her a feminine governor of that law, can she be both a governess and a genuinely manless woman? Since she cannot be a subversive, can she at least be a radical spinster? The novel *Parents and Children* explores this question with a wider range of nurturing and educating spinsters. Compton-Burnett gives us two contrasted sets of characters: Emma Hatton and Bertha Mullet as nursemaids, Miss Mitford and Miss Pilbeam as governesses. Each spinster has a different relation to the institution and to the discourse that shapes it.

Emma Hatton represents what Julia Kristeva calls the "semiotic chora"—that discontinuous, anarchic, laughter-filled space where both desire and signification are still without discrete objects, that realm of potentially fulfilled desire before the child becomes immersed in the "symbolic function of paternal discourse" (133, 138). Although Hatton does not give birth to the children, she does mother them, and her mothering gives her a kind of influence not available to the actual mother, Eleanor. It is Hatton who guides the children from the disruptive amorphous state of objectless desire to the government of the father and his discourse. "Emma Hatton was a short, square woman of an age which had never been revealed, but revealed itself as about fifty-five, with a square, dark face, large, kind hands, deep, small, dark eyes, stiff, iron-grey hair, and a look of superiority, which was recognized and justified. She was a farmer's daughter, who saw the training of children as her vocation and therefore pursued it. Honor and Gavin regarded her as the centre of their world, and Nevill expended on her the force of a nature diverted by nobody else" (37). By becoming the central object of their desire, the nursemaid brings the children into the realm of potential discourse, and in the process they become the object of her desire. She may be the center of their world when they are young, but only because they are also the center of hers. The institution requires that the children displace a single male as the object of her desire, and this places her in a state akin to manlessness, a state nevertheless framed by the government of the father. Thus, we see that the educating spinster, rather than having no object of desire (a state of existence that is in actuality impossible to live out), actually gains those objects granted her by the father. She must practice a continuous deferral of self-determined desire, which would be directed toward objects determined by herself, by redirecting that desire toward objects inseminated by the father's desire. This matronly but imposing, mysterious woman, Hatton, thus exerts a silent influence within the household. Her warm presence is everywhere felt and even occasionally acknowledged. Therefore, as Peterson points out, "in spite of similar work situations, the stereotype of the downtrodden, pathetic governess stands in sharp distinction to that of the warm, jolly nanny who won the affection of her charges and often the sincere regard of her employers" (9). Because the nanny's work is more clearly mothering rather than educating and because she nurtures the children from the innocent state of satiated desire into the more treacherous realm of the father's law of language and repressed desire, she holds a less ambiguous place in the household. Even as she replaces the actual mother, her economic value is more easily justified as relieving the mother's arduous charge.

Nevill, the youngest child, who still clings to the semiotic realm, is so dependent on Hatton that it would be accurate to say that his umbilical cord is still uncut. Under her protection, he remains a free spirit, able to talk gibberish whenever he wants—though we soon discover that his semiotic language has its own meaning, which comments powerfully on the patriarchal discourse of his elders. To be Hatton's favorite is not necessarily a help, and it can easily prove a hindrance. James is the perfect instance of this phenomenon. "His dependence on Hatton at Nevill's age had exceeded his brother's, and still went beyond anyone else's. If Hatton could have betrayed a preference, it would have been for him; and it sent a ray of light through his rather shadowed life to remember that at heart she had one" (48). James's life is shadowed by the weakness of his own ego. He is a fragile boy, unable to compete well within the family or at school, self-conscious, awkward, introverted. He still yearns for the semiotic realm of boundless discourse and desire far beyond the age when it is socially acceptable, and so he attempts to substitute romantic books for Hatton's protection. James, so awkward in the normal world of boys and sports, "was a boy who could only learn from a woman in his home," and so, for the slightest reasons, he stays at home to study with his sisters under Miss Mitford rather than fulfilling his proper place in the institution (47). "James lived to himself like Nevill, but with less support, so that his life had a certain pathos" (48). We sense strongly that James's isolation and his suffering will only intensify as he grows, for he will not fit into an institutionalized world where a relentless will to power must replace the seemingly innocent and secure world of Hatton's bosom.

Leaving Hatton's nursery for the family parlor is like leaving nature for civilization and its discontents. Despite the pervasive influence of Hatton, the farmer's daughter, and despite her apparent connection to nature's realm, she is as much a part of the institution as any of the others and as vulnerable to the discourse that institutes and limits it. She sees her vocation as the training of children, and this is exactly what she does. Whatever power she has is limited by all the other complexities of discursive structure and social reality. Therefore, when Eleanor says that "'Hatton will rule the house in the end'" (54), it is ironic, for Hatton's rule is as duplicitous as Miss Gibbon's assent. She can rule only insofar as the children are ruled by her and only insofar as the children are not ruled, like James, by the father's law. Even as the children internalize her, they go beyond her. Indeed, her role is to carry them beyond her, to move them successfully from herself as the focus of boundless desire to the institution as the structure of bound desire.

Bertha Mullet, Hatton's assistant, "looked up to [Hatton] and bowed to her rule" (37), but her sympathies lie with the children themselves. She plays with them in a way Hatton does not. She talks not so much to them as with them. She is almost a child herself. Therefore, she could never take Hatton's place, but she has made a place of her own in the children's desires. "She would sometimes push up her cheeks towards her eyes, and entertain the children with a representation of this creature [which she is imitating in the scene]" (36–37). Mullet's relation to her superior, to herself, to the children, and to the institution is capsulized in this one comment: "'I do think Hatton does talk beautifully,' said Mullet, in a tone that seemed a reproach to the existing social order. 'As pointed and as finished as any lady'" (41). She views Hatton in much the same way as Nevill does, and like Nevill her position is protected by Hatton. She can remain a woman-child, a playmate for the children, almost untouched by the institution, by discourse, or by the pains of unfulfilled desire. Her comment, potentially subversive, is actually diffused by the nature of her discursive function. Although she is not as innocent as Nevill, her discourse is taken as unseriously. Wedded to Hatton's realm, to the nursery, she possesses its child-like liberties without also possessing the liberty a woman could aspire to in an ideal manless state.

Because Miss Mitford refuses to teach the youngest children, the Sullivans find it necessary to acquire an extra governess, Miss Pilbeam. What Miss Mitford already knows, Miss Pilbeam seems unlikely to learn. Like Miss Gibbon, Miss Mitford has managed her position in the margins of discourse well, but Miss Pilbeam seems headed for a rougher course in life. We sense this from the very beginning when Honor, an extremely precocious and candid girl, remarks, "'I have had two governesses. . . . I know the tricks of the trade'" (41). Unfortunately, the same cannot be said for Miss Pilbeam. She is an example of a governess who has a difficult time governing her own private space and so will have a difficult time governing the children.[4] Like Miss Gibbon—and, as Ursula points out, like all governesses—she is not well educated, but unlike Miss Gibbon, she may never learn to use whatever personal knowledge she can glean to compensate for her lack of academic knowledge. Instead of being content with the rhetoric of assent and living peacefully within the limits of discourse and desire, Miss Pilbeam asserts herself, expresses her will to speak as the power to will; ironically her self-willing discursiveness only makes her more vulnerable to the institution and to desire than Miss Gibbon and Miss Mitford are.

Miss Pilbeam's "qualification for teaching was her being presumed to know more than young children, and she was required to produce no others" (81). Honor and Gavin, her two older pupils, immediately pick up on her incompetence, as she reveals herself to them in the same way the Mowbray daughters think that Miss Gibbon has revealed herself:

> "You can do a good deal with threepence a week," said Miss Pilbeam.
> "Did you have as much when you were a child?" said Gavin.
> "Yes, that is what I used to have."
> "Could your father afford to give it to you?"
> "Yes he used to manage that."
> "Then why do you have to be a governess?"
> "Well, I want more than that now."
> "How much do you have?" said Honor, with her eyes and her hands engaged with her pen, and her voice sounding as if it barely detached itself.

"You know you should not ask that question."
"You asked us how much we had." (84)

It is only the first day and already Miss Pilbeam is in trouble. It is not only that Honor is so precocious but also that Miss Pilbeam is so unself-governing. It is clear who will have the upper hand. When Eleanor comes in to check on the new governess, Gavin unwittingly blurts out that Miss Pilbeam has to read the lesson "'out of the book herself,'" implying that she does not possess the knowledge contained within the book. Honor immediately covers for the governess: "'He said Miss Pilbeam was reading from the book. We are to answer questions afterwards.'" Under Honor's tutelage, Miss Pilbeam may "'perhaps . . . begin to make progress'" (86). As Miss Pilbeam reveals her personal life—her desires and illusions—to the children, she becomes vulnerable to them (especially to Honor). Instead of Miss Pilbeam's controlling her potential power by acknowledging her vulnerable position within the hierarchy the way Miss Gibbon and Miss Mitford do, she attempts to impress the children with life outside the Sullivan family. When Gavin asks whether her father is a gentleman, instead of mimicking or evading the obvious implication, she asserts, "'He is an educated man. He passed very hard examinations.'" But Gavin is not nonplussed: "'But he doesn't earn enough for you not to be a governess.'" Miss Pilbeam responds, "'He likes me to do something useful.'" Gavin goes on to insist, "'But teaching isn't useful unless you know enough to teach.'" Miss Pilbeam, trying to salvage the situation, retorts, "'I know enough to teach you'" (87). But once again she is on shaky ground, for even if she does know enough to teach him—which is doubtful—she does not know enough to control him.

Miss Pilbeam prides herself on her usefulness, but the children have a much better sense of her utility. When Eleanor states that Miss Pilbeam is a "'useful person in two households'" (unlike live-in governesses) and that she hopes Honor will grow to be like the governess, Honor, after looking appropriately surprised, comments, "'No, I don't think so. If people are useful, it is only nice for other people, and not for them'" (86). Even if Miss Pilbeam isn't conscious of her extraneous position as a governess, Honor is. Honor is also conscious of the spinster's larger social superfluity. After Miss Pilbeam informs the children that her father is going to remarry, they have an extended conversation about her prospects in a new homelife. They ask her whether it makes her hate her father, whether her stepmother will put her out.

> "No, I don't think she will do that," said Miss Pilbeam, with a smile.
>
> "You would laugh on the other side of your face, if she did."
>
> "Miss Pilbeam would live here with Hatton and Mullet," said Nevill.
>
> Honor and Gavin looked at each other, and burst into laughter at this estimation of Miss Pilbeam's place.
>
> Miss Pilbeam looked towards the window.
>
> "I am 'he'; you are 'she'; Miss Pilbeam is 'it'," said Gavin, to his sister, seeming to receive an impetus from Nevill's words.
>
> Miss Pilbeam turned sharply towards him.
>
> "I suppose your father will like your stepmother better than you," said Honor, quickly. (268)

This episode perfectly captures the precariousness of Miss Pilbeam's position. She may think she is better off than Hatton and Mullet, but actually she is not. Her use to her father is at least as precarious as Hatton's use to Mr. Sullivan. Gavin cleverly mimics Nevill's innocent semiotic language to satirize Miss Pilbeam's actual place within the father's symbolic realm of law. Miss Pilbeam, manless and useless, becomes an "it" once her father remarries. Honor quickly counters the attack Miss Pilbeam is about to make and once again puts the governess in her place. Thus, Miss Pilbeam's ostensible utility in her own home comes under the relentless scrutiny of an observant child. The governess's utility in the Sullivan household also comes under Honor's scrutiny. When Miss Pilbeam suggests that because Honor is so quick she might help Gavin catch up, Honor responds, "'No, I don't teach people,' . . . implying a difference between her experience and Miss Pilbeam's" (88). By entering the arena of competitive discourse with the children rather than existing in the margins of discourse—in the silences—Miss Pilbeam forfeits her greatest advantage. Not only does she become a victim of her own words, a hostage to her own desire, but also she is terrorized by the children, whose institutional power is so much greater than hers despite the fact that her job is putatively to govern them. In other words, "'she can't stand on her own legs'" (90), as Honor notes when the governess threatens to call Mrs. Sullivan in to fend off the children's rudeness.

Miss Mitford doesn't have to make such threats. She comes perhaps as close as possible to being a radical spinster, a genuinely manless woman, within the confines of a life devoted to educating in the father's home, although even she cannot be a subversive governess. She exerts her influence not to enhance her noninstitutional power and certainly not to subvert the institution but rather to enhance the privacy of her space, the government of her own discourse and desire. "She was a person of reading and intelligence, but preferred a family to a school, and knew that by taking a post beneath her claims, she took her employers in her hand. She held them with unflinching calm and without giving any quarter, and criticism, after she had met it with surprise and had not bent to it, had not assailed her. Eleanor was hardly afraid of her, as she did not feel that kind of fear, but she hesitated to judge or advise her, and seldom inquired of her pupils' progress except of the pupils behind her back" (47). Unlike Miss Pilbeam, Miss Mitford protects her privacy and recognizes how to exploit her spinsterhood and her knowledge; unlike Miss Gibbon, she refuses to become symbolically married to the father even though she must submit to the father's institutional power. Like Miss Gibbon and unlike Miss Pilbeam, she appreciates her marginal position and uses it for the sustenance of her own contentment. "She was a fairly satisfied person, with a knowledge of books which was held to be natural in her life, and a knowledge of people which would have been held to be impossible, and was really inevitable" (65). Miss Mitford is the most contented character in the novel. When all the other characters are buffeted by the traumatic events, she remains unmoved and unaffected.

Her aloofness troubles the family. They call her incessant reading an "extravagance" because it indicates how much her inner life is detached from theirs. Isabel comments, "'Mother says she wonders you have time to read them all.'" Miss Mitford responds, "'Does she? . . . I never forget the claims of my own life'" (79). Her detachment enables her to cultivate her own limited desire but does not threaten her capacity to earn her bread. She orders books by the post twice a week and reads newspapers; it is even a mystery how she can afford them (106–7). But because Miss Mitford knows exactly where she stands, the children cannot use her desire against her.

> "You are as afraid of Mother as we are, Mitta," said Venice.
>
> "Not quite. She has no affection for me, and that puts me outside her power. But I am afraid of her, of course. I am a sensitive, shrinking creature at heart."
>
> "Would you mind if she—?"
>
> "Dismissed me? Yes. . . . " (80)

Because Miss Mitford knows the difference between institutional power (her capacity to be dismissed) and the noninstitutionalizable power of discursive desire, she can live a content and secure life even within the context of her vulnerable position as an educating spinster.

Miss Mitford has chosen to work in a home rather than a school. She could not make such a decision if she were motivated by a desire to subvert the patriarchal institution. It is not that the girls' school is any less the product of patriarchal discourse, but that in the boarding school, educating spinsters occupy an anomalous space inside the institution that exercises its power over them. Schoolmistresses perform the same function as governesses, as we see so well in a novel like *More Women than Men,* but within the context of a feminine community the chance for liberties, if not liberty and liberation, is amplified. The schoolmistress, if she so chooses, is more at liberty to fashion her own discourse and even to use that discourse to attempt an assault on the institution she is supposed to be nurturing in her teaching. Compton-Burnett's schoolmistresses do not, however, choose to become subversive in the Miss Brodie fashion. Like all her characters, they are more concerned with surviving than with rebelling, more concerned with simply managing the willfulness of discursive desire than with breaking out of its limits.

In *Ivy: The Life of I. Compton-Burnett,* Hilary Spurling points out how the novelist was fond of posing as "the mousy, innocuous, insignificant governess" in the presence of both her friends and strangers (370). To Compton-Burnett, the demeanor of the governess represents a way of living, an ideal condition of wise contentedness to which the marginal manless woman is best able to aspire. Educating spinsters may some day exploit their knowledge to lord over old married men, but their lording will be the same old game except with a different set of players. From Compton-Burnett's perspective, bemused restraint is better than monopolizing the game. As readers, we learn to appreciate this condition, and we become educated by another kind of educating spinster, the unmarried "lady novelist," who, through her own delimiting discourse, brings us to understand the sources of knowledge, the treachery of desire, and the limits of discourse itself.

NOTES

1. Significantly, the first question Bowen asks Compton-Burnett in his interview concerns her unusual reliance on dialogue (165). Hutchinson analyzes the authorial worldview that can be inferred from these "walls of

words," a worldview in which "the surface is the reality, or at least the only reality available to us" (84). See also Sarraute.

2. During the period portrayed in Compton-Burnett's novels, the question of "surplus" women became a burning issue. For the sociohistorical implications of this controversy, see Jeffreys, especially ch. 5, and Vicinus, ch. 1. Auerbach also discusses this issue and the conflict between the portrayal of these "surplus" women in Victorian arts and their actual social conditions (ch. 4).

3. For a good discussion of feminine education and status, see Vicinus, especially 166–77. The irony of Miles's position becomes clear once we recognize his true relation to work. As Liddell points out, "The male tyrants [in Compton-Burnett's fiction] are all country gentlemen living on inherited property which they have done nothing to augment; nevertheless they resent in the young their unproductiveness" (24). Miles is actually no more productive than his daughters and a great deal less productive than Miss Gibbon, who at least contributes to society by earning her own bread.

4. In his survey of Compton-Burnett governesses, Liddell offers a different view of Miss Pilbeam. He sees her as "an unpretending young woman" who "manages to defend her ground" (64). I suppose if we consider the odds against her, this characterization makes sense, but in comparison with Miss Mitford the characterization seems much too generous.

WORKS CITED

Auerbach, Nina. *Women and the Demon: The Life of a Victorian Myth.* Cambridge: Harvard University Press, 1982.

Bowen, John. "An Interview with Ivy Compton-Burnett: BBC Programme, Sept. 17, 1960." *Twentieth-Century Literature* 25 (1979): 165–72.

Compton-Burnett, Ivy. *A Father and His Fate.* 1957. Oxford University Press, 1984.

———. *A God and His Gifts.* 1963. New York: Penguin, 1983.

———. *A House and Its Head.* 1935. New York: Penguin, 1958.

———. *More Women than Men.* 1933. London: Allison and Busby, 1983.

———. *Parents and Children.* 1941. New York: Penguin, 1970.

Hutchinson, Joanne. "Appearances Are All We Have." *Twentieth-Century Literature* 25 (1979): 183–93.

Jeffreys, Sheila. *The Spinster and Her Enemies: Feminism and Sexuality, 1880–1930.* London: Pandora, 1985.

Kristeva, Julia. *Desire in Language: A Semiotic Approach to Literature and Art.* Ed. Leon S. Roudiez. New York: Columbia University Press, 1980.

Liddell, Robert. *The Novels of I. Compton-Burnett.* London: Gollancz, 1955.

Peterson, M. Jeanne. "The Victorian Governess: Status Incongruence in Family and Society." *Suffer and Be Still: Women in the Victorian Age.* Ed. Martha Vicinus. Bloomington: Indiana University Press, 1972.

Sarraute, Nathalie. "Conversation and Sub-Conversation." *The Art of I. Compton-Burnett.* Ed. Charles Burkhart. London: Gollancz, 1972.

Spurling, Hilary. *Ivy: The Life of I. Compton-Burnett*. New York: Columbia University Press, 1986.

Vincinus, Martha. *Independent Women: Work and Community for Single Women, 1850–1920*. Chicago: University of Chicago Press, 1985.

Woolf, Virginia. *A Room of One's Own*. New York: Harcourt, Brace and World, 1929.

SUSAN KATZ

Writing for "Monie": The Legacy of the Spinster to E. M. Forster

> . . . he believed that she had paid homage to the complexity of life.
> —E. M. Forster, *Where Angels Fear to Tread*

As a fatherless boy in a close matriarchal household, E. M. Forster was treated to an unusually rich experience of canny, self-sufficient women. When Forster was left an only child at the age of one-and-a-half, no fewer than four husbandless relatives clustered around him and his widowed mother Lily. The pair was briefly joined by Lily's closest friend, Mamie Synnot, the widow of a relative of Forster's father, but Mamie soon left because of her excessive devotion to the baby who, in Forster's biographer's terms, "was the lifeline for two shipwrecked women" (Furbank 2: 122). Constant attention was lavished on Forster by his Aunt Laura Forster, whose home eventually descended to Forster, and by his maternal grandmother, whom Forster adored because she was "'so shrewd, downright, and gay'" (Furbank 2: 28). And Forster's great-aunt Marianne Thornton, a wealthy spinster prophetically nicknamed Aunt Monie, dispensed to Lily and her son large doses of advice and, in her will, a generous portion of her fortune. It may be tempting to infer from our knowledge of Forster's homosexuality and his reputation as a misogynist (Furbank 2: 175) that Forster had rebelled against the coddling and baby-worshipping of these "'stacks of females'" (Furbank 1: 88). Literary critics have tended to see the feminine environment in which Forster was raised as personally and artistically disabling to him or as the source of an Oedipal conflict which Forster resolved only through writing.[1] But textual evidence suggests that the young E. M. Forster absorbed the informing values of his novels from these many nurturing female relatives, and in his later, nonfictional works—most explicitly in *Marianne Thornton* (1956)—he acknowledges that unmarried women bestowed on him a legacy which was both material and spiritual.

The tensions, perhaps contradictions, in Forster's characterizations of unmarried women in the early novels, particularly in *Where*

Angels Fear to Tread (1905) and *A Room with a View* (1908), betray a mingling of hostility and gratitude in Forster's relationships with his female caretakers. After exhausting the possibilities for expressing his concerns in novels with the writing of *A Passage to India* (1922–24), Forster turned to other narrative forms, the last of which was what he termed a "domestic biography" of his Aunt Monie. The expressed objective of this work, entitled *Marianne Thornton,* was to acknowledge his debt to his great-aunt for the bequest in her will, which he regarded as "the financial salvation of my life" (*Marianne Thornton* 324–25). But a subtext of the biography is that Forster had also inherited from his Aunt Monie and the other unmarried women in his family the humane sensibility that inspired his novels. That Forster finally wrote a family history from the point of view of this spinster great-aunt indicates that the mature E. M. Forster had grown to acknowledge his affection and respect for the women in his family, who might have been overpowering but also had awakened in him—by the example of their devotion to him and to each other—a reverence for human relations. In 1937, Forster paid even his mother—friend, traveling companion, and in her old age, millstone—her due in a letter to a friend: "'Although my mother has been intermittently tiresome for the last thirty-years . . . I have to admit that she has provided a sort of rich sub-soil where I have been able to rest and grow'" (Furbank 1: 217). Collectively, all of these unmarried relatives created an environment that was a "sort of rich sub-soil" for Forster, who ultimately attributed his personal values and artistic accomplishments to his feminine heritage.

Marianne Thornton is composed of four parts—"Daughter," "Sister," "Aunt," and "Great-Aunt"—corresponding to Monie's roles. Beyond delineating the ancestral ties between Marianne Thornton and himself, Forster establishes in the biography a spiritual kinship with his spinster great-aunt. Forster's personal history of Monie is also, in part, a record of the family's weakening grip on their home, Battersea Rise. The house, which Forster emblematized in *Howard's End* (1910), and Marianne Thornton herself emerge from the biography as the two most formative influences on the author's imagination. As a consequence of a family quarrel, the sixty-year-old Marianne was expelled from Battersea Rise, a dislocation which she described as "'such a mixture of going to be married and going to die'" (201). Forster, who was "also deprived of a house myself" (205), identified with Aunt Monie's rooting herself in a locale and experiencing her deracination as a critical rite of passage. Marianne's resiliency in forming a new establishment, without marrying or dying but by taking in her niece as a companion, displays the self-command that characterizes Forster's most compelling unwed heroines, particularly Caroline Abbott in *Where Angels Fear to Tread.*

Marianne Thornton was herself a species of writer, having been educated by her father in current political affairs and economics and, when she was fifteen years old, appointed his amanuensis. While hers was an indirect form of authorship, Marianne cultivated during her apprenticeship the informed opinions and authoritative prose style which later characterize her own diaries and letters. Her youthful travelogues from which Forster quotes testify to Marianne's individualism and broadmindedness toward those who were not of her class or nationality. When Forster reflects on Monie's legacy to him, he associates the financial bequest with his career as an author, for the £8,000 Forster inherited from her was applied first to his education and then, indirectly, to his writings: "After Cambridge I was able to travel for a couple of years, and travelling inclined me to write" (324–25). Forster concludes his portrait of Marianne Thornton by defining himself as a product of her generosity: "But I am thankful so far," Forster proclaims, "and thankful to Marianne Thornton; for she and no one else made my career as a writer possible, and her love, in a most tangible sense, followed me beyond the grave" (324–25). While Forster portrays himself as the fulfillment of Aunt Monie's ambitions for him, we also can see that through Forster Marianne Thornton may have accomplished her own aspirations of authorship.

Most important, one can detect in *Marianne Thornton* that it was from the unmarried women in his family that Forster had absorbed his attitudes and ideals, his tone and his temperament. For example, the sentiments of Aunt Monie's New Year's Day note to her eight-year-old grandnephew, "Many happy returns of the day dearest Morgan—that is what everybody is wishing themselves and everybody they love, but we cannot make ourselves or other people happy by only wishing it—we must try to make them so. . . . " (320), are echoed in the governing principle of *Howard's End,* Forster's injunction to "only connect." Aunt Mamie, too, displays a sensibility and ironic wit in the passages Forster quotes, which he obviously admired and apparently emulated. Her wondrous pleasure in the mysteries of the universe, which Forster obviously shared, can be heard in her speculations about heaven: "'Won't it be exciting, won't it be fascinating to *know,* and I have an idea that one or two who might expect to be very highly placed may have some surprises'" (313). Without Forster's saying so, one senses that some of Mamie's maxims, such as "'I do prefer people who are untruthful through sympathy to those who are truthful through hardness'" (313), provided the standards by which Forster governed himself and his fictional characters. By documenting the life of Marianne Thornton and thereby tracing the history of several generations of his family, Forster articulates his own spiritual concerns and directly acknowledges unmarried women as the source of his most cherished values.

In the early fictional works, however, Forster projects onto spinsters his uneasiness about the generosity of his benefactresses. Through the heroines of *Where Angels Fear to Tread* and *A Room with a View,* Forster explores the complex motives behind feminine selflessness and devotion. On one level, the self-commanding Caroline Abbott and the manipulative Charlotte Bartlett would seem to express Forster's resentment of controlling women; yet, when he encircles a heroine like Caroline Abbott in a mystical glow by which she illuminates the way of others toward ease and happiness, perhaps Forster was commemorating those women who had indulged and encouraged him. The unwed heroine seems to have loomed large in Forster's imagination, for despite his stated intention that "the object of [*Where Angels Fear to Tread*] is the improvement of Philip" (149), Caroline Abbott, who "was originally meant to turn out smaller and different" (150), is the spiritual center of the novel. Unmarried heroines are also agents of the central relationships in each of these novels, and they perform a therapeutic function, healing the injured feelings and severed ties of the principal characters. Although the superficial appearance of Forster's spinsters—their drabness, intrusiveness, self-pity, and self-effacement—is drawn from conventional representations of old maids in nineteenth-century British literature, the stereotyped figure of the self-abnegating spinster expands into a psychologically and symbolically complex character in the course of Forster's narratives. In his characterization of the unwed heroines of two novels and the nonfictional *Marianne Thornton,* Forster dramatizes with increasing subtlety that even if unmarried women lack social status, certain spinsters may possess another kind of authority, issuing from their wisdom and self-knowledge. At the same time these heroines are transformed by experience (change or growth is a rare occurrence among fictional spinsters prior to Forster's), they, in turn, transform or, in Forster's term, transfigure the experience of other characters and, ideally, that of the reader.

In *Where Angels Fear to Tread,* Caroline Abbott's integrity and insight culminate in Forster's beatification of her. The clarity of Caroline's responses to her fellows—particularly her compassion and her candid admission of sexual desire—radiates outward, humanizing those who are sensitive enough to value the intensity of her emotional commitments. Forster thus reconceives the spinster as a heroine who is no longer a dependent within her own family or society but, rather, possesses within herself a gift that is hers to bestow on others: an appreciation of truth, beauty, and love. Charlotte Bartlett's emergence as the heroine of *A Room with a View* is more oblique, more enigmatic, and, finally, more compelling. While Charlotte appears to be an insidious figure in Lucy's life, Forster also suggests that by consciously and unconsciously manipulating Lucy, Charlotte guides her toward a true understanding of love. At the same time, Charlotte herself comes to an honest reckoning with her own limitations. If one agrees with George Emerson's speculation that Miss Bartlett maneuvered his reunion with Lucy, one can interpret Charlotte's behavior as her having surmounted her own condition of sublimated desire. Whereas Charlotte at first appears to be a caricature of a quirky old maid whose actions and utterances are all symptoms of her repressed sexuality (a "flat character" in Forster's terminology), Forster's more enlightened view of celibacy enables him to invest Charlotte Bartlett, as he does Caroline Abbott, with the empathy and wisdom that facilitate love. Forster's own experience with unmarried women enabled him to modify the conventional type of spinster and introduce into fiction an unwed heroine who recuperates the value of truth, beauty, and happiness.

Forster's characterization of Miss Abbott in *Where Angels Fear to Tread* unsettles the literary stereotype of the old maid. Instead of being peripheral and inconsequential, Caroline Abbott emerges as the heroine of the novel by exemplifying a moral ideal that inspires reverence and restores meaning. By enacting a noble standard of conduct—generosity, compassion, candor, and devotion—she transcends, and enables others to transcend, the lovelessness and hypocrisy of English society. Through Caroline Abbott, Forster also demonstrates that unrequited love can be enriching, rather than disabling, and that there are other experiences besides marriage by which an author can signify the personal growth and social value of a heroine. Such a broad view of spinsterhood enabled Forster, as early as 1905, to modify the conventional heterosexual love plot, which he later abandoned altogether. By resisting romantic closure for this novel, by situating an old maid at the center of narrative, and by making her the vehicle for the novel's moral concerns, E. M. Forster credits the unmarried woman with a more therapeutic role than she had previously enjoyed in fiction.

Forster initially presents Caroline Abbott from the point of view of those who do not inquire into character too deeply—members of Sawston, the British community in the novel, and Caroline's acquaintances, such as Philip Herriton, who had always perceived her as "good, quiet, dull, and amiable, and young only because she was twenty-three: there was nothing in her appearance or manner to suggest the fire of youth. All her life had been spent at Sawston with a dull and amiable father, and her pleasant, pallid face, bent on respectable charity, was a familiar object of the Sawston streets" (16). Everyone infers from Caroline's status as unwed daughter and caretaker of her father that she can be typecast as vacuous and complacent. Her face is a "familiar object" because Caroline is a legible type to the Sawstonites, and everyone assumes that an unexceptional appearance such as hers cannot mask either mystery or passion. But the task of the novel, in large part, is to foil this reflexive dismissal of such figures as Caroline Abbott. As Caroline emerges from behind her pleasant, pallid face as a committed, intelligent, and noble woman, the Herritons first dismiss her as a lunatic, then patronize her as a novelty, and eventually revere her as a goddess. But Caroline evades these categorizations as well, for in Forster's reconception of the old maid, miraculous healing powers do not isolate her yet again—as a witch or a sorceress—but signify her attainment of a mortal ideal: sympathy, integrity, and love.

The novel is structured around the therapeutic powers of its heroine. It opens with Mrs. Herriton administering a dose of Caroline Abbott to her widowed daughter-in-law Lilia by sending them to Italy together, for she believes that "no one could live three months with Caroline Abbott and not be the better for it" (7). In Forster's ironic plot, however, Mrs. Herriton's smug expectations of Caroline's improving influence are fulfilled by not her daughter-in-law but her son, Philip Herriton, Caroline herself, and, by extension, the reader. In Italy, Lilia falls in love with and has a brief unhappy marriage to Gino, a young Italian, and dies giving birth to their son. Her former mother-in-law dispatches her disaffected son Philip and her fanatical daughter Harriet to Monteriano to "save" the baby, whom Caroline has also set out to reclaim from his father. When all three Sawstonites converge on Monteriano, a series of confrontations and cultural clashes occur between the stiff, conventional British and the earthy, vital Gino. Eventually, Caroline's insight into Gino and her influence over Philip enable them to concede Gino's worthiness as a father and the arrogance of their own claims. But Harriet, who is immune to Caroline's influence, abducts the baby, who is killed as the Herritons' and Caroline's carriages collide on the road out of Monteriano. In the pivotal scene of the novel, after the baby has been killed, Gino beats Philip nearly to death, but Caroline saves both Philip and Gino by initiating a reconciliation that transforms the violence between them into love and kinship. The novel's ending, in which Philip confesses his love for Caroline, and Caroline declares her sexual attraction to Gino, completes the healing process at work in the novel. From the tattered lives of the anguished Gino and the cynical Philip, Caroline salvages meaning, for "she was determined to use such remnants as lie about the world" (139). Caroline's resourcefulness is sacred, since she can bind "remnants" into wholes.

Caroline diagnoses the malady that infects the Sawstonites as hypocrisy and disaffection. Having taken a draught of Italy, Caroline explains, she has been cured of her own English prejudices and has expelled the "deadening" influence of Sawston. "'All that winter I seemed to be waking up to beauty and splendour and I don't know what,'" she reveals to Philip, "'and when the spring came, I wanted to fight against the things I hated—mediocrity and dulness and spitefulness and society'" (61). Clearly, the Herritons had underestimated Caroline's complexity, so when Caroline explains her support of Lilia's marriage as, in part, a condemnation of Sawston's values, she reveals to Philip and to the reader unanticipated depths. She declares that she "'hated the idleness, the stupidity, the respectability, the petty unselfishness,'" which Philip corrects to "'petty selfishness.'" But she insists on "petty unselfishness," explaining, "'I had got an idea that everyone has spent their lives in making little sacrifices for objects they didn't care for, to please people they didn't love; that they never learnt to be sincere—and, what's as bad, never learnt how to enjoy themselves'" (60). Beneath her apparent complacency, Caroline exercises a critical intelligence, condemning the bad faith underpinning such pretenses of self-sacrifice. She deplores the detachment—the lack of passionate devotion to people or ideas—that characterizes her compatriots. Caroline's encounters in Italy also demonstrate that her criticism of society is not a form of defeatism but an avowal of faith in individuals to invest their own lives and the lives of others with pleasure and dignity.

Philip, too, suffers from social malaise, but his critical stance is a retreat from rebellion into aestheticism. When Caroline concedes that the failure of Lilia's marriage is a measure of the strength of social convention, Philip articulates the theories in which he finds refuge: "'Society *is* invincible to a certain degree. But your real life is your own, and nothing can touch it. There is no power on earth that can prevent your criticizing and despising mediocrity—nothing that can stop you retreating into splendour and beauty—into the thoughts and beliefs that make the real life—the real you'" (62). But Caroline sees this "retreat" into such abstractions as splendor, beauty, thoughts, and beliefs as complicity with society; Caroline instead advocates an ethos of engagement, of individual acts that abolish mediocrity, hypocrisy, and joylessness.

Caroline rouses Philip out of submitting to circumstances by forcing him to confront the moral dilemma surrounding Gino's baby: "'Do you want the child to stop with his father, who loves him and will bring him up badly, or do you want him to come to Sawston, where no one loves him, but he will be brought up well?'" (120). She seeks to transmit to him her own integrity, which demands commitment to a course of action rather than submission to fate. "'Settle which side you'll fight on,'" she insists. "'But don't go talking about an "honourable failure," which means simply not thinking and not acting at all. . . . You told me once that we should be judged by our intentions, not by our accomplishments. I thought it a grand remark. But we must intend to accomplish—not sit intending on a chair'" (120). Moreover, Caroline argues the necessity of having convictions instead of relinquishing control by letting circumstances govern our choices: "'There's never any knowing—which of our actions, which of our idlenesses won't have things hinging on it for ever'" (123). Caroline's resolve distinguishes her from the Herritons, from Sawston society, and allies her with the instinctive, passionate Gino, who is, in fact, the only character who readily intuits Caroline's exceptionality, deeming her, unlike any other woman of his acquaintance, "'simpatico'" (39). This compassion and indomitability are not portrayed as an eccentricity of Caroline's but as earnestness that counters the false pride of Sawston. In opposition to Mrs. Herriton's lies to her family and to herself about her motives for rescuing the baby, and without telling her father her real destination, Caroline journeys to Monteriano to further her notion of justice, defiantly explaining to Philip, "'If you are here to get the child, I will help you; if you are here to fail, I shall get it instead of you'" (86). Her singlemindedness is thus not caricatured as a narrow idée fixe but is commended as an effectual moral stance.

In the pivotal scene of the novel, in which Caroline sets out to convince Gino to relinquish the child but upon seeing Gino with his son is converted into Gino's advocate, Caroline's openness to new impressions erases her last traces of bigotry (chapter 7). Watching the father wash his son, she is humbled; father and son cease being a moral cause and recall her to their human bond. To Caroline, "This was something too remote from the prettiness of the nursery. The man was majestic; he was part of Nature; in no ordinary love scene could he ever be so great" (111). This scene on the loggia, when Philip approaches and sees the family assembled as "the Virgin and Child, with Donor," mocks Philip's impulse to aestheticize things and celebrates Caroline's ability to sanctify the mundane. Caroline's response to Gino, in turn, conditions Philip's acknowledgment that Gino's love for his son is a claim superior to the Herritons' pride. Caroline thus presents a vision to Philip that effects his conversion; Philip is awakened by the scene to the primal connections between human beings, and he recognizes the urgency of creating relationships with those we cherish.

Philip is made whole by realizing that Caroline has, indeed, transcended the banal Sawston existence and has ascended to inspiring heights of self-awareness and self-acceptance. Caroline's capacity for consoling, healing, and harmonizing people fills the emotional and spiritual void in Philip's life. His vision of her transforms her into a divine personage:

> All through the day Miss Abbott had seemed to Philip like a goddess, and more than ever did she seem so now. . . . Her eyes were open, full of infinite pity and full of majesty, as if they discerned the boundaries of sorrow, and saw unimaginable tracts beyond. Such eyes he had seen in great pictures but never in a mortal. . . . Philip looked away, as he sometimes looked away from the great pictures where visible forms suddenly become inadequate for the things they have shown to us. He was happy; he was assured there was greatness in the world. There came to him an earnest desire to be good through the example of this good woman. He would try henceforward to be worthy of the things she had revealed. Quietly, without hysterical prayers or banging of drums, he underwent conversion. He was saved. (138–39)

Philip's "interpretation" of Caroline is mediated through art; to him the "great picture" of Caroline holding the grieving Gino to her breast represents a noble ideal. While Philip perceives Caroline in secular terms as a goddess, he can comprehend Caroline's redemptive powers only through the vocabulary and iconography of Christianity. "Full of infinite pity and full of majesty," Caroline is figured as the Madonna, though not the Madonna of Philip's half-mocking tag to the earlier scene on the loggia, "Virgin and Child, with Donor." Now he sees before him the Madonna della Misericordia, the Mother of Mercy, which figures Caroline as a symbol of even more potent female power. This image of clemency, eventually declared heterodox by the church, "omitted Christ altogether and inspired veneration for the Virgin for her own sake, suggesting that her mercy, directly given, could save sinners" (Warner 327). Forster inspires awe for his heroine by alluding to this image which celebrates the "Virgin's autonomous sovereignty" (Warner 327–28). Less threatened by a powerful virgin than the church fathers were, Forster characterizes his heroine as an agent of salvation.

Caroline declines Philip's deification of her, however, resisting his impulse to desexualize and dehumanize her. Instead, she emphatically asserts her own humanness by unashamedly admitting her love and sexual desire for Gino. Declining to have it "legitimized" in a more exalted form, she boldly declares, "'I'm in love with Gino—don't pass it off—I mean it crudely—you know what I mean'" (145). And since she means sex, she demands that Philip "'get over supposing I'm refined. That's what puzzles you. Get over that'" (147). By flaunting her own corporeality, she paradoxically appears yet more superhuman to Philip, since her rejection of conventional morality makes her seem divine: "As he spoke she seemed to be transfigured, and to have indeed no part with refinement or unrefinement any longer. Out of this wreck there was revealed to him something indestructable—something which she, who had given it, could never take away" (147). Caroline has become whole through her encounter with Gino, and she, in turn, transmits the ideal of spiritual integrity to Philip.

The triangular romance between Gino, Caroline, and Philip should not be read as an emblem of frustrated desire, however, because each of these characters is "saved" by his or her love for the other. Forster's original title for the novel, *Rescue,* exemplifies how Forster uses everyday acts and secularized language to express his faith in the ability of individuals to be the salvation of their fellows.[2] While each of the actual "rescue" missions after Lilia and the baby is thwarted, Caroline and Philip are "saved" by the consoling embrace of another. The wounds of Gino and Philip are healed by Caroline, and Caroline finds consolation in the emotional bond she forms with Philip and Gino.

One of Forster's definitions of love, "emotional communion, this desire to give and get, this mixture of generosity and expectation" (*Aspects of the Novel* 51), is realized in the unconsummated romances in the novel. By positing an ideal of love in which the union is sanctified by emotional, rather than sexual, reciprocity, Forster creates an exemplary relationship in which those who remain unwed can achieve fulfillment. In this way, Forster represents an alternative to sexual love and invents a way in which singleness need not be construed as deprivation. Philip is transformed by the experience of his unrequited love for Caroline: "This episode, which she thought so sordid, and which was so tragic for him, remained supremely beautiful. To such a height was he lifted, that without regret he could now have told her that he was a worshipper too" (147–48). For her, the opportunity to confide her love for Gino to Philip is a consummation of sorts; hereafter she and Philip are joined in the pronoun "they," united in the task of saving Harriet from the bits of dirt which, literally and figuratively, fly in her eyes and obscure her vision as they travel homeward. In this act, the sacred quality of Caroline's generosity finds a practical outlet in Harriet, for now the love of Caroline and Philip, which does not exhaust itself in the beloved, extends toward and, ideally, envelops the unredeemed. Forster thus employs a form of narrative closure that exalts humane action rather than romantic conquest as a heroic ideal.

According to P. N. Furbank, E. M. Forster stopped writing novels after *A Passage to India* (1924) because "being a homosexual, he grew bored with writing about marriage and the relations of men and women" (2: 32). But *Where Angels Fear to Tread,* by redefining heroism as the ability to transfigure or spiritually enrich the life of another and by casting an old maid as a transcendent figure, is an innovative, if not radical, departure from the traditional plot, themes, and characterization of domestic romance. Moreover, Forster equates the spinster with figures of inspiring wisdom and redemptive power. Caroline Abbott's ability to heal wounds, save souls, and transfigure experience is expressly likened to the protective role of the Virgin Mary. But her role in the text, as the one who restores order and invests the life of those she encounters with fresh meanings, allies her with the author. In *Two Cheers for Democracy* (1951), Forster defends the value of art "because it has to do with order, and creates little worlds of its own, possessing internal harmony, in the bosom of this disordered planet" (59). In *Where Angels Fear to Tread,* the spinster is an artist whose vision of harmonious friendship restores order and creates a sanctuary within this disordered planet.

Charlotte Bartlett, the unwed heroine of *A Room with a View,* is also said to "have worked like a great artist" and, like Caroline Abbott, uses her artistry to usher others out of her own "cheerless, loveless world" into a world of beauty and love (78). Miss Bartlett appears to be Forster's caricature of an old maid, and on the manifest level of the narrative she is ridiculed. But while the pantheistic, sensualist Mr. Emerson is heralded as the champion of a union between his love-struck son George and Miss Bartlett's cousin and charge Lucy Honeychurch, Forster reveals through George Emerson that Charlotte should also be credited as an agent of romance. At the end of the novel, on their honeymoon in Florence, George speculates to Lucy "'that your cousin has always hoped. That from the very first moment we met, she hoped, far down in her mind, that we should be like this—of course, very far down. That she fought us on the surface, and yet she hoped'" (209). The phrase "far down in her mind," or at an unconscious level, indicates the psychological density with which Forster conceived Charlotte Bartlett. In fact, by giving Miss Bartlett centrality over the more conspicuously attractive figures of Lucy Honeychurch and Mr. Emerson in reading *A Room with a View,* one can see that by appearing to conform to the literary tradition of situating a seemingly inconsequential spinster on the periphery of the community of characters in the novel, Forster deflects notice away from the powerful agency of his unwed heroine. Instead of impeding the action in the novel or the growth of the heroine—as the old maid often does in nineteenth-century fiction and appears to do in this novel—Charlotte Bartlett actually mobilizes the plot, facilitates the romantic closure, and recuperates the value of love, beauty, and the sensual pleasure she professes to deplore.

The contradiction at the core of Charlotte Bartlett is expressed through her signal stance: apologetic self-assertion. Much of the comedy behind this character (and, historically, in stereotypical characterizations of spinsters) issues from her profuse efforts to accommodate everyone and, in so doing, cause inconvenience everywhere. But Charlotte Bartlett resists being genuinely inconsequential, unlike the sisters Alan who are summoned and dismissed at everyone's whim, by making inconsequence a force with which to reckon. When she arrives at the Honeychurches' without change for the driver's fare, for example, in a frenzy of self-effacement Charlotte makes herself the center of attention. (The success of her strategy, and of Forster's execution of it, can be gauged by how she remains much more vivid and memorable than almost any other character after we finish the novel.) Charlotte's paradoxical trait propels the plot of *A Room with a View:* she maneuvers Lucy's romance with George because her stated principles are undermined by her unconscious motives.

The narrative structure of *A Room with a View,* punctuated by "coincidental" encounters, justifies George's suspicion that his union with Lucy is the fulfillment of Charlotte's unconscious wish to make this match. One example of the propulsive effect on the plot of what appears to be merely another comic glimpse of Charlotte Bartlett occurs at the picnic when Charlotte relinquishes her mackintosh square to Lucy:

> "The ground will do for me. Really I have not had rheumatism for years. If I do feel it coming on I shall stand. Imagine your mother's feelings if I let you sit in the wet in your white linen." She sat down heavily where the ground looked particularly moist. "Here we are, all settled delightfully. Even if my dress is thinner it will not show so much, being brown. Sit down, dear; you are too unselfish; you don't assert yourself enough." She cleared her throat. "Don't be alarmed; this isn't a cold. It's the tiniest cough, and I have had it three days. It's nothing to do with sitting here at all." (66)

By criticizing Lucy for being too unselfish and for not asserting herself enough, Charlotte asserts her own selfish desire for the square and for the privacy of Miss Lavish's company, thereby manipulating Lucy into yielding them both to her; in acquiescing to Charlotte's demands, Lucy ends up in George's embrace. To what degree, one wonders, was Charlotte aware that by expelling Lucy from her company she might be propelling her into George's arms? The plot of *A Room with a View* is full of such "coincidences," which underscore the causal relationship between Charlotte's pretense of self-effacement and the accomplishment of Lucy's romance. A more circuitous instance is when Cecil reads aloud Eleanor Lavish's description of George and Lucy's kiss on the Italian hillside. Despite Charlotte's professed indignation at George's presumptuousness and the vow of silence she had extracted from Lucy, Charlotte had registered and recounted the scene at its full worth. After severing the bond between George and Lucy, she reconstructs and immortalizes it. Miss Lavish's novel, the product of two spinsters' voyeuristic enjoyment of youthful passion, regenerates that passion by inspiring George to recall the earlier embrace—and to repeat it.

The narrative structure of *A Room with a View*—the recollection or recurrence of several episodes featuring Miss Bartlett—also indicates that even the repressive presence of Charlotte Bartlett perpetuates the love between Lucy and George. When Lucy and George embrace on the hill in Fiesole, Charlotte's voice shatters the serenity of the moment, and she is a blight on the landscape: "The silence of life had been broken by Miss Bartlett, who stood brown against the view" (68). Later, back in England, Lucy takes her fiancé to "the Sacred Lake" where, Lucy recalls, "'I bathed here, too, till I was found out. Then there was a row.'" "'Who found you out?'" Cecils asks. "'Charlotte,' she murmured. 'She was stopping with us. Charlotte—Charlotte'" (107). Charlotte, who stops all pleasure when she stops with the Honeychurches, is invoked immediately before Cecil asks Lucy's permission for their first kiss. But the conjunction of Charlotte's name and Cecil's cool, clumsy kiss recalls George Emerson and forces Lucy to compare Cecil's formal courtship with George's spontaneous embrace. Charlotte, as the inhibiting figure in these recollected scenes, now inspires the leap in Lucy's imagination from the static English pond to the erotic Italian hillside. Lucy's memory is triggered by Charlotte, and the once repressive figure now awakens Lucy to her own passionate nature.

Finally, Charlotte acts as a monitory figure who steers Lucy away from her own solitary existence. Lucy's underestimation of her cousin's insightfulness, which the reader shares to some degree, is calculated by Charlotte Bartlett, whose circuitous discursive style also obscures the directness of her perceptions and motives. Lucy overlooks the complexity of her cousin when she misinterprets her as, "Happy Charlotte, who, though greatly troubled over things that did not matter, seemed oblivious to things that did; who could conjecture with admirable delicacy 'where things might lead to,' but apparently lost sight of the goal as she approached it" (55). Perhaps Charlotte intentionally creates in Lucy "the sensation of a fog" (12), for Charlotte seems to be clearer than Lucy about what matters and how to achieve it. Always in a flurry of ineffectual movement, Charlotte nevertheless penetrates to the motives behind Lucy's superficial gestures. For example, when Charlotte and Lucy flee from the Emersons to Rome, Lucy embraces Charlotte in a rush of affection, and the narrator remarks, "Miss Bartlett returned the embrace with tenderness and warmth. But she was not a stupid woman, and she knew perfectly well that Lucy did not love her, but needed her to love" (77). Immediately afterwards, simperingly apologetic, Charlotte retreats into "her favourite role, that of the prematurely aged martyr" (77).

The dialogue that follows, Charlotte's catalogue of her own inadequacies, appeared in "Old Lucy," the first draft of the novel, but what had prompted it in the earliest version was not Lucy's spontaneous affection but Lucy's unpleasantness: "But Lucy was very disagreeable and said so many unpleasant things that Miss Bartlett *was obliged to return to* the role that suited her best—that of the prematurely aged martyr" (emphasis added).[3] This passage implies that Charlotte was obliged to play the martyr because it was efficacious, and the phrase "the role that suited her best" could mean either that this role was the one in which she appeared to best advantage or, more likely, that it was the one that served her purposes most effectively. What is made explicit in the draft, but can only be inferred in the final version, is that Charlotte's martyrdom is a calculated foil to Lucy. By affecting martyrdom, Charlotte displays her most unlovable self, thus accomplishing her largely unconscious ambition of provoking Lucy's rejection of her.

Before Lucy can reject Charlotte's example, however, Lucy has to acknowledge their kinship. From the early drafts of *A Room with a View,* known as "Old Lucy" (1901–2) and "New Lucy" (1903), one can detect how Lucy and Charlotte, on the surface antithetical heroines, were conceived by Forster to have a certain similitude, a fundamental likemindedness, which makes the possibility of Lucy's repeating Charlotte's fate a more plausible threat. The plot of "Old Lucy" hinges on a more trivial incident than does *A Room with a View:* virtually confined within the pensione in Florence, Miss Bartlett offends Lucy by mistakenly assuming that Lucy had received a marriage proposal from the hero, Mr. Arthur. By implying that Lucy has stained her reputation by dallying with Mr. Arthur, Charlotte causes the quarrel which forces Lucy's departure to Rome. The pretext on which Lucy parts from Miss Bartlett is as flimsy as the story is trite, but this draft includes one remarkable scene, omitted from the final version, which reinforces the bond between the cousins. Describing Lucy's preparations for leaving, the narrator informs us, "When Lucy settled to <part from> /leave/ Miss Bartlett she did not realize when it would be most painful. The parting of the two ladies had nothing difficult in it. They rolled <asunder> /away/ like billiard balls. But the parting of their clothes was an excrutiating operation, similar to the rending asunder of live flesh" (67). The consanguinity of Miss Bartlett and Lucy is literalized in the clothing imagery, and a certain symbiosis is established by their divvying up umbrellas, Baedekers, and, since in this draft they share the same surname, handkerchiefs "all lettered B, who owned how <much> many?" (68). The common ownership of certain possessions symbolizes the mutual identification or potential interchangeability of the cousins. The narrator reflects that "Lucy never forgot the days she spent in Miss Bartlett's room, endeavouring to disentangle their clinging shrieking agonised bleeding clothes" (68). Not merely melodramatic overwriting, this sentence insists on the inseparability of the spritely young woman and the self-sacrificing spinster, an affinity which is suppressed in *A Room with a View* until Lucy's pledge of celibacy. In this more explicit version, Forster indicates that one kernel of his story is the kindred spirit binding these apparently antipathetic women.

In *A Room with a View,* Lucy despises Charlotte, but when she returns to England and becomes engaged to Cecil, she clearly has internalized Charlotte's bleak outlook. Defending Cecil's cynicism to her mother and trying to reconcile herself to him, Lucy resorts to a series of platitudes: "No one is perfect, and surely it is wiser to discover the imperfections before wedlock," to which the narrator remarks, "Miss Bartlett, in deed, though not in word, had taught the girl that this our life contains nothing satisfactory" (134–35). After Lucy breaks her engagement to Cecil, Mrs. Honeychurch cautions Lucy that she resembles cousin Charlotte in "'the same eternal worrying, the same taking back of words'" (193). To cast such a pall over the vivacious Lucy, "[Miss Bartlett] had worked like a great artist; for a time—indeed, for years—she had been meaningless, but at the end there was presented to the girl the complete picture of a cheerless, loveless world in which the young rush to destruction until they learn better—a shamefaced world of precautions and barriers which may avert evil, but which do not bring good, if we may judge from those who have used them most" (78–79). Before the point of view in this passage shifts from Lucy to the narrator, Lucy experiences Cousin Charlotte as "a great artist" in her portrayal of life as dismal and hazardous. Indeed, Lucy allies herself with Charlotte Bartlett, according to the narrator, by denying her love for George:

> She gave up trying to understand herself, and joined the vast armies of the benighted, who follow neither the heart nor the brain, and march to their destiny by catch-words. The armies are full of pleasant and pious folk. But they have yielded to the only enemy that matters—the enemy within. They have sinned against passion and truth, and vain will be their strife after virtue. . . .

> Lucy entered this army when she pretended to George that she did not love him, and pretended to Cecil that she loved no one. The night received her, as it had received Miss Bartlett thirty years before. (174)

Lucy dissolves into Forster's famous "muddle" because she denies the truth of her own emotions. But if Charlotte is the one who had recruited Lucy as a self-deceiving sinner, Charlotte's own perception of the truth saves Lucy from "the enemy within." Charlotte's real artistry lies in her presenting an image of the world—by whispering precautions and erecting barriers—that eventually inspires Lucy to defect from "the vast armies of the benighted" and to extinguish the Charlotte Bartlett within herself.

Here the novel begins to work in two directions: while Forster characterizes Charlotte Bartlett as a querulous prude the passionate Lucy must repudiate, Forster also dramatizes that it is the inhibited spinster's intuition and vicarious enjoyment of Lucy's sensual desires that facilitate the consummation of romantic love. To reunite Lucy with George, Charlotte has to commit a sacrifice of self: she must admit her own errors of judgment, her own shortcomings, and the unsuitability of her own benighted existence for Lucy. At the same time Charlotte had been drawing Lucy into the darkness of her own existence, the spirit Lucy exhibits, which had been dormant in Charlotte for thirty years, has been roused. George later observes to Lucy that Charlotte had reunited them by ushering Lucy into the Reverend Beebe's study to encounter Mr. Emerson because "'the sight of us haunted—or she couldn't have described us as she did to her friend. There are details—it burnt. I read [Miss Lavish's] book afterwards. She is not frozen, Lucy, she is not withered up all through'" (209). Even if Charlotte is a compendium of catchwords and lies, beneath it all, George insists, she sees the truth and "'far down in her heart, far below all speech and behavior, she is glad'" (209). "Below all speech and behavior," in her unconscious actions, Charlotte does express generosity and compassion. The ending of the novel implies that by facilitating Lucy and George's union, Charlotte has achieved the ideal exalted beyond even love in the novel: truth. Mr. Emerson voices the principles that we can only infer Charlotte has apprehended: "'We fight for more than Love or Pleasure: there is truth. Truth counts, Truth does count'" (204). By steering Lucy toward Mr. Emerson, Charlotte also enables Lucy to acknowledge what Mr. Emerson calls "the holiness of direct desire" (204), which Charlotte had learned from the example of Lucy and George. At the same time that Charlotte Bartlett is "perhaps Forster's greatest comic creation" (Cavaliero 94)—and we do enjoy wincing at her every accommodating self-denial—she also achieves nobility as a heroine, because she musters the self-knowledge and generosity to transform her unconscious wish for Lucy's happiness into a conscious act.

An interesting piece of evidence that Forster knew Miss Bartlett would be misunderstood but intended her to be credited with largess surfaces fifty years after the publication of the novel in Forster's cynical account of the subsequent lives of his characters entitled "A View with No Room." Forster reports that "Miss Bartlett left [the George Emersons] with what she termed her little all. (Who would have thought it of Cousin Charlotte? I should never have thought anything else.)" (210). Charlotte's self-deprecating act of generosity, the common underestimation of Charlotte, and the author's superior conviction in his character's unwavering generosity reinforce the subtle execution of Charlotte Bartlett's heroism in *A Room with a View.*

Forster's characterization of unmarried women in the novels served as a working through of those tensions that we may too hastily assume were disabling to a young man raised within a community of women. By the time he wrote *Marianne Thornton,* Forster was able to steer himself directly to the essence of his feelings for those humane, unconventional, self-possessed women who Forster believed "had paid homage to the complexity of life."[4] In so doing, he reconceived the unmarried woman—in life and in literature—as a purposive and inspiriting figure and recast her in the role of the heroic spinster.

NOTES

1. Glen Cavaliero, for example, argues that Forster "used the domestic background which threatened him as a man to establish himself as an artist." But he then retracts this theory and argues, conversely, that "Forster has been castigated for not breaking free from maternal bonds; but at the deep level of artistic conscience he may have known that he was right to stay with them" (59).

Oliver Stallybrass speculates that one of Forster's letters, explaining that he had cancelled a trip to Greece because of his mother, reveals that Forster's characterization of Charlotte Bartlett in an early draft of *A Room with a View* is "among other things a projection of his resentment, tinged with self-contempt, at his continuing failure to detach himself from his mother's apron-strings!" (Introduction, *Lucy Novels* 85).

2. Stallybrass, Introduction, *Where Angels Fear to Tread* ix. John Colmer explains Forster's pervasive use of religious diction in the novels as "an expression of that widespread attempt in a secular age to invest life with meaning and significance by using religious terminology to describe heightened states of being. . . . At moments of intense emotion or as the result of visionary experiences, Forster's characters are granted a view that transfigures the details of ordinary life" (57).

3. E. M. Forster, "Old Lucy," *Lucy Novels* 49. In quoting from the manuscripts, I followed Stallybrass's practice of including both the words deleted and those included in the various manuscript versions of the novel.

4. Philip Herriton's observation about Caroline Abbott in *Where Angels Fear to Tread* (89).

WORKS CITED

Cavaliero, Glen. *A Reading of E. M. Forster.* London: Macmillan, 1979.

Colmer, John. *E. M. Forster: The Personal Voice.* London: Routledge and Kegan Paul, 1975.

Forster, E.[dward] M.[organ]. *Aspects of the Novel.* New York: Harcourt, Brace and World, 1927.

———. *Howard's End.* Abinger edition of E. M. Forster, vol. 4. Ed. Oliver Stallybrass. London: Edward Arnold, 1973.

———. *Marianne Thornton: A Domestic Biography.* New York: Harcourt, Brace, 1956.

———. "New Lucy." *The Lucy Novels: Early Sketches for A Room with a View.* Abinger edition of E. M. Forster, vol. 3a. Ed. Oliver Stallybrass. London: Edward Arnold, 1977.

———. "Old Lucy." *The Lucy Novels.* Abinger edition of E. M. Forster, vol. 3a.

———. *A Room with a View.* Abinger edition of E. M. Forster, vol. 3. Ed. Oliver Stallybrass. London: Edward Arnold, 1977.

———. "A View with No Room." *Observer* and *New York Times Book Review* July 27, 1958. Rpt. as appendix, Abinger edition of *Room.*

———. *Two Cheers for Democracy.* Arbinger edition of E. M. Forster, vol. 2. Ed. Oliver Stallybrass. London: Edward Arnold, 1972.

———. *Where Angels Fear to Tread.* Abinger edition of E. M. Forster, vol. 1. Ed. Oliver Stallybrass. London: Edward Arnold, 1975.

Furbank, P. N. *E. M. Forster: A Life.* 2 vols. New York: Harcourt Brace Jovanovich, 1977.

Stallybrass, Oliver. Introduction. *The Lucy Novels.* Abinger edition of E. M. Forster, vol. 3a.

———. Introduction. *Where Angels Fear to Tread.* Abinger edition of E. M. Forster, vol. 1.

Warner, Marina. *Alone of All Her Sex: The Myth and the Cult of the Virgin Mary.* New York: Vintage, 1976.

Sybil Oldfield

From Rachel's Aunts to Miss La Trobe: Spinsters in the Fiction of Virginia Woolf

No twentieth-century woman writer had greater cause to praise spinsters than had Virginia Woolf: the motherless daughter found alternative mothers and positive life-models among single women right up to her death. But Virginia Woolf's creative life between 1910 and 1940 coincided with a *Zeitgeist* that became increasingly contemptuous and hostile toward spinsters,[1] and there is a corresponding tension in her fiction between her desire to do justice to her own life-enabling relationships with single women and her, perhaps unconscious, temptation to collude with the currently dominant negative stereotype.

The first "significant spinster" in young Virginia Stephen's life was her forty-year-old Greek teacher, Janet Case. "How I loved her, at Hyde Park Gate, and how I went hot and cold going to Windmill Hill; and how great a visionary part she played in my life, till the visionary became a part of the fiction, not of the real life" (*Diary*, July 19, 1937). Not only did Janet Case introduce Virginia Stephen to Sophocles' *Antigone*, the foundation text of her lifelong antimilitarism, but she also spurred her former pupil to participate in feminist political struggle.[2] Janet Case grew into a significant, lifelong friend: "No-one, not Leonard even, knows how much I have to thank Janet for" (Letter to Margaret Llewelyn Davies, July 11, 1937). "[To] sit by her side when she knew that death was near was to be taught once more a last lesson, in gaiety, courage, and love."[3]

Even more emotionally necessary to the young Virginia Stephen was Violet Dickinson, the generous, stable, protective Quaker aristocrat whom Virginia Stephen called "My Woman" in letter after letter between 1902 and 1908. It was Violet Dickinson who best helped her recover from her second suicidal breakdown, in 1904, and who then encouraged her to write and found a publishing outlet for her earliest literary essays.[4] And it was typhoid-stricken Violet Dickinson to whom Virginia Stephen lied about Thoby's recovery to keep her closest friend alive: "We want you more and more. I never knew till this happened how I should turn to you and want you with me when no-one else could help . . . I think of you as one of the people . . . who make it worth while to live and be happy" (Letter, December 18, 1906).

Yet another influential, although much older, spinster was Leslie Stephen's Quaker sister, Caroline, at whose quiet, Cambridge home Virginia Stephen would hear eloquent and sometimes profound talk about the private soul and the public world. "One could not be with her without feeling that after suffering and thought she had come to dwell apart, among the things which are unseen and eternal and that it was her perpetual wish to make others share her peace."[5] The irreverent niece would often laugh at her aunt, "the Quaker trumpeting like an escaped elephant on the stairs" (Letter to Violet Dickinson, October 22, 1904), but she could also find herself admitting that this same aunt, nicknamed "Nun," was "a kind of modern prophetess, . . . charming and wise and humane . . . a remarkable woman I always feel when I see her" (Letters to Madge Vaughan and Violet Dickinson, July 2, 1906). It was Caroline Stephen, author of *Quaker Strongholds* and *The Light Arising,* who bequeathed to her niece the income for a "room of [her] own."

Finally in this early period, and less positive though also important, was young Virginia Stephen's close encounter with the forceful spinster Mary Sheepshanks, then acting principal of Morley College, who engaged her as a voluntary worker to teach evening classes to working men and women between 1905 and 1907. Mary Sheepshanks was an extraordinarily able, trenchant feminist and educationist, who, despite feeling Virginia Stephen's irresistible charm, did not scruple to criticize her protégée's wilder flights of fantasy substituting for history: "Sheepshanks showed wolf's fangs" (Letter to Violet Dickinson, June 29, 1905). Unfortunately, Mary Sheepshanks was going through a particularly dark period in her life just then, and Virginia Stephen's own vulnerability to manic depression made her fiercely allergic to the older woman's self-pity and self-hate. Nevertheless, she still had reason to be grateful to Mary Sheepshanks, both for giving her a function when she was feeling rudderless and for introducing her to a world that she otherwise would never have encountered—the world of ardent but undereducated working-class men and women.

This profound and variegated personal debt to spinsters at the outset of Virginia Stephen's writing life was reinforced by her reading. Her earliest review essays show her constructing an inner chronology of eighteenth- and nineteen-century literary women, including Anna Seward, Elizabeth Carter, Lady Hester Stanhope, Elizabeth Hitchener, Dorothy Wordsworth, Jane Austen, Maria

Edgeworth, the Brontës, and Christina Rossetti. It was these English literary spinsters who (together, of course, with Elizabeth Barrett Browning, George Eliot, and Elizabeth Gaskell) made Virginia Stephen feel less isolated.[6]

Working against all that positive firsthand experience, whether actual or literary, of strongly individual, gifted, and intensely feeling single women was the negative popular stereotype of the spinster that was current just then. "Spinsters had to face the fact that they were a nuisance to everybody, because there was no provision for them to be independent of a man's help in an economy set up by males for males."[7] No provision, that is, for upper-middle-class females. It was axiomatic that such women were life-denied and therefore life-denying. It was above all for her *barrenness* that the spinster was found wanting before World War I. During that age of rival imperialisms when young males were soon to be hurled at one another till their death, it was vital to maintain the supply of young.[8] The most "advanced" theorists of sexology were stressing the procreative function of women to the exclusion of any other. "Woman's special sphere is the bearing and rearing of children."[9] "Procreation is their proper element."[10] Childless spinsters were nothing more than the "waste products of our female population."[11] "What is the good of all these spinsters?" asked young Rebecca West in *The Freewoman,* July 11, 1912. No wonder some single women became convinced of their own worthlessness and malignancy. "The spinster . . . is the failure, the barren sister, the withered tree, . . . our social nemesis," wrote a spinster in the first number of *The Freewoman,* November 23, 1911. In literature, Granville Barker's six Miss Huxtables in *The Madras House* (1912), E. M. Forster's beetle-like Charlotte Bartlett in *A Room with a View* (1908), and his Harriet Herriton who actually destroys a baby in *Where Angels Fear to Tread* (1905) are typical. Only the spinster novelist F. M. Mayor dug deeper and found in her *Third Miss Symons* (1913) not the unloving, petty-minded spinster of caricature but a truly tragic human being, wasted because not wanted.[12]

Where then did Virginia Stephen stand in her portrayal of middle-aged and elderly single women in her first novel, *The Voyage Out,* begun in 1907 and redrafted many times while she herself was still a single woman? Spinsters play such a minor part in *The Voyage Out* that their presence has often been overlooked altogether. Indeed, Virginia Woolf's own vagueness about Rachel's aunts is mirrored in her uncertainty about what to call them—Aunt Bessie in chapter 1 becomes Aunt Lucy and Aunt Eleanor in chapter 2, then

Aunt Lucy and Aunt Katie in chapter 14, and finally Aunt Lucy and Aunt Clara in chapter 16. What matters about the aunts is not their individuality but their corporate being, expressing shared values in a shared life. At first that shared life is rendered unsympathetically. They have brought up their niece "with excessive care," protecting her from any knowledge of sex, and Aunt Lucy is caricatured for "her nervous hen-like twitter of a laugh" as she evades Rachel's questioning about her feelings (ch. 11). From that episode Rachel learned a negative and depressing lesson: "It appeared that nobody ever said a thing they meant, or ever talked of a feeling they felt" (ch. 11). In other words, the aunts had transmitted a fear of the emotional life and, instead of sincerity, had taken refuge in meaningless proprieties of word and deed—a typical "old maidish" inheritance. Their trivial, nondescript lives are further evoked in chapter 11: "They are probably buying wool. . . . They tidy their drawers a good deal."

A hundred pages later, Rachel, and therefore her creator and the reader as well, suddenly see these same aunts in a quite different light—their lives become serious and worthy of respect. Challenged by her lover, Terence Hewet, to try to describe what he calls "the curious silent unrepresented life" of women that had been "going on in the background all these thousands of years" while the man's view got represented instead, Rachel has something of a revelation as she ponders the life of her aunts:

> They were very much afraid of her father. . . . He was good-humoured towards them, but contemptuous. . . . She had always taken it for granted that his point of view was just, and founded upon an ideal scale of things where the life of one person was absolutely more important than the life of another, and that in that scale they were of much less importance than he was. But did she really believe that? . . . it was her aunts who influenced her really. . . . She reviewed their little journeys to and from Walworth, to charwomen with bad legs, to meetings for this and that, their minute acts of charity and unselfishness which flowered punctually from a definite view of what they ought to do, their friendships, their tastes and habits; she saw all these things like grains of sand falling, falling through innumerable days, making an atmosphere and building up a solid mass, a background. . . . And there's a sort of beauty in it—there they are at Richmond at this very moment building things up. . . . It's so unconscious, so modest. And yet they feel things. They do mind if people die. Old spinsters are always doing things . . . it [is] very real. (ch. 16)

Through reviewing and revaluing her aunts in this way, Rachel frees herself from being dominated by a conventionally patriarchal, utilitarian point of view, articulating instead the primacy of the inner life and its web of affections and obligations—"it was her aunts who influenced her really."

Rachel's aunts live several thousand miles away from the main action of *The Voyage Out*, but in the foreground of the novel there is another modest-but-real, civilized-because-kind spinster—the fifty-year-old English teacher, Miss Allan, with her sturdy climbing legs and pleasant, heavily lined face. She and her sister (left behind in England) have had to be the strong ones in their family, supporting the financial failure of a brother without allowing that fact of life to make them either bitter or self-pitying. Unlike Rachel's aunts, the Allans' lives are not restricted to the private sphere. Miss Allan wears a Suffrage Society button, and her sister succinctly reports to her in a letter giving the latest news from that struggle: "Political prospects *not* good, I think privately, but do not like to damp Ellen's enthusiasm. Lloyd George has taken the Bill up, but so have many before now, and we are where we are; but trust to find myself mistaken. Anyhow we have our work cut out for us . . . " (ch. 14). Miss Allan's "we" here, of course, refers to all the "excellent women"—energetic and politically aware, crusading for their right to citizenship.

Why is Miss Allan in this novel at all? She is totally unlike Rachel in her definiteness of both task and point of view, yet Rachel suddenly yearns to get close to her "for it seemed possible that each new person might remove the mystery which burdened her" (ch. 19). But they never do get close despite all Miss Allan's intelligence, humor, and real goodwill. She had been schooled by her hard life into reticence, and since the younger woman is inarticulate for other reasons, "there was nothing to be done but to drift past each other in silence" (ch. 19). Miss Allan thus contributes her mite to the novel's theme of the (near) impossibility of human communication. At one point Miss Allan even becomes, unjustly, one of the many people exemplifying for Rachel the meaninglessness of life. But at the end of the novel it is the pointless, premature death of Rachel herself that converts Miss Allan to a recognition of the meaninglessness of human effort. She, whose whole lifework has been to transmit what she had cared for to younger minds, had looked to the Rachels to continue for her. But now "she felt very old this morning, and useless too, as if her life had been a failure, as if it had been hard and laborious to no purpose. She did not want to go on living. . . . There did not seem to be much point in it at all, one went on, of course one went on . . . " (ch. 26). Virginia Woolf's depiction of English spinsters in *The Voyage Out* thus evolves from initial cliché and condescension to an acknowledgment of their depth in "Souls that appear to have no depth at all / To vulgar eyes."[13]

The main characters in Virginia Woolf's second novel, *Night and Day* (1919), are two spinsters in their late twenties whose repeated question to themselves is: "To marry or not to marry?" or, conversely, "To stay single or not to stay single?" There did seem to be a particularly drastic life-choice that had to be made by educated women in the years just preceding World War I—either an independent life entirely given over to one's chosen work or marriage.[14] To Virginia Woolf's Katherine Hilberry, however, the situation at first looked rather different since she was one of the last survivors of nineteenth-century upper-class daughterhood: "[She] was a member of a very great profession which has, as yet, no title and very little recognition. . . . She lived at home. She did it very well, too" (ch. 3).

Not only is Katherine responsible for all the household affairs but she has to be the parent of her own mother, Mrs. Hilberry, who "would have been perfectly able to sustain herself if the world had been what the world is not" (ch. 3). For Katherine, therefore, continued single life means an indefinitely extended daughterhood: "We are daughters until we become married women."[15] The prospect is so unfulfilling that she actually allows herself to become engaged to an uncongenial, conventional-minded dilettante simply "to have a house of my own" (ch. 16). She breaks off that false commitment to spurious "independence," having realized that what she really wants is not to marry anyone but "to go away by herself, preferably to some bleak northern moor, and there study mathematics and the science of astronomy" (ch. 18). She envies her friend Mary Datchet for "living alone and having your own things" and for being engaged—without an engagement ring (ch. 21). By the end of this (very long) novel, however, Katherine is so overpowered by passionate love that she decides to share her loneliness with Ralph Denham, promising to marry him. Whether that passion will turn out to be compatible with her first passion for mathematics and astronomy we never learn.

The other spinster, Mary Datchet, is a more original character in literary history in that she is one of the first women in English fiction whose work is her absorbing interest in life. She "liked to think herself one of the workers . . . winding up the world to tick for another four-and-twenty hours. . . . She felt . . . that she was the centre ganglion of a very fine network of nerves which fell over England" (ch. 3). Mary Datchet also comes to know passionate love (also for Ralph Denham), but she acknowledges it to herself only when it is too late. So far, so conventional—the spinster has to renounce personal happiness. But that is not the end of Mary Datchet. Despite feeling barren and intolerably alone, she turns herself into a full-time professional political worker for radical social reform and discovers that work, rather than love, is truly her salvation. What is still more original is this portrayal of Mary's transformation from an unfledged young woman into a "serviceable human being" is that she comes to make the astonishing discovery that she does not love Ralph anymore (ch. 31), thus finishing off the fictional cliché of the spinster with a permanent, unassuageable, secret affair of the heart. Mary actually pities Katherine Hilberry for not being able to see what she herself now feels to be the unromantic truth about Ralph Denham.

There are two things missing from Virginia Woolf's portrayal of Mary Datchet, however, which prevent it from being a great landmark in the literary history of the spinster. First, there is no precise, vivid re-creation of what Mary's political work really means to her. Why does she have to be so actively committed to the struggle for adult suffrage? What sort of England is it that she dreams may be born out of her movement for democratic radical reform and the taxation of land values? The trouble is that although Virginia Woolf had very considerable respect for "public women" like Margaret Llewelyn Davies and Pippa Strachey—of whom Mary Datchet may be a younger version—she could never wholeheartedly share their total commitment to political action or political organization. One is reminded of George Eliot's letter to Mrs. P. A. Taylor in July 1878, where she declares, "My function is that of the aesthetic, not the doctrinal teacher . . . not the prescribing of special measures."[16] Mary Datchet's hardheaded, reformist political activism was precisely the kind of work that Virginia Woolf could not render convincingly from the inside. Second, for whatever reason, Virginia Woolf does not allow Mary to have what so many of the outstanding women of the early twentieth century did have—a longstanding "marriage of true minds" with another woman.[17] Mary's emotional depth and complexity are thereby diminished. Perhaps the basic problem with Mary, however, is that she shares with every other character in *Night and Day* a certain lack of vitality, symptomatic, very possibly, of the author's incomplete psychological recovery between 1917 and 1919 after her severe mental breakdown. We are told, not shown, that Mary Datchet is sane and pleasant, strong and gentle; but she never possesses her own characteristic "voice," whether silent or speaking. It is not enough to be told to look up at Mary—in both senses of the phrase—working away at her papers in her lonely lamplit room.

Mrs. Dalloway (1925) is a much more successful novel than *Night and Day,* but its most memorable spinster is hardly a positive life-model. We first meet Miss Kilman through the eyes of Clarissa Dalloway, who can see nothing in her daughter's history tutor but a hideously ugly, bitter, hard-done-by humbug of a religious zealot in a smelly raincoat. Miss Kilman is feared and hated by Clarissa partly because of her influence over Clarissa's daughter and partly because she undermines Clarissa's ability to like herself. One hundred pages later Miss Kilman is allowed her point of view about Clarissa, but it does not win us over to her side. Miss Kilman is ruthlessly reductive in her judgmental assumption of social and moral superiority: "[Mrs. Dalloway] came from the most worthless of all classes—the rich with a smattering of culture" (136). Since we have learned by now that there is a complex, vulnerable human being underneath Clarissa's veneer of the society lady, Miss Kilman's condemnation falls to the ground, blunt edged and harmless. Clarissa Dalloway is not "worthless"; it is the judges of "worthlessness" who need a wide berth. True, Miss Kilman had once suffered real social persecution because of her integrity—her refusal on principle to join in German-baiting or in denying her own German extraction during World War I—but now she is incapable of any honesty about herself or others. She tells herself that she does not envy Clarissa, but she is corroded with envy; she tells herself that she pities Clarissa, while all the time she is really longing to make her suffer: "If she could have felled her it would have eased her. But it was not the body; it was the soul and its mockery that she wished to subdue; make her feel her mastery. If only she could make her weep; could ruin her; humiliate her; bring her to her knees crying, 'You are right!'" (138).[18]

Her name notwithstanding, it is not men Miss Kilman hates but another woman—the mother of her beloved pupil. Miss Kilman plays the same role in Clarissa Dalloway's life that Dr. Bradshaw plays in the life of Septimus Smith. Both of them endanger the sacred "privacy of the soul" with their need to bend others to their will. The reader is relieved to learn that seventeen-year-old Elizabeth Dalloway is not in fact possessed in spirit by praying sessions with Doris Kilman, as her mother fears, but breaks free. The repulsive sight of Miss Kilman fingering the last two inches of a chocolate éclair, opening her mouth to swallow it down, then wiping her fingers, and washing the tea around in her cup is not mitigated by her agony at feeling herself repulsive to Elizabeth at that moment (145). It is not enough, it seems, for a fictional character to suffer for a reader to feel sympathy; only something positively endearing, however slight, can elicit that, and there is nothing endearing about Miss Kilman. There are other spinsters in *Mrs. Dalloway*—old Miss Perry with her one glass eye, formerly an intrepid explorer botanizing in the Himalayas; Milly Brush, Lady Bruton's devoted companion always in the background; Ellie Henderson, the pathetic, odd-woman-out at Clarissa's party. But the spinster one remembers, the "archetypal spinster," is Miss Kilman sweating in her green mackintosh.

How vital is it to the characterization of Doris Kilman that she is a spinster? Unfortunately, it would seem that at this particular point in her writing Virginia Woolf did endorse the vulgar consensus: because ugly in body, a spinster; because a spinster, ugly in soul. It is not unfeminist to portray a hate-filled woman with a need for power, but it is unfeminist to portray such characteristics as the necessary product of heterosexual failure. Miss Kilman felt that she had begun "with this indignity—the infliction of her unlovable body which people could not bear to see. Do her hair as she might, her forehead remained like an egg, bald, white. No clothes suited her. She might buy anything. And for a woman, of course, that meant never meeting the opposite sex. Never would she come first with any one" (142). Hence her other appetites—for power and for food. It is an all-too-vivid rendering of an unpleasant stereotype that was becoming more and more powerful.

Sheila Jeffreys places this increasing hostility toward spinsters within an ideological context of intensifying antifeminism during the 1920s:

> The sexologists assumed that there was a sexual instinct or drive and that if this instinct did not find its appropriate outlet in sexual intercourse, then women would suffer from "repression" and "thwarted instincts," which would cause them to be "bitter," "man-hating," "destructive," "fanatical," "kill-joys," a "threat to civilisation.". . . [Ludovici's *Lysistrata or Woman's Future* (1924)] was concerned about "surplus women," the 2 million women in excess of men in the pop-

> ulation in Britain. He feared that, because these "surplus women" had not access to sexual satisfaction with men, the women's "thwarted instincts" would find some destructive outlet. . . . The dangerous effects of "thwarting" the "instincts" according to Ludovici was that women would compensate with the "lust of exercising power" . . . woman movements were "largely led either by spinsters or else by unhappy married women."[19]

Perhaps the blatantly antifeminist animus in such attacks on the spinster enlightened Virginia Woolf. Perhaps she convicted herself of bad faith toward all the beloved single women in her own life. Perhaps she was influenced by the contrast with a very different fictional spinster, Mary Jocelyn, the heroine of *The Rector's Daughter* by F. M. Mayor, which she and Leonard had just published at the Hogarth Press in 1924. (Rosamond Lehmann was to call Mary Jocelyn "a kind of touchstone for feminine dignity, intelligence and truthfulness.")[20] For whatever reason, Virginia Woolf was never to pillory a spinster qua spinster again. But she was, very briefly, tempted.

The holograph manuscript of *To the Lighthouse* (1927) reveals that Virginia Woolf's first idea for her artist/observer of the Ramsays was to have been a fifty-five-year-old, "rather fluttered," "old maid," named Miss Sophie Briscoe, who had "spent much of her life sketching" nice hedgerows and thatched cottages.[21] The very next page of the holograph (dated September 3, 1925), however, substitutes a *thirty-three-year-old* Lily Briscoe, who, though humble, does not absolutely abase herself before Mr. Ramsay's mental powers and for whom the struggle to paint is a serious matter. Indeed, as Lyndall Gordon has pointed out, it is Lily Briscoe's consciousness that finally comes to dominate the whole novel.[22] We cannot be certain just why there was a metamorphosis from feeble butt to independent-minded, creative, loving analyst. Possibly it was through her sister and her sister's friends (including the unmarried women painters Carrington, Brett, Nan Hudson, and Ethel Sands) that Virginia Woolf had come to know too many women seriously committed to their painting for her to be comfortable about patronizing a lady sketching prettily at her easel.[23] Would she not be colluding with the Charles Tansleys of this world: "Women can't paint, women can't write"?[24]

Virginia Woolf needed a "real" artist, however unrecognized, to raise the question of how to represent truth about life and the relationship between things in a formally satisfying way. She also wanted to include her own, daughter-as-adult's response to the Ramsays. Lily therefore had to be young enough to be Mrs. Ramsay's daughter but old enough to be free of her domination.

Lily Briscoe wins the reader's trust as a reliable interpreter from the moment we are inside her. We relish her humor that keeps the alarming aberrations of a waving, shouting Mr. Ramsay in proportion; we respect her intense concentration on what she is trying to paint—"looking, straining, till the colour . . . burnt into her eyes"—and we recognize her honesty in not tampering with the unfashionable vividness of what she sees (pt. 1, sec. 4). We know her to be intelligent and loving, and "skimpy Lily Briscoe," "poor Lily Briscoe" is therefore not skimpy or poor at all. It is Lily who perceives that Mr. Ramsay is wearing his wife to death, Lily who recognizes that his egotism, constantly ministered to, has made him a tyrant, Lily who identifies and frees herself from Mrs. Ramsay's powerful will, Lily who senses when Mrs. Ramsay is drained and needing help at the dinner party, Lily who is sensitive to the tragedy of the younger children beaten down emotionally by their cormorant father, and Lily, the survivor, who is left to ask, "What does it mean then, what can it all mean?" (pt. 3, sec. 1).

Lily Briscoe had to be a spinster for two reasons. First, Virginia Woolf was able to invert the usual negative, clichéd concomitant of spinsterhood—the spinster's lack of relationship with a man—and to concentrate instead on Lily's positive preoccupation with a woman. Second, by juxtaposing the childless artist Lily and the fertile mother Mrs. Ramsay, Virginia Woolf could, very simply, demonstrate that there is more than one kind of creative lifework for a woman.

What Lily herself feels for Mrs. Ramsay is both the motherless daughter's aching loss and the grown woman's desire to be one with another woman. She is both child and would-be lover as she sits on the floor, "with her arms around Mrs. Ramsay's knees, close as she could get, smiling to think that Mrs. Ramsay would never know the reason of that pressure," longing for intimacy (pt. 3, sec. 6).[25] One of the most poignant and probably most piercingly autobiographical passages Virginia Woolf ever wrote renders Lily's desolation and emptiness as she allows herself to feel at last the full impact of Mrs. Ramsay's death: "To want and not to have, sent all up her body a hardness, a hollowness, a strain. And then to want and not to have—to want and want—how that wrung the heart and wrung it again! Oh Mrs Ramsay! she called out silently, to that essence which sat by the boat, that abstract one made of her, that woman in grey. . . . 'Mrs Ramsay!' she said aloud, 'Mrs Ramsay!' The tears ran down her face" (pt. 3, sec. 6).

But another part of Lily Briscoe, the part that "liked to be alone . . . liked to be herself" (pt. 1, sec. 9), has to stand up to Mrs. Ramsay, resist her magnetic will to pull her into the vortex of marriage, and instead keep herself to her other passion, the compulsion to paint—"the one thing one did not play at" (pt. 3, sec. 2). The novel ends with Lily's consummation. For a second she sees it clearly, draws a last unifying stroke in the center, and then lays down her brush in exhaustion, having had her vision. In fact, Lily has had not one vision but a series of visions, all connected with Mrs. Ramsay and all needing Lily's unique power to see. First, she had seen how life, made up of little separate incidents which one lived one by one, became curled and whole like a wave (pt. 1, sec. 9). Then followed her rapt contemplation of William Bankes's adoration of Mrs. Ramsay's beauty, a rapture so self-authenticating and sublime that it temporarily silenced all Lily's questioning about life: "It was love, she thought, . . . distilled and filtered; love that never attempted to clutch its object; but, like the love which mathematicians bear their symbols, or poets their phrases, was meant to be spread over the world and become part of the human gain" (pt. 1, sec. 9). At that moment Lily Briscoe exemplified what the philosopher G. E. Moore meant when he wrote "the appreciation of a person's attitude towards other persons, . . . to take one instance, the love of love, is far the most valuable good we know."[26] Lily Briscoe tried to express her sense of Mrs. Ramsay's beauty, her mysterious, solid, comforting mass, through a purple triangular shape on her canvas, a shape that corresponds, one feels, to what Mrs. Ramsay herself had felt to be her innermost identity—her "wedge-shaped core of darkness" (pt. 1, sec. 2). After Mrs. Ramsay's death, Lily realizes that Mrs. Ramsay had in fact managed to give shape to life, "making of the moment something permanent, . . . [creating] little daily miracles, illuminations," which instead of the great revelation, are all that we can hope to have (pt. 3, sec. 4). Out of her great love and her great need, Lily manages to summon Mrs. Ramsay back from the dead; she sees her once again sitting in her chair by the step and is able to finish the picture. By not succumbing to Mrs. Ramsay's "Marry, marry," little Brisk has held fast her own creative vision and given Mrs. Ramsay herself a kind of immortality.

The Pargiters: A Novel Essay, begun in October 1932 and abandoned the following February, contains the two "lost" spinsters of Virginia Woolf's fiction, Eleanor Pargiter and Lucy Craddock. It might seem that the former was not lost at all since she becomes one of the main characters in *The Years* (1937), but there are far too many other characters in *The Years* and far too many fragmented snatches of their thoughts and inconsequential talk for Eleanor Pargiter to emerge—for this reader at least—as anything more than a dimly sensed stalwart "presence." In chapter 1 of *The Pargiters*, however, Eleanor had been given vivid imaginative life. Her inner voice was far more emphatic in that first version. The sentence "'Delia is a selfish little pig' Eleanor [thought]" (ch. 1) is deleted in *The Years*, and her forceful "She did wish people wouldn't" in *The Pargiters* (ch. 1) later becomes flattened into "She wished people would not" (1880 sec.). In *The Years* we are told that Eleanor "had her dreams, her plans, of course; but she did not want to discuss them" (1880 sec.). In *The Pargiters*, however, Eleanor had spelled out her dream: "I should take a room, somewhere . . . in a poor neighbourhood: and I['d] pull down all these awful slums and—well, start things fresh,—if I had the money" (ch. 1). Finally, Eleanor's conspiracy with her brother Morris reaching right back to their childhood was evoked in *The Pargiters* but omitted from *The Years*. In 1935 two more large sections of *The Years* were actually excised just before publication, and once again the character of Eleanor was diminished. In this final version of the 1917 section of *The Years* we have one of Eleanor's many unfinished, interrupted sentences: "I was thinking as I came along in the bus." The excised passage had actually gone on to give us Eleanor's thoughts about the war and England and her own sense of frustrated effort over housing, starved as she had been of funds.[27]

Of course, Virginia Woolf herself knew all that she later decided to delete about Eleanor Pargiter, but her common reader cannot know. It seems a great pity because if Virginia Woolf had kept more closely to her original treatment of Eleanor outlined in *The Pargiters*, then the force of Eleanor in old age (ripping apart the newspaper photo of a fat Fascist leader in the 1930s and exclaiming, "Damned—bully!") would have been greatly intensified. We might have had a Woolfian counterpart of that other Eleanor, the great British and international woman politician of the 1930s—Eleanor Rathbone M.P. (and spinster).[28]

The other "lost" spinster from *The Pargiters* is Miss Craddock, Kitty Malone's history tutor, who was perhaps created to atone for Miss Kilman. In the fourth chapter and fifth essay of *The Pargiters*,

Virginia Woolf gives Kitty's relationship with Lucy Craddock something of what she herself had felt for Janet Case:

> Kitty counted the days between one lesson and another. She treasured every word of praise that Miss Craddock gave her; she invested all Miss Craddock's relations with glamour, kept every note she had from her; and left a pot of white azaleas at her lodgings once when she was ill. . . . Kitty . . . when she fell in love with Miss Craddock was falling in love with something which seemed to her wonderful, new, exciting—the disinterested passion for things in themselves; so that however much she scamped her history, she knew that history to Miss Craddock was a thing to starve oneself for; to drudge after; to love for itself. (fifth essay)

But *The Pargiters* was abandoned, and Janet Case was never to read her former pupil's attempt at a tribute to "the women who teach women." Neither, of course, was she ever to read the obituary Virginia Woolf wrote for her in *The Times,* July 22, 1937, which described her as "a rare teacher and a remarkable woman." In that note Virginia Woolf testified to her teacher's gift both for making Greek literature live and for connecting it with the politics of the day: "In her way she was a pioneer; but her way was one that kept her in the background, a counsellor rather than a champion, listening to the theories of others with a little chuckle of merriment, opening her beautiful veiled eyes with a sudden flash of sympathy and laughter, but for herself she wanted no prominence, no publicity."

It was Janet Case, and women like her, who gave Virginia Woolf her vision of The Outsider she delineated in *Three Guineas* (1938). Outsiders were, and are, all those women who have worked for little or no pay and for no recognition but simply for the sake of the work itself. This disinterestedness is their contribution to "freedom, equality and, peace"[29]—what Virginia Woolf meant by "civilization." *Three Guineas* is, among other things, a celebration of those life-models, outsiders in their own time, who achieved great things for other people. It includes a great roll call of English spinsters—Mary Kingsley, Anne Clough, Mary Astell, Emily Davies, Florence Nightingale, Philippa Strachey, Sophia Jex-Blake, Harriet Martineau, Octavia Hill, Charlotte Brontë, Gertrude Bell, and Margaret Llewelyn Davies—among still more explorers, educators, writers, doctors, and social reformers hidden in the notes.

It was high time spinsters should be championed in the 1930s, because the popularization of Sigmund Freud's theories and D. H. Lawrence's mystical elevation of heterosexual intercourse had brought the image of the spinster down to its nadir. It was her virginity rather than her barrenness or her perverted lust for power that stigmatized the spinster now. If heterosexual intercourse is the only path to human maturity and fulfillment, the spinster, by definition, must be sexually retarded and psychologically subnormal for life:

> Today, there is a far worse crime than promiscuity: it is chastity. On all sides the unmarried woman today is surrounded by doubts cast not only upon her attractiveness or her common sense, but upon her decency, her normality, even her sanity. The popular women's magazines, short-story writers, lecturers and what not are conducting a campaign which might almost be called the persecution of the virgins. . . . Seriously, it takes considerable vanity, self-respect and periodical inoculations of flattery for the un-married woman . . . to stand up to the world today.[30]

Fortunately for unmarried women, at least one of their number did have "considerable vanity, self-respect and periodical inoculations of flattery" at that time—Dame Ethel Smyth, the last significant spinster in Virginia Woolf's personal and creative life. Ethel Smyth's incomparable vitality, her humor, and her total honesty were deeply necessary to Virginia Woolf, no matter how much she might laugh or groan at the older woman's relentless pursuit of her ear and heart. Ethel Smyth symbolized for Virginia Woolf the indestructibility of women's spirit of creativity and resistance; she was "one of the ice breakers, . . . the window smashers . . . the armoured tanks."[31] As well as being a superb, passionate, and tireless friend, she was also the first woman to compose music on a large scale and one of the first women to write a confessional autobiography. Just thinking of Ethel Smyth gave Virginia Woolf courage. She was Virginia Woolf's "uncastrated cat, challenging the world, yet divinely compassionate of its . . . infirmities" (Letter, October 12, 1940). It was Ethel to whom Virginia Woolf wrote on February 1, 1941, a few weeks before her death: "I would like to ask, quite simply, do you still love me? . . . Do love me."

There is, surely, more than a touch of Ethel Smyth, the composer of both comic and tragic operas, in Virginia Woolf's last fictional spinster, Miss La Trobe, with her

> passion for getting things up. . . . [her] wonderful energy. . . . [her] look of a commander pacing the deck. . . . Her abrupt manner, stocky figure; her thick ankles and sturdy shoes. . . .
>
> "Music!" she signalled, "Music!" . . .

> Down came her hand peremptorily. "Music, music," she signalled. . . .
>
> . . . she was one who seethes wandering bodies and floating voices in a cauldron, and makes rise up from its amorphous mass a re-created world. . . .
>
> . . . She brandished her script. Music began. . . . [32]

At last, with Miss La Trobe in *Between the Acts,* Virginia Woolf transcended the belittling category of spinster altogether. Miss La Trobe is defined not by her nonrelation to a man or men but by her own vision and by her own passion, which happens to be for an actress who has just left her. She is autonomous but not nonrelational. In the earliest typescript version of the novel *Pointz Hall* (dated August 1938), Miss La Trobe had been given an improbable past, including an illegitimate baby at eighteen and a hatshop. Two years later, in the summer of 1940, Miss La Trobe had turned into a very masculine lesbian with a closer affinity to the tobacco-smoking, beer-drinking village men in the pub than to other women: "Nature had made her more than half a man herself. . . . She didn't care . . . how she 'degraded' her class (middle) or her sex (female). Or even remembered one or the other. She sat there like a man, her arms akimbo, her mug before her, staring out of her deep set blue eyes. . . . Though the women had nothing but the very plainest terms for her. The men knew that Bossy was after something."[33] By the final typescript of *Pointz Hall* in November 1940, Virginia Woolf was less crudely explicit, choosing instead a more generalized, even uncertain comment: "Nature had somehow set her apart from her kind"—her kind including both men and women (432). Yet it was both men and women Miss La Trobe was specially gifted to see and hear, better perhaps than they could themselves: "There was the high ground at midnight; there the rock; and two scarcely perceptible figures. Suddenly the tree was pelted with starlings. She set down her glass. She heard the first words" (*Between the Acts* 147).

What finally matters about Miss La Trobe is that she alone is she. Without her—the perpetual Outsider/Outcast/Witch/Artist/Observer—there would have been no pageant, no attempt to bring people together to make them see, if only for a moment, that "we all act all parts" (137) and that "each is part of the whole" (133). Miss La Trobe has to pay in blood at times for her compulsion to get her vision across—"A failure. Another damned failure" (72)—but she also has her moments of glory, especially when nature, in the shape of cows or a summer shower, comes down and takes her part. After the pageant is over, only old Bart understands: "She don't want our thanks, Lucy" (141). What she wants is a drink and the oblivion in which to dream her next production.

This tale of Virginia Woolf's fiction thus ends with a figure who makes all the old rigid and patronizing sexual stereotyping quite obsolete. It is appropriate, then, that Virginia Woolf's very last description of a "real-life" spinster, written when southern England was awaiting Nazi invasion, should have been full of amazement and delight as she chronicled "old Miss Green aged 60 letting herself down out of the Rectory window in shorts to show us how, when we're on fire, . . . hanging by her toenails and descending with a jump" (*Letters* and *Diary*, July 1940).

NOTES

1. See Sheila Jeffreys, *The Spinster and Her Enemies: Feminism and Sexuality, 1880–1930* (London: Pandora, 1985), and Doan, Introduction, herein.

2. See Virginia Stephen's letter to Janet Case, January 1, 1910, offering to address envelopes for the Adult Suffragists, in Virginia Woolf, *The Flight of the Mind: The Letters of Virginia Woolf, 1888–1912*, vol. 1, ed. Nigel Nicholson (London: Hogarth Press, 1975) 421.

3. Letter to Margaret Llewelyn Davies, *Leave the Letters Till We're Dead: The Letters of Virginia Woolf, 1936–1941*, vol. 3, ed. Nigel Nicholson (London: Hogarth Press, 1980); Virginia Woolf's Obituary for Janet Case, *The Times*, July 22, 1937. Note Lyndall Gordon's point in *Virginia Woolf: A Writer's Life* (New York: Oxford University Press, 1984) that it was Janet Case who had given young Virginia Stephen essential moral support in her resistance to her stepbrother's sexual advances (85).

4. See Ellen Hawkes, "Woolf's Magical Garden of Women," *New Feminist Essays on Virginia Woolf*, ed. Jane Marcus (London: Macmillan, 1981) 39.

5. Virginia Stephen's obituary for Caroline Stephen in *The Guardian*, April 21, 1909, rpt. in the endnotes to Jane Marcus, "Thinking Back through Our Mothers," *New Feminist Essays on Virginia Woolf*. See also the very interesting essay by Jane Marcus, "The Niece of a Nun," *Virginia Woolf: A Feminist Slant*, ed. Jane Marcus (Lincoln: University of Nebraska Press, 1983).

6. See Virginia Woolf, *The Essays of Virginia Woolf, 1904–1912*, vol. 1, ed. Andrew McNeillie (London: Hogarth Press, 1986).

7. Ruth Adam, *A Woman's Place* (London: Chatto and Windus, 1975) 18.

8. See Anna Davin, "Imperialism and Motherhood," *History Workshop* 5 (1978): 9–56.

9. Havelock Ellis, *Man and Woman*, 1894, quoted in Jeffreys 129.

10. Iwan Bloch, *The Sexual Life of Our Time*, 1909, quoted in Jeffreys 138–39.

11. Walter Heape, *Sex Antagonism*, 1913, quoted in Jeffreys 144.

12. See Sybil Oldfield, *Spinsters of This Parish: The Life and Times of F. M. Mayor and Mary Sheepshanks* (London: Virago, 1984), ch. 8. *The Third Miss Symons* was reissued in 1980 as a Virago Modern Classic.

13. William Wordsworth, *The Prelude,* 1805, bk. 12.

14. The necessity to choose between a profession and marriage was taken as axiomatic in the period before the general use of contraception and was reinforced by a "marriage bar" in the British civil service and many education authorities. See Vera Brittain, *Women's Work in Modern England* (London: Noel Douglas, 1928), ch. 4.

15. Virginia Woolf's first short story, "Phyllis and Rosamond," 1906, rpt. in Virginia Woolf, *The Complete Shorter Fiction of Virginia Woolf,* ed. Susan Dick (London: Hogarth Press, 1985).

16. George Eliot, *The George Eliot Letters, 1878–1880,* vol. 7, ed. Gordon Haight (New Haven, Conn.: Yale University Press, 1955) 44.

17. For example, Margaret Llewelyn Davies and Lillian Harris, Sophy Sanger and Maud Allen, Esther Roper and Eva Gore-Booth, Dr. Hilda Clark and Edith Pye, Eleanor Rathbone and Elizabeth McAdam, Jane Harrison and Hope Mirrlees.

18. *Mrs. Dalloway* (London: Hogarth Press, 1960). Rachel Bowlby in *Virginia Woolf: Feminist Destination* (Oxford: Blackwell, 1985) suggests that Miss Kilman's anger may be a caricature of the anger of the frustrated Charlotte Brontë heroine—an anger Virginia Woolf found destructive of art and humane living.

19. Jeffreys 172–73. Cf. Carroll Smith-Rosenberg, "Politics and Culture in Women's History," *Feminist Studies* 6, (1980): "The period 1890–1920 saw a concerted male attack upon the legitimacy of [the] world of female identification and solidarity" (63).

20. Oldfield 283. See also ch. 12 for a discussion of *The Rector's Daughter*'s spinster heroine.

21. Virginia Woolf, *To the Lighthouse: The Original Holograph Draft,* ed. Susan Dick (Toronto: University of Toronto Press, 1982; London: Hogarth Press, 1983) 29–30.

22. Gordon 198.

23. See Wendy Baron, *Miss Ethel Sands and Her Circle* (London: Peter Owen, 1977). Mark Gertler is quoted describing Ethel Sands as "an old and thin virgin" and as "a rich, ugly and elderly spinster, cultured and friendly" (101). Virginia Woolf sought and respected Ethel Sands's response to *To the Lighthouse.*

24. Cf. Desmond MacCarthy's agreement with Arnold Bennett that women are inferior to men in intellectual power and that they always will fall short of the highest creative achievement of men, combated by Virginia Woolf in her letters to the *New Statesman,* October 9 and 16, 1920, rpt. as Appendix 3 to *The Diary of Virginia Woolf, 1920–1924,* vol. 2, ed. Anne Olivier Bell (London: Hogarth Press, 1978).

25. Cf. Adrienne Rich, *Of Woman Born* (London: Virago, 1977) 227–28.

26. G. E. Moore, "The Ideal," *Principia Ethica* (1903; Cambridge: Cambridge University Press, 1960), ch. 6, sec. 122.

27. See Grace Radin, "'Two Enormous Chunks': Episodes Excluded during the Final Revisions of *The Years*," *Bulletin of the New York Public Library* 80 (Winter 1977): 221–51. This bulletin includes an essay by Jane Marcus much more positive about *The Years* than this critic feels able to be. Woolf's *The Pargiters: A Novel Essay* was published as *The Pargiters: The Novel-Essay Portion of The Years*, ed. Mitchell A. Leaska (New York: New York Public Library and Readex Books, 1977; London: Hogarth Press, 1978).

28. Eleanor Rathbone (1872–1946) was the leading campaigner for a state wage for mothers, which Virginia Woolf advocated in *Three Guineas*. See Eleanor Rathbone, *The Disinherited Family*, ed. Suzie Fleming (Bristol: Falling Wall Press, 1986). She was also the champion of unenfranchised girls and women throughout the British Empire as well as being the unofficial M.P. for all the world's refugees and a leading anti-Fascist. See Mary Stocks, *Eleanor Rathbone* (London: Gollancz, 1949).

29. *Three Guineas*, ch. 3. See also the spinster references in Brenda Silver, *Virginia Woolf's Reading Notebooks* (Princeton, N.J.: Princeton University Press, 1983) 215–314.

30. Winifred Holtby, "Notes on the Way," *Time and Tide*, May 4, 1935, rpt. in Paul Berry and Alan Bishop, eds., *Testament of a Generation: The Journalism of Vera Brittain and Winifred Holtby* (London: Virago, 1985).

31. Virginia Woolf, typescript of a speech before the London/National Society for Women's Service, January 21, 1931 (a corrected version of which became "Professions for Women"), published in Virginia Woolf, *The Pargiters: The Novel-Essay Portion of The Years*, ed. Mitchell Leaska (London: Hogarth Press, 1978) xxvii–xxxxiv. For Ethel Smyth's feelings about Virginia Woolf, see Jane Marcus, "The Snow Queen and the Old Buccaneer," *Virginia Woolf Miscellany* 9 (1977): 4–6.

32. *Between the Acts* (1941; London: Penguin, 1953) 145, 48, 88, 108, 126. It should be noted that another possible life-model for Miss La Trobe was Ellen Terry's daughter, the stage designer and producer Edy Craig. See Julie Holledge, *Innocent Flowers: Women in the Edwardian Theatre* (London: Virago, 1981), pt. 3.

33. Virginia Woolf, *Pointz Hall: The Earlier and Later Typescripts of Between the Acts*, ed. Michael Leaska (New York: University Publications, 1983) 176–77.

PART THREE

Excellent Women

Dale M. Bauer

The Politics of Collaboration in *The Whole Family*

> We cannot always help ourselves in the matter of our relations. Some are born relatives, some achieve relatives, and others have relatives thrust upon them.
>
> —John Kendrick Bangs's "Tom Price" in *The Whole Family*

The politics of collaboration in *The Whole Family* (1908) might be best explained by the humorist John Kendrick Bangs, one of the contributors: it was, for the twelve authors involved, a process of having relations thrust upon them (although they were paid for their troubles). They were forced to deal with familial rivalry, indeed with sexual and authorial jealousy.

This collaborative novel, as Alfred Bendixen writes in his fine introduction to it, was to be—according to William Dean Howells who conceived the project—"a realistic portrait of a typical American family 'in middling circumstances, of average culture and experiences'" (xii). I want to begin with the title, *The Whole Family,* in challenging the essentializing notions of the family offered first by Howells and with varying assent and dissent by the collaborators. Mary Wilkins Freeman, for one, disrupts this whole familial configuration, this totalizing picture of "the American family," by introducing a sexually vibrant and transgressive spinster. The spinster delays the conventional marriage plot and thereby forces us to confront the alternative plots for women offered in *The Whole Family.*

The novel ostensibly concerns Peggy Talbert's engagement and marriage, but it quickly turns to the question of sexuality and desire in the family when Mary Wilkins Freeman develops the spinster aunt character, Elizabeth Talbert, who claims Peggy's fiancé is actually in love with her and not Peggy. From that point on, as Alfred Bendixen observes, "the plot increasingly focused on family misunderstandings and family rivalries, which were mirrored by the artistic rivalries of the authors" (xxvi). These rivalries become the occasion for the authors' ideological claims about "normal" family life and the containment of sexuality; each author wrote one family member's perspective—from Howells's father to Phelps's married daughter—but Howells thought they all ought to focus on the details of the engagement, not Freeman's spinster. This essay will address the themes of family life as the twelve authors (all under contract at Harper's) address them: the battle over the representation of the spinster; the changing family structure under capitalism, including reproduction and production; and relations among women, within and across generations. John Crowley writes that the novel is characterized by shifting points of view, a mark of the "modernist" text (112–13). My point is not that this is a modernist text or a realist one, as Howells would have the novel. Rather, the authors establish themselves in the system of competition—not collaboration—and profit making that characterizes publishing.

Let me make a momentary digression to an appeal for spinsterhood found in an unlikely place—Catharine Maria Sedgwick's 1827 novel *Hope Leslie.* Not only does Sedgwick address the possibility of intermarriage between Faith Leslie, an English settler in Puritan New England, and one of her Indian captors, but also she makes a plea for spinsterhood as a legitimate form of lived experience. After Hope Leslie marries Miss Downing's first love, Miss Downing "returned to New England," where her

> hand was often and eagerly sought, but she appears never to have felt a second engrossing attachment. The current of her purposes and affections had set another way. She illustrated a truth, which, if more generally received by her sex, might save a vast deal of misery: that marriage is not *essential* to the contentment, the dignity, or the happiness of woman. Indeed, those who saw on how wide a sphere her kindness shone, how many were made better and happier by her disinterested devotion, might have rejoiced that she did not. (quoted in Freibert and White 146)

Sedgwick applauds the social usefulness of the unmarried woman. Moreover, this passage sheds a curious light on the nineteenth-century ideology of separate spheres: marriage, as Hannah Webster Foster writes in *The Coquette,* is "the tomb of friendship," for marriage restricts the spheres in which women might work and live (quoted in Freibert and White 36). Miss Downing has a larger sphere of influence, indeed power, by remaining unmarried and practicing her "disinterested devotion." In fact, remaining outside of the marriage market promises a way to subvert a rigidified nineteenth-century culture.

This digression might help explain Freeman's positioning of the spinster in the "whole family." While a married woman *might* be economically better off (though this is not necessarily true in the novel), Freeman's spinster knows precisely what is traded for this economic security. Freeman's spinster need not be sexually proper—or sexual property—because she does not look for a husband. In the course of this essay, I will show how the "spinster" is a construct which the authors—each responding to Freeman's construction of a nonstereotypical "old maid"—seek to define in a battle for control. This sexually vital spinster contrasts with the image of the frigid, man-hating stereotype Sheila Jeffreys convincingly details in *The Spinster and Her Enemies.* Elizabeth Talbert is the obverse, according to the way others see her: lascivious, aggressive, awful. According to Jeffreys, the spinster demonstrated a "growing lack of interest in clothes, lack of 'sex attraction' and indifference to men" (95). Elizabeth recognizes the stereotype but clings to the notion that the old maid has "ceased to exist. Sometimes I wish she were still existing and that I carried out her character to the full" (35). On the contrary, only when Alice Brown sends Elizabeth packing to New York where she is to make a career does the family's spinster represent the stereotype. Either through production or reproduction, then, each family member must contribute to the family business, "the Works."

In this context, Michele Barrett's analysis of the ideology of familialism as the basis for "women's oppression today" is useful: "The family-household constitutes both the ideological ground on which gender difference and women's oppression are constructed, and the material relations in which men and women are differently engaged in wage labour and the class structure" (211). Since Elizabeth Talbert is on the margins of the family, engaged in neither production nor reproduction, the family to which the spinster is attached disciplines her for failing to marry. Under the gaze of the family, the spinster is held accountable for her outré sexuality and her pink dress. Elizabeth's unwillingness to allow Peggy's marriage to take place and her desire to force Harry Goward (the fiancé) to reveal his sexual dalliances demonstrate her forestalling of the reproduction of patriarchal relations. She throws off the concept of dependence for an "in-dependence," a relation to the family that allows her to work within its structure (as Sedgwick's Miss Downing does) without being forced into silence. To be a spinster, then, is not to be an outsider but to work within the family to alter it.

Our first view of Elizabeth Talbert comes in Howells's opening chapter, "The Father." The neighbor, Ned Temple, who earlier had an affair with Elizabeth but does not remember her family name, describes spinsters in a general fashion: "My wife inferred from the generation to which her brother [Cyrus Talbert] belonged that [Elizabeth] had long been a lady of that age when ladies begin to be spoken of as maiden. . . . From the general impression in Eastridge we gathered that Miss Talbert was not without the disappointment which endears maiden ladies to the imagination, but the disappointment was of a date so remote that it was only a matter of pathetic heresay, now" (19). The spinster from the beginning is a matter of speculation, of rumor, and is generally circumscribed by these reactions. But Elizabeth refuses such inscription, refuses to be constrained by gossip. She does not protect her reputation from the imaginations of the neighborhood but instead compels a place in those imaginations by insisting that Harry Goward is interested in her first and Peggy second. Freeman's spinster, then, is open about her sexuality, which is not "of a date so remote." In fact, she refuses to mediate her sexual desires through the family, where desire is restructured and reordered so that it does not violate family order.

The father—Cyrus Talbert—explains his own view of women and old maids: "'You see, I've always had the idea that women, beginning with little girls and ending with grandmothers, ought to be brought up as nearly like their brothers as can be—that is, if they are to be the wives of other women's brothers. It don't so much matter how an old maid is brought up, but you can't have her destiny in view, though I believe if an old maid could be brought up more like an old bachelor she would be more comfortable to herself, anyway'" (23). There are two conflicting messages here. On the one hand, the father's view seems perfectly liberal: women ought to be brought up as men are. In fact, if they were brought up like men, even the old maids (a destiny which cannot be predicted in childhood or adolescence) would more likely be self-sufficient and comfortable. Talbert implies that men are brought up to be independent and autonomous, while women are trained to be dependent and relational. On the other hand, his view of education for women is contradictory. If women were raised as men are, then they might be independent. But that independence is exactly what frightens the family about the maiden aunt, who prefers her autonomy and authority. Talbert suggests that such education is for "other women's brothers," so that women's education is in service of the homosocial exchange of women between men. Talbert cannot imagine equality in education, for that would threaten his hierarchy of sexual difference. Coeducation, for Cyrus, depends on the acknowledged inferiority of women and a cultural assurance that women will remain in the home. (All the more reason that Charles Edward's and Lorraine's desires to go to Europe must be kept in check; the father cannot risk their coming back with notions like Elizabeth's.)

Cyrus Talbert glosses over Peggy's attendance at a coeducational school: "'I said to my wife that I didn't see how, if a girl was going to get married, she could have a better basis than knowing the fellow through three or four years' hard work together. When you think of the sort of hit-or-miss affairs most marriages are that young people make after a few parties and picnics, coeducation as a preliminary to domestic happiness doesn't seem a bad notion'" (6). Education prepares women for marriage in the way that Elizabeth Talbert's "culture" (her informal education in Europe) does not. Again, "hard work together" at college serves as a context for love and social arrangements, love being entirely dependent on the ability of two people to produce. Education, then, is part of the disciplinary structure that keeps women in line.

The second chapter is Freeman's and introduces the aunt's view of herself, one which comes into conflict with her family's view of her. To her, the label "spinster" is acquired only once she comes to Eastridge, the family's home. She explains: "Here I am the old-maid aunt. Not a day, not an hour, not a minute, when I am with other people, passes that I do not see myself in their estimation playing that rôle as plainly as if I saw myself in a looking-glass. It is a moral lesson which I presume I need. I have just returned from my visit at the Pollards' country-house in Lancaster, where I most assuredly did not have it" (30). Elizabeth recognizes that the image of the spinster her family would like her to reflect is a "moral lesson." Others—the Pollards, for instance—do not need to remind her of her unmarried status, for it does not reflect on their family. Her desires do not correspond to the family's, just as Freeman's did not jibe with Howells's notion of the plot. All the more reason, then, that the threat to Peggy's marriage, which Elizabeth's claims about Harry pose, must be eliminated. If Peggy weren't to marry Harry, she might be a spinster as well. This is the threat of marginalization, embodied in the spinster, which the culture holds up as a Medusan image to unmarried women. Elizabeth, who refuses the mirror which culture holds to her, does not turn into stone, however. The spinster thus represents a danger to the patriarchal domestic ideology which the whole family is enlisted to protect.

Of course, this domestic arrangement—the bourgeois family—does not benefit everyone. Lorraine, the daughter-in-law who is married to Charles Edward, hates and rejects the family more than Elizabeth does (perhaps because her movements are even more constrained and disciplined than Elizabeth's). Her mother-in-law expresses horror at the fact that Lorraine has not made the bed by ten in the morning, even though Lorraine claims that she always makes the bed before she sleeps in it again. To the mother, Lorraine fails at her domestic work and, hence, fails the family. Lorraine's first thought in Mary Stewart Cutting's chapter on her is telling: "I have never identified myself with my husband's family" (80). Despite this self-chosen alienation, or perhaps because of it, Lorraine is silenced in the big house, although the family is shocked by her "influence" on their son (83): "I never talk at all any more when I go over to the big house, for I can't seem to without horrifying somebody" (84).

Clearly, it is not just the spinster who horrifies the family with her talk of sexual desire and transgressions. The daughter-in-law also horrifies because she has influence, although no voice of her own, silenced as she is by the glances she gets at the house and by her economic dependence. Because Elizabeth forgoes the economic dependence of marriage, there is no blackmail to silence her. Lorraine and Peter (Lorraine renames her husband because she hates "Charles Edward," inherited from generations) hope to go to Paris with the money he will inherit, for Peter also hates "that way of living he's been always used to, with its little, petty cast-iron rules and regulations, and the stupid family meals, where everybody is expected to be on time to the minute" (87). Nevertheless, Lorraine has to make an internal vow "never [to] open [her] mouth again, while [she lives] here, about *anything* [she was] interested in . . . " (86). Thus, the family effectively regulates its members by forcing them into internal, never external, revolt. The family decides what is "'necessary'" and rules on all desires, institutionalizing them in the family form. Lorraine and Elizabeth, then, share a transgressive desire. As Lorraine herself says, "Miss Elizabeth Talbert is a howling swell; she only just endures it here" (92).

Elizabeth Talbert, however, does more than just endure; she overthrows the custom of silence, insisting that she have a voice in the family and resisting cooptation. Elizabeth renames her situation: "They [the family members] do not know that today an old-maid aunt is as much of an anomaly as a spinning-wheel, that she has ceased to exist, that she is prehistoric, that even grandmothers have almost disappeared from off the face of the earth. In short, they do not know that I am not an old-maid aunt except under this blessed mansard-roof, and some other roofs of Eastridge, many of which are also mansard, where the influence of their fixed belief prevails" (33).[1] The old-maid aunt is now of the breed of "new women" of independence. Only where tradition dies hard, and there is a particular investment in maintaining the family as a regulatory institution, does the old maid exist as a fossil, a relic, a testament to the way things were—and judged according "to what people think [she is], rather than what [she actually is]" (31). Such is the family's nostalgic desire for the place spinsters used to have in culture. Elizabeth is displaced and disruptive, since she deafens her ear to the voice of culture.

After her "tragedy" of lost love, Elizabeth does not mourn. The family has its judgment—directed against the woman who lost her man—for that occasion, too: "They all unanimously considered that I should dress always in black silk, and a bonnet with a neat little tuft of middle-aged violets, and black ribbons tied under my chin. I know I am wicked to put on that pink gown and hat, but I shall do it. . . . Thank fortune, I have a sense of humor" (45). The portrait of the mourning woman sounds surprisingly like Mlle. Reisz in Kate Chopin's *The Awakening*, but there is a crucial difference. Elizabeth means it as a joke; her family wants her to dress her "age," which she translates as mourning. Elizabeth's revolt is like Edna Pontellier's in *The Awakening* insofar as it is "wicked": "'By all the codes which I am acquainted with, I am a devilishly wicked specimen of the sex,'" Edna says in chapter 27 (138). In both cases, what is oppressive is not patriarchy in the abstract so much as the assumption that desire can be encoded only in the family, as a natural site of fulfillment.

Despite her sense of humor, Elizabeth condemns the socialized weakness that comes with being feminine: "What a woman I am! I mean, how feminine I am! I wish I could cure myself of the habit of being feminine. It is a horrible nuisance; this wishing to consult with somebody when I am worried is so disgustingly feminine" (47–48). Elizabeth wants to throw off not only the construction of the spinster but also the socialized behavior which comes with being "feminine." Her lived experience of the feminine clashes with the discursive systems that, as Janice Doane and Devon Hodges argue in *Nostalgia and Sexual Difference*, "have so long attempted to naturalize the place of 'woman'" (107). Elizabeth's is a response to the devaluation of the feminine.

Part of this novel—Mary Heaton Vorse's chapter on the grandmother—is a lament of this feminization since the grandmother is nostalgic for the past, when women were hardworking without having to go to college. For instance, the grandmother blames the evils of the age on women's conspicuous leisure and the move away from women's work and industry at home:

> Machinery has put a stop to many of our old occupations, and the result is a generation of nervous women who haven't a single thing in life to occupy themselves with but their own feelings, while girls like Peggy, who are active and useful, have nothing to do but to go to school and keep on going to school. If one wanted to dig into the remote cause of things, one might find the root of our present trouble in these changed conditions, for Cyrus's sister, Elizabeth, is one of these unoccupied women. Formerly in a family like ours there would have been so much to do that, whether she liked it or not, and whether she had married or not, Elizabeth would have had to be a useful woman. . . . (62–63)

The grandmother easily identifies the "present trouble" as a result of Elizabeth's unemployment around the house; her leisure, not her spinsterhood, is the source of the trouble. For the grandmother, the rise of industrial capitalism is at odds with the preservation of the family. This is not to ignore the grandmother's collusion in the family's repression of sexuality. By blaming Elizabeth for family troubles, the grandmother can ensure Peggy's future marriage to Harry Goward. Moreover, her meddling in family affairs is just compensation for the fact that in the new leisure state she, too, has nothing to do. Hers is a nostalgia for a precapitalist household, for the supportive mode of relations between women in the home (as Carroll Smith-Rosenberg describes them in "The Female World of Love and Ritual"). According to the grandmother, the competition and anger against Elizabeth would not exist if the women—equally employed in the home—belonged to a female network. The capitalist household, on the contrary, leads the grandmother to hate Elizabeth, who has more freedom than the married women have. The capitalist familial relation thus leads to competition among women for status, a competition which for Smith-Rosenberg did not exist before the "changed conditions" to which the grandmother refers. As Michele Barrett argues, "It seems clear that feudal relations of production tied the whole household rather than the individual to socially productive labour and that there was therefore a less sharp distinction between the labour of men and women" (177). Cyrus Talbert is no feudal lord or laborer; he is a manufacturer of ice pitchers, among other things. I would therefore argue that the spinster, or Freeman's manifestation of her, was invented in the nineteenth century, coincident with the change from household production to production at "the Works."

The women's work at home—done by the mother, the grandmother, the married daughter Maria, and, to a lesser extent, Lorraine—differs sharply from Peggy's college work (considered by Cyrus and Grandmother to be preparation for marriage and a way to idle away one's productive time). Elizabeth's leisurely visits to friends are profoundly at odds with the rest of the family's obligations. The capitalist household thus produces not only a division of labor between men and women but also fierce divisions among women in the household. (Maria also complains about her duties in the household, contrasting them with Peggy's and Alice's. Maria argues for Peggy to be sent to school because she herself feels an injustice about having to work in the home and wants to spare Peggy her bitterness.) Again, Barrett is useful here: "The accompanying ideological processes [in the separation of home and workplace for the family] have involved the establishment of the privatized domestic area of 'the home' as the particular province of women and of 'femininity' and maternalism. Women have become dependent upon the male wage in capitalism and this mediated dependence upon the wage is circumscribed by an ideology of emotional, psychical and 'moral' dependence" (179). We can observe such dependence in Maria's gratefulness to Tom Price, her husband, for straightening out the scandal when she leaves for New York with Dr. Denbigh so that Denbigh can flirt with Elizabeth and, in the process, scare Harry back to Peggy. Only Elizabeth holds out for moral and psychic independence, against the wishes of the women around her who have already colluded with the system.

The grandmother complains that Elizabeth is "a case of arrested development" and has failed to enter into women's mature dependence on the male wage (68). Another complaint against Elizabeth is that she shares Cyrus's house and considers it is as much hers as Mrs. Talbert's, but she does not do any of the domestic labor Mrs. Ada Talbert does. The grandmother wishes Elizabeth would marry to avoid hurting the family's reputation and to avoid her influence—"an atmosphere of criticism"—to which the young Alice is vulnerable (69). Alice thinks, "As for Aunt Elizabeth, she is lovely sometimes, and the way she remembers things that happened when she was young is simply wonderful. She knows how girls feel, too, and how they suffer when they are like Dr. Denbigh says I am—very nervous and sensitive and high-strung" (102). These two forces—conservative domesticity and Elizabeth's "new women" ideology—battle for Alice's allegiance. No wonder, then, that the grandmother accuses Elizabeth of boredom, of lack of productive work, and avoids the question of an older woman's sexuality. It is a question the whole family begs.

That almost all of the characters try to tame Elizabeth demonstrates their fear of her power and the need to assert what the authors consider to be "natural" and domesticated sexuality. Mrs. Temple, married to Elizabeth's old flame, throws a temper tantrum when she believes Elizabeth is out to steal her husband. Elizabeth responds by teaching Mrs. Temple, whom Elizabeth considers to be a perfect bourgeois housekeeper, to fix her hair like Elizabeth's to be more alluring to Ned Temple. Elizabeth's notion is that "'any man would rather have his wife look well than his house'" (55). Elizabeth is a source of sexual knowledge, to which the repressed family must appeal when Peggy's engagement is in crisis. Peggy especially fears Elizabeth, as though the unmarried woman represents a pollution or plague which the innocent Peggy might catch. Peggy's first notion is to hide from her aunt, but she overcomes it, regaining her civility in the act of overcoming any social danger. She thinks, "I don't know what I thought Aunt Elizabeth could do to me, but I felt safe" (277). This safety comes only when she feels under the protection of Stillman Dane's (her future husband's) wing. Peggy fears, most of all, people pointing at her and labeling her a spinster, the image of sexual "disappointment" (283). In fact, the last two sections of the novel—in the voices of Peggy and a friend of the family—force the novel into a strange and unsettling closure. But I will come to that later.

Henry James's section, "The Married Son," is the most curious, not for what it says about Elizabeth but for its refusal to come to terms with the spinster. James might have mentioned her only slightly, but it is clear he challenges Freeman (that is, Elizabeth) in the chapter he writes. For instance, James's Charles Edward/Peter is ambivalent about his wife Lorraine; he confesses he writes in his journal to work her off (147), to shed himself of her influence. Only his mother understands the absurdity of life in America, by which James means the incongruence of a place so thoroughly "modern" and yet, at the same time, a "dense wilderness of nocturnal terrors" (145), where no consciousness or a serious literary recognition of truth may grow (158). The soil is too thin, as James had argued in his *Hawthorne*. Where can one get "true culture," if one is an eligible female, a bachelor, or an aspiring writer/painter? Europe, of course, where Peter and Lorraine are headed, where Henry James and a host of other American writers went before the war to get culture (176). Significantly, Elizabeth Talbert also had gone, only to return a woman with a larger notion of the world than that circumscribed by the family in Eastridge. James's Peter describes Elizabeth as a "prowling" woman (166), but in fact James, who comes after Freeman in order of composition, gobbles up the literary territory with *his* themes, arresting the development of Freeman's issue about the spinster's sexuality.[2]

As I have already argued, Lorraine's alienation from the family most closely resembles Elizabeth's. That is not to say, however, that the married son and the men in the family are not repressed and tamed too. The ideology of the family serves to keep everyone in line and at home so that Paris—both Lorraine's and Charles Edward's goal—is beyond the pale of the necessary. If Charles Edward sees Elizabeth as Archne-like, "'spinning a web,'" he sees himself as caught, if not by Elizabeth then by the family (268, 145). Hating the family, Charles Edward and Lorraine conspire to do something "'desperate'" and in the meantime "consort, so far as in our deep-dyed hypocrisy we do consort, with the rest of the Family, that we have Sunday supper with the Parents and emerge, modestly yet virtuously shining, from the ordeal . . . " (148). James's section, like few others, demonstrates the deep hatred for the conventions of bourgeois family life and its constrictions, especially those which cause "the strange stultification of the passions in us, which prevents anything ever from coming to an admitted and avowed head" (165).

Strangely, Elizabeth awakens the married son's anger. She is the only member who does not stifle her passions or her discourse about them, but he still wants to "administer" a "dose" of humility to Elizabeth, a cure for her prowling (166, 167). Instead of uniting to resist the family, the local source of power repressing them both, they become rivals, which serves to draw off their alienated protests. The married son realizes that "real" things never are discussed in the family, for the business of the family is to substitute a representation of the "happy family" for a real contradiction—the son's ambivalent feelings toward the family. Peter Gay writes in *The Bourgeois Experience: The Education of the Senses* that the family was "a fertile breeding ground for sexual rivalries" (444), such as the one between Peter and Elizabeth (and, as Bendixen points out, between Freeman and James).

It is no accident that the name of the hotel to which Tom and Maria Price go after the pairing off in New York is The Happy Family; it is also no accident that the novel is called *The Whole Family* rather than *The Happy Family.* The Happy Family is itself a site of representation, a place created and sold to bourgeois consumers, just as *The Whole Family* is a representation. Henry James's married son summarizes the effect of such representations of the family: "the more we pig together round about [Father] the more blandly patriarchal we make him feel" (167). We might say, then, that the purpose of the family is to preserve this image of bland and unchallenged patriarchalism over and against the contradictions and anger brewing in each member of the family.

Elizabeth Stuart Phelps's married daughter does not dismiss the spinster as the married son does. In fact, Maria Price, the household manager and orchestrator of Peggy's destiny, believes that she has underestimated Elizabeth: "I ought to have fathomed her. It never occurred to me that she was deep enough to drop a plummet in" (187). Maria's goal is to ensure that Peggy marries; Elizabeth, as I have argued, wants to disrupt this patriarchal plot. Maria shares her grandmother's point of view of Elizabeth: "She always has had, she always must have, she always will have, the admiration of some man or men to engross her attention. She is an attractive woman; she knows it; women admit it; and men feel it. I don't think Aunt Elizabeth is a heartless person; not an irresponsible one, only an idle and unhappy one" (194–95).

Maria's distrust of Elizabeth stems from her belief that "the economic pressures of capitalism turned busy, independent women into narcissistic, sentimental consumers," as Doane and Hodges claim about Ann Douglas's lament of the feminization of American culture (Doane and Hodges 59). Rather than celebrate the liberation of the spinster, Maria can only complain that women must begin to think about other women, to fathom them as agents of their own destiny. What happens when women are no longer the center of domesticity? Elizabeth's sexual desire is a threat to Maria's ability to manage the family household because desire is antithetical to management, to the family interest. What Stendhal says about love in Boston is true of the family's account of desire: "'Young American girls in the United States are so imbued and fortified with rational ideas that love, the flower of life, has deserted their youth. In Boston a girl can quite safely be left alone with a handsome stranger, in the certainty that she will think of nothing but the income of her future husband'" (quoted in MacCannell, xiii). Desire has been sublimated for management, for familial control, with Maria as the main advocate of dependence on one's husband.

What, then, can we make of the strange destiny which Alice Brown, who writes Peggy's section, reserves for Aunt Elizabeth? Lyman Wilde, Elizabeth's old suitor, has led the handicraft movement and has been a vital influence on Lorraine's marriage, not to mention on the opera season. Elizabeth comes home announcing her engagement; Alice Brown rewrites that ending. Brown has Lyman send Elizabeth a letter claiming that he "owed everything . . . to her" and that "he was taking refuge with an English brotherhood to lead, for a time, a cloistered life instinct with beauty and its worship, but that there as everywhere he was hers eternally" (270–71). Peggy sentimentalizes the letter, believing it unforgettable and "most beautiful." But Brown puts an end to Elizabeth's sexuality, her recuperation from her old tragedy, and her future.

After this letter, Elizabeth gets another one—this time from the spiritualist Mrs. Chataway (her card reads "Magnetic Healer and Mediumistic Divulger")—and appears in black, the same costume she had foresworn as the uniform of her spinster state, "like some sister of charity" (291). Elizabeth announces that she will join Mrs. Chataway in "'a connection which will lead to the widest possible influence for her and for me'" (291). With her "enormous magnetism," Elizabeth will become a spiritualist, her sexual energies diverted into a more lucrative trade (291). The whole family is about this alienation of desire. Charles Edward, Lorraine, Elizabeth, and even the mother try to resist the commodification of desire. This is the struggle taking place in the novel, from the time Lyman Wilde decides not to marry Elizabeth so that he can "build a nest" before marriage, thereby losing her. This ideology of familialism is reinforced when, through the interference of the friend of the family—the great Gerritt Wendell, a peace correspondent for a famous newspaper (Henry Van Dyke's irony is not missed when we consider his character's role as orchestrator of the marriage)—Peggy marries Stillman Dane, her old psychology professor who has quit teaching because of his inheritance. Peggy, "a well-bred angel," has been domesticated and saved from the clairvoyant spinster, not to mention James's alienated Bohemian brother (307).

The clairvoyant spinster is a strange and powerful image to conclude Freeman's creation. Elizabeth is sent away to New York, a suitable place for clairvoyants, and her sexuality remains mystified. The denial of her own sexuality has given her the magical power to see others' desires. As long as her "energies" correspond to the whole family's business mentality, then Aunt Elizabeth does not pose a threat. As Jackson Lears points out in *No Place of Grace,* the arts and crafts revival at the turn of the century had much to do with the revival of spiritualism and medieval cults. Crafts leaders were "harbingers of bourgeois values" (76) as well as advocates of the simple life, such as the one Lyman would find in the English brotherhood. We can assume that when Lyman "vanished into thin air" after a quarrel with Elizabeth, he is off to lead this "simple life" (47). He is variously referred to as a painter (88) and as "'the most *radical* and *temperamental* leader in the great handicraft development,'" who is "'opposed to machines'" and printing, preferring a return to script and scriveners (221). In short, Lyman represents a force in the novel that must be banished. Lears calls this a "republican moralism," contrasting it with the "new culture of consumption" (77) for which the father mass produces items at "the Works": "The deep dissatisfaction with labor-saving devices and bourgeois notions of comfort, the lust for 'hard reality' and the deification of work, all suggested that the Arts and Crafts movement had religious overtones . . . as a faint, unconscious protest against an emergent secular civilization based on material consumption" (96). The possibility of Lyman Wilde's joining forces with Elizabeth portends too much. His discontent with modernism and the culture of consumption which the Talbert industry represents parallels Elizabeth's liberation from the family through supernaturalism and mysticism. Both are part of the antimodernist movement at the turn of the century. In both cases, Lyman and Elizabeth want to turn away from the complacent, self-congratulatory family to an alternative social arrangement.

Who controls representation controls social power. In the novel, indeed in the politics of collaboration itself, who controls "plot"—what Howells's Cyrus calls the "destiny" of the character—determines in large part the form and ideology of the text. Every contributor after Freeman must confront the spinster and Freeman's representation of her. There are no easy answers, given that each contributor deals with the aunt as a form of narrative power. By making her into an object of scorn, James, Vorse, and Bangs all try to objectify and stereotype her—as critical, as spurious (139), as useless, as lascivious. Bangs's Tom Price believes that Elizabeth "seems to regard all men as her own individual property" (136), a curious claim since the grandmother, Maria, and even the father consider the spinster part and parcel of the family property. Freeman disrupts those stereotypes by allowing Elizabeth a subjectivity of her own. There is no final word about the spinster in the novel because of the politics of collaboration, often an unhappy collaboration with authors unwilling to address the narrative effect of Elizabeth on the family. There is no easy binary of supporters and detractors of the spinster in the novel. The issues of commodity, utility, and housework itself complicate the question of sexuality and the family. What I can say in conclusion, however, is that this text demonstrates the cultural unconscious at work in subverting the order of the whole family and opening it up—through Freeman's character—to an attack from within its ranks. In that vein, James and Freeman share this cultural unconscious and a drive for disordering the family, for altering the material (James) and sexual (Freeman) relations of the family. Freeman and James are more relatives than strangers.

NOTES

1. And if Elizabeth renames her situation, in another sense Mary Wilkins Freeman renames the novel itself by giving names to most of the novel's characters. Strictly speaking, the novel often verges on incoherency because each author would wrest control of the plot by redefining the characters and their situation. James, in fact, wanted to finish the novel for Jordan (the Harper editor), fearing no doubt that his own chapter would not properly influence the subsequent chapters/authors. What mitigates the novel's incoherence, however, is the way Freeman's chapter succeeded in establishing the terms of the subsequent debate.

2. For a discussion of this point, see Crowley 112–13.

WORKS CITED

Barrett, Michele. *Women's Oppression Today: Problems in Marxist Feminist Analysis*. London: Verso Editions, 1980.

Bendixen, Alfred. Introduction. *The Whole Family*. By William Dean Howells et al. New York: Ungar, 1986.

Chopin, Kate. *The Awakening*. New York: Penguin, 1984.

Crowley, John. "The Whole Famdamnily." *New England Quarterly* 60 (1987): 106–13.

Doane, Janice, and Devon Hodges. *Nostalgia and Sexual Difference*. New York: Methuen, 1987.

Freibert, Lucy M., and Barbara A. White, eds. *Hidden Hands: An Anthology of American Women Writers, 1790–1870*. New Brunswick, N.J.: Rutgers University Press, 1985.

Gay, Peter. *The Bourgeois Experience: Education of the Senses*. New York: Oxford University Press, 1984.

Jeffreys, Sheila. *The Spinster and Her Enemies: Feminism and Sexuality, 1880–1930*. London: Pandora, 1985.

Lears, Jackson. *No Place of Grace*. New York: Pantheon, 1981.

MacCannell, Juliet Flower. *Figuring Lacan: Criticism and the Cultural Unconscious*. Lincoln: University of Nebraska Press, 1987.

Smith-Rosenberg, Carroll. "The Female World of Love and Ritual." *Disorderly Conduct: Visions of Gender in Victorian America*. New York: Oxford University Press, 1985.

CATHERINE KENNEY

Detecting a Novel Use for Spinsters in Sayers's Fiction

Dorothy L. Sayers often asserted that her goal as a mystery writer was to bring the genre back into the mainstream of English literature by allying the modern detective story with the great Victorian novels of mystery and sensation, especially the work of Wilkie Collins.[1] As one of detective fiction's most influential critics during its so-called Golden Age, Sayers also argued that establishing such a link with tradition was necessary for any crime literature to outlive its immediate time.[2] Now, more than a half-century after the publication of her final novel, it is possible to claim a kind of permanence for her work. Sayers's fiction continues to attract new generations of readers, and she is considered a dominant figure in the development of the mystery genre by most of its latter-day critics and practitioners.[3] One of the reasons for her novels' durability is their emphasis on the status of women, particularly as that status relates to the choice of marriage or spinsterhood. Sayers's novels are filled with spinsters and other "unattached" women, as well as images of good and bad marriages, which highlight her preoccupation with the marriage question. Thus, her work is linked not only to the tradition exemplified by Collins and Dickens but also to the considerable body of English fiction devoted to elucidating female experience and scrutinizing the institution of marriage, most notably Jane Austen's novels and Charlotte Brontë's *Jane Eyre.*

In Sayers's third novel, *Unnatural Death* (1927), the women's question comes to the fore. This book presents one of her most successful minor characters, Miss Alexandra Katherine Climpson, the sprightly and appealing spinster-sleuth who is introduced in a chapter boldly entitled "A Use for Spinsters." Interestingly, the novel itself was called "The Case of the Three Spinsters" in an early draft.[4] This working title indicates that, on some level, Sayers intended the novel to be a consideration of spinsterhood, although exactly who these three particular spinsters were is unclear, for there are many unmarried women in the book.[5] Yet the completed novel, which may include characters that differ from the ones Sayers originally planned, does revolve around the murder of one spinster by another. It seems fair to say that these two principals, in addition to Miss Climpson, represent the "Three Spinsters" of Sayers's original idea, playing as they do the central roles of murderer, victim, and detective.[6] The subject of spinsterhood and the character of the spinster-sleuth are particularly apposite to the narrative of *Unnatural Death* because its murder plot emerges from relationships involving different kinds of spinsters. This integration of story, theme, and character shows Sayers moving toward the kind of truly organic unity that her finest fictions would achieve. The effort is not wholly satisfactory here, and indeed at times appears clumsy, but this novel is a necessary preamble to the more polished structure of *Murder Must Advertise* (1934) and to *The Nine Tailors* (1934) and *Gaudy Night* (1935), which represent supreme accomplishments in this type of unity and rank among the greatest mystery stories ever written.

The epigraph of the chapter introducing Miss Climpson explains Sayers's preoccupation with the spinster type: "There are two million more females than males in England and Wales! [The year is 1927.] And this is an awe-inspiring circumstance."[7] Dorothy Sayers had herself been awed by this circumstance. In the turbulent years between her move to London in 1920—as a brilliant young woman full of literary ambition and longing for excitement—and the composition of *Unnatural Death,* Sayers had struggled to find suitable work as well as a mate. During this time, she experienced two traumatic love affairs, one of which left her with a child, born in 1924. Her authorized biographer, James Brabazon, cites persuasive evidence of her overwhelming desire to marry, which seems to have reached crisis proportions during this period. Just two months shy of her thirty-third birthday in 1926, the novelist, who supported herself by working as a copywriter at England's largest advertising agency, married Oswald Arthur Fleming, a Scottish journalist and nerve-scarred World War I veteran with whom she seems to have had little in common (Brabazon, ch. 8–10). The turmoil and frustration of these years provided the domestic backdrop for her 1926 novel of marital discord and betrayal, *Clouds of Witness.* The upheaval in her personal life certainly must also have influenced her next book, *Unnatural Death,* a novel which considers marriage and its alternatives, just as its author had been considering these questions in her own life. Like others of her generation in England, Sayers faced the two-pronged challenge of a severe shortage of marriageable men, brought about by the carnage of World War I, at the very time of increasing emancipation for women, especially educated women like herself.

In Lord Peter Wimsey's Cattery—the detective agency masquerading as a typing bureau where Miss Climpson and other self-supporting single women are employed—the novelist addresses the problem of "superfluous women" in her society. As Lord Peter explains:

> "Miss Climpson . . . is a manifestation of the wasteful way in which this country is run. Look at electricity. Look at water-power. Look at the tides. Look at the sun. Millions of power units being given off into space every minute. Thousands of old maids, simply bursting with useful energy, forced by our stupid social system into hydros and hotels and communities and hostels and posts as companions, where their magnificent gossip-powers and units of inquisitiveness are allowed to dissipate themselves or even become harmful to the community, while the ratepayers' money is spent on getting work for which these women are providentially fitted, inefficiently carried out by ill-equipped policemen. . . . My god! it's enough to make a man write to *John Bull.* And then bright young men write nasty little patronising books called 'Elderly Women,' and 'On the Edge of the Explosion'—and the drunkards make songs upon them, poor things." (*Unnatural Death,* ch. 3)

Wimsey argues repeatedly that giving useful employment to such "superfluous women" is not just an act of charity toward them but a service to society. The Cattery is thus the first significant dramatization of Sayers's doctrine of work—the central theme that emerges from her entire canon—which is based on the conviction that every human being not only deserves but needs "a proper job." By a proper job, Sayers means work that is suited to the worker, work that is both worth doing and well done.[8]

Miss Climpson is brought on stage in *Unnatural Death* because she is better at some types of investigation than either Wimsey or the police—better *because* she is a woman and has learned to notice certain things and to negotiate the minefield of personal relationships that so often explodes into novels, as well as murder *anglaise.* Sherlock Holmes enjoins us to appreciate the "great issues that may hang from a bootlace," a task of no great difficulty for the intelligent female of the species, whose small domestic frame has often limited her to the scrutiny of such minute detail and whose survival has often depended on it. In the spinster-sleuth, Sayers takes another stereotypically female activity, gossip, and rarifies the potentially destructive habit into an art and science. Accustomed to the role of confidante the spinster so often fulfills in fiction, and presumably in life, Miss Climpson makes a graceful, unobtrusive investigator who is able to "ask questions which a young man could not put without a blush."[9] When such an innocuous-looking "elderly spinster"[10] appears on the scene, "of course she asks questions—everyone expects it. Nobody is surprised. Nobody is alarmed. And so-called superfluity is agreeable and usefully disposed of" (*Unnatural Death*, ch. 3). Miss Climpson has thus found a "good job" in the real sense of the term. As Sayer asserts in the 1938 essay "Are Women Human?," "The only decent reason for tackling any job is that it is *your* job, and *you* want to do it" (*Unpopular Opinions* 109). Through Miss Climpson and the Cattery, Sayers comments on a serious social problem of her day; with typical confidence and panache, she suggests a commonsensical solution to the predicament of women for whom a wasteful and inefficient world seems to have no use. This is the first glimmering of the Dorothy Sayers that would emerge a decade later in the essays of incisive social criticism.[11] It also adumbrates the kind of social commentary that was to inform her best novels dealing with contemporary society and the women's question, *The Documents in the Case* (1930) and *Gaudy Night*.

When Sayers created Miss Climpson, she brought a traditional detective type into the postwar world. Women crime-solvers had been a feature of detective fiction as early as 1861, when W. S. Hayward's *The Revelations of a Lady Detective* recounted the experiences of a fictional female sleuth at Scotland Yard.[12] Hayward's Mrs. Paschal, like the members of Wimsey's Cattery, took up the job of detecting "as an escape from the dreadful alternative of genteel poverty" (Craig and Cadogan 15), the most likely alternative for both spinsters and widows. While the idea of a female detective might have been the sheerest fantasy in the Victorian period, by November of 1918 twenty-five women had been appointed to the London Metropolitan Police, in ample time to prepare Sayers's Inspector Parker to deal with a female detective. In their historical survey of women in crime fiction, Patricia Craig and Mary Cadogan note that another variation on the type, which they call the "elderly-busybody" female detective, was created in 1896 by the first of a long line of women detective novelists, the American Anna Katharine Green (11). Women have thus figured significantly in the development of detective fiction, as both writers and detectives, almost from the beginning. Given this fact, in addition to the considerable female readership for mysteries, it is not surprising to find the form addressing issues of particular concern to women. For reasons discussed below, an unmarried woman has had a special place in the history of this genre.

By the time Sayers wrote *Unnatural Death,* she was surely aware of the convention of the female detective and its variant, the spinster-sleuth, since she was already immersed in research for her proposed critical-biographical study of Wilkie Collins.[13] In fact, her study of Collins must have strongly influenced her in this area, because she particularly admired his subtle analysis of the predicament of Victorian women, once declaring him to be the "most genuinely feminist of all the nineteenth century novelists."[14]

Although Agatha Christie's Miss Marple is no doubt the most famous representative of the spinster-sleuth tradition, it is important to note that Miss Climpson predated her by three years.[15] Exemplifying the differences between Sayers and Christie—two writers who are often inappropriately compared—Miss Climpson is a more rounded and sympathetic character than Miss Marple, and the stories in which she appears focus more on the realistic portrayal of character and social milieu than upon the slick mechanism of the detective plot that was Christie's forte. This is to say that Sayers was working in a genuinely novelistic tradition, while Christie used narrative simply as a way of structuring the detective puzzle.[16] Even though neither of their spinster-sleuths has an official status or aegis for her inquiries, Miss Climpson is firmly supported by the wealth and social position of Lord Peter Wimsey—an important concession to realism, given her time and place. How any amateur becomes involved in the investigation of a crime is a perennial problem in detective fiction, a problem that often strains credibility to the limit. Lord Peter himself must wrestle with his amateur status as a crime-solver, but as his employee, Miss Climpson is unassailably professional, a privileged place indeed for a woman of her generation. No self-appointed busybody snooping among unwitting neighbors, Miss Climpson's proper job is detection. It is clear, in fact, that this "most faithful of sleuths" (*Unnatural Death,* ch. 16) is a thoroughly businesslike woman who appreciates the responsibilities and perquisites of her job (ch. 22). By working for Wimsey, she and the other "superfluous women" employed by the Cattery gain access to the hierarchical power structure of society, an access usually barred to their gender. Shrewd and deliberate, Miss Climpson would have chosen the law as her profession had she been born a generation or two later (ch. 3), but her intelligence is well used in her position as Peter Wimsey's strong auxiliary. Miss Climpson typifies "the woman detective [who] stands out as the most striking, and the most agreeable embodiment of two qualities often disallowed for women in the past: the power of action and practical intelligence" (Craig and Cadogan 246).

Miss Climpson's character is so strong and interesting, in fact, that in *Unnatural Death* she tends to steal the show. Certainly this book's most vivid and memorable scenes center on her, as she interrogates villagers, examines her own highly bred Christian conscience, and comments on the varieties of female experience reflected in these pages. The richly comic and thoroughly human character of Miss Climpson is an indication of Sayers's novelistic abilities and her movement toward writing a traditional English novel, a genre distinguished by memorable "minor" characters that are often its most striking feature.

Miss Climpson is dramatized chiefly through her letters, with their effusive enthusiasm and wild emphases. These letters reveal that Sayers has really penetrated Miss Climpson's mind, as she had never inhabited Lord Peter's mind in the earlier novels.[17] The result is fiction that is both more believable and more subtle. Since Sayers had been working on her study of Wilkie Collins during the mid-1920s, it is possible that she was deliberately experimenting with the epistolary form, which Collins had used to great effect in *The Moonstone* (1868). (In 1930, she would write her own stunning epistolary novel, *The Documents in the Case*.) But equally important is the sense that Miss Climpson is so real because she reflects a deeply felt part of Dorothy Sayers's experience. As James Brabazon says, albeit with too little recognition of Peter Wimsey's representing an essential part of Sayers's personality, "Wimsey was fabricated for a purpose—Miss Climpson came from the heart" (128).

Sayers's access to Miss Climpson's mind is often exploited for comic effect, as in the description of the spinster-sleuth's realization that "'if Mary Whittaker were to marry, she would marry a rabbit.' (Miss Climpson's active mind quickly conjured up a picture of the rabbit—fair-haired and a little paunchy, with a habit of saying, 'I'll ask the wife.')" (*Unnatural Death*, ch. 16). Like the endless "twaddle" of her letters to Lord Peter, Miss Climpson's seemingly irrelevant flow of ideas here is a clue not only to the character of Mary Whittaker, who is the novel's villain, but to the solution of the mystery as well. At a turning point in the novel, we are made privy to Miss Climpson's struggles with the moral implications of detection, a fact which elevates the work from simple detective story to the realm of fable.[18] Finally, with Huck Finn–like irony, she decides to risk going to hell anyway: "'Well,'" said Miss Climpson, "'if this is a sin I am going to do it, and may I be forgiven'" (*Unnatural Death*, ch. 22). Though what happens to her soul as a result of this action is never clear, the detective in her is richly repaid: "From these few fossil bones [the scattered words and phrases written down by an anguished young woman preparing for confession], Miss Climpson had little difficulty in reconstructing one of those hateful and passionate 'scenes' of slighted jealousy with which a woman-ridden life had made her only too familiar. . . . Humiliating, degrading, exhausting, beastly scenes. Girls' school, boarding-house, Bloomsbury-flat scenes. . . . Silly *schwarmerei* swamping all decent self-respect. Barren quarrels ending in shame and hatred" (ch. 22). Perhaps Dorothy Sayers had herself experienced or witnessed such scenes; she seems painfully aware of, and frightened by, the destructive tension created by inharmonious sexual relationships—especially when, in the absence of useful work, those relationships become the focus of life.

Miss Climpson is by nature "an active woman" who becomes anxious and depressed when she is "condemned to inactivity" (*Unnatural Death*, ch. 22). Without her intelligence and resolve, as well as the salubrious "outlet" of the Cattery, she might have become the pathetically ridiculous, and ultimately dangerous, frustrate typified by Agatha Milsom in *The Documents in the Case*. Her sex drive and need for useful occupation sublimated in inexplicable cravings, bizarre avocations, and wild fantasies, Miss Milsom encourages the destructive tension in the Harrison household that culminates in adultery and murder.[19] Yet Miss Climpson, who has found her proper job, turns her spinster status into an advantage, because it frees her from the tedium and routine of family duties.[20] Since she is elderly, and thus presumably beyond the marriageable years, Miss Climpson is also protected from the suspicion of sexual motivation for her investigative activities. In this way, she is similar to most of the great male detectives, who tend to be either asexual, in the Holmesian mold, or at least do not mix romance with detection.[21]

Yet Miss Climpson is "a spinster made not born—a perfectly womanly woman" (*Unnatural Death*, ch. 16), her creator appears anxious to tell us, perhaps to differentiate her clearly from the two generations of lesbians who generate the novel's mystery plot. Unlike these women, who have aggressively rejected the company of men, Miss Climpson is no man-hater; her relationship with Lord Peter is one of great warmth and mutual respect. The assumption is that Katherine Climpson would have chosen marriage as certainly as she would have chosen the law, but history made both choices impossible for her; her sleuthing is the best job she can make of her life given the circumstances.[22] To readers in the latter part of the twentieth century, this may not be a sympathetic position for Sayers to take on the subject of marriage, but it is the position she also took in her own life; in some ways a conventional person, she seems to have concluded that a marriage of compromise was preferable to no marriage at all.

In contrast to Miss Climpson, the spinster "made not born" who would have chosen a conventional married life, there are the novel's two lesbian couples who represent, in turn, happy and unhappy matches between females from two different generations of Englishwomen. Exemplifying the old order, Miss Agatha Dawson, whom Miss Climpson comes to regard as "a remarkable old lady" (*Unnatural Death*, ch. 12), is heartlessly murdered by her ruthless niece, Mary Whittaker, perhaps the most wicked of Sayers's villains. The actions of Mary Whittaker, a nurse who takes advantage of her privileged relationship with a patient who is also her loving aunt, suggest she "thought that anyone who inconvenienced her had no right to exist."[23] Her murder of Miss Dawson, which is motivated by money, sets off a string of other killings, including the murder of a young woman whom Whittaker has manipulated into self-effacing and humiliating devotion. Whittaker's material greed extends into a kind of emotional greed, the rapacious possessiveness that masquerades as love. She thus represents what is for Dorothy L. Sayers one of the most flawed human actions, that of turning another person into one's job. (This is the flaw underlying the actions of the Shrewsbury Poison Pen in *Gaudy Night*.) Contrasted with the deception and hideous artifice of Mary Whittaker is the bracing and appealing image of her victim's partner, as she is remembered by a loyal old retainer who was in her employ for fifty years:

> "A rare young lady she was in them days. . . . Straight as a switch, with a fine, high colour in her cheeks and shiny black hair—just like a beautiful two-year-old filly she was. And very sperrited. Wonnerful sperrited. There was a many gentlemen as would have been glad to hitch up with her, but she was never broke to harness. . . . Well, there is some creatures like that. I'ad a terrier-bitch that way. Great ratter she was. But a business woman—nothin' else. . . . The Lord makes a few on 'em that way to suit 'Is purposes, I suppose." (ch. 12)

"A business woman—nothin' else" describes not only Clara Whittaker but Miss Climpson herself. Whereas old Miss Whittaker was a good horsewoman, Mary Whittaker is a bad nurse, a fact suggesting her moral corruption. Having suitable work and serving that work well are sympathetic traits in Sayers's characters generally, and her insistence on the central place of work in human life remains one of the most liberating aspects of her treatment of women and their experience.[24]

Without such suitable employment, people become dangerous to themselves and others: "A human being *must* have occupation, if he or she is not to become a nuisance to the world," Sayers once warned (*Unpopular Opinions* 110). These "nuisances" may take the form of petty irritations and gossip; they may escalate into emotional vampirism; their apex is the destruction of peace and order in the act of murder.[25] The need for productive work is a curious and yet oddly fitting theme for a detective story, a form that tends to flourish among leisured classes. The genre itself may, in fact, be regarded as one of the games invented by civilized people to occupy time, to provide innocuous employment for those who might otherwise become nuisances to their world.

The use of the spinster-sleuth is a striking example of the tendency of detective fiction to mirror the concerns and experience of its time, in this case, the changing status of women and their quest for fulfilling work. Specifically, the character type suggests a way of capitalizing on the growing economic burden of women who had become superfluous or redundant—to use the more contemporary but equally cruel adjective—since the mid-nineteenth century, when the detective story was born. Casting a spinster in the role of detective may, in our day, appear conventional, even trite. Is the spinster-sleuth just another variation on the old joke about the old maid seeking excitement in the threat of violence? Perhaps the murder mystery itself, with its titillating and faintly erotic insinuations of forbidden action and information, is just a stylized sublimation of the sex drive. Detection at least constitutes an acceptable instrument for probing into other people's lives and psyches—dangerous territory for a form often described as "cozy." It is interesting that today, when being an unmarried woman does not necessarily imply spinsterhood or virginity, the female detectives created by writers like Amanda Cross, P. D. James, and Lady Antonia Fraser may be unmarried, but one would not likely call them spinsters—except, perhaps, in the narrowly legal sense of the word.

Yet Sayers's use of the spinster may appear more stereotyped than it actually is. As the novels present Miss Climpson, it is her rational mind, rather than any patronizing notion of "women's intuition," which makes her a good detective.[26] Like Wimsey and Holmes before her, Miss Climpson "reads" experience. She once maintained, correctly, that she knew the accused in a murder trial was innocent, not because of any factual evidence presented but because the person's "demeanour [which was calm and open] was part of the evidence" (*Strong Poison,* ch. 4). Such deduction may appear to be intuition or guesswork, especially to those not literate in the language of appearances, but it is actually the product of a person who has learned to interpret experience in its smallest, most subtle details.

When in *Strong Poison* (1930) Sayers introduces Harriet Vane, who is an educated woman like herself, she introduces another variation on female experience and the marriage question. Unlike Miss Climpson and the many unskilled women who need work, Harriet Vane is well equipped to take care of herself, by herself. Like her creator, she is a successful detective novelist and Oxford-educated scholar. She has satisfying work, enough money to support herself (*Have His Carcase,* ch. 1). Should she remain unmarried, then, or fall into the marriage trap? Must marriage be a trap for her, since she can enter into it freely, without the conventional economic and social motives? Sayers weaves these two strains together in a most ingenious way: she makes Climpson and the Cattery responsible for saving Vane's life, thereby suggesting the necessary interdependence of all women. It is the tough-minded Miss Climpson who, as a jury member, forces a retrial for Harriet Vane when she is falsely accused of murdering her lover. The relationship between Climpson and Vane thus reiterates a common fictional motif. As Nina Auerbach has observed, "In both art and life we find intense alliances between the old maid and the fallen woman, each in her own way an exile from woman's conventional family-bounded existence" (151). Though Sayers may not agree with the judgment, society treats Vane as a "fallen" woman in the aftermath of her lover's death. As the crucial juror in Vane's trial for murder, Miss Climpson dramatizes the "reclamation of fallen women [which] was one of the few respectable activities available to philanthropically minded Victorian spinsters" (Auerbach 153). The relationship between these two women suggests a powerful realism in Sayers's characterization of Miss Climpson, who was, after all, a product of the Victorian era and an embodiment of its values of duty, propriety, and enterprise.

At the end of *Strong Poison,* with Vane free both legally and financially, the focus turns to her dilemma of choice, which is the basis of both *Have His Carcase* (1932) and *Gaudy Night*. In the latter novel, she chooses to marry, but this is just one in a series of choices, as *Busman's Honeymoon* (1937) makes clear. In each of these novels, significant spinsters and other unattached women appear, imaging different female proclivities and predicaments: the pathetic, aimless spinsters and widows of *Have His Carcase;* the spiteful, man-hating mantrap, Miss Hillyard, of *Gaudy Night;* the desperate Aggie Twitterton of *Busman's Honeymoon*. Against these lost women are pitted the considerable strengths of Miss Climpson herself, as well as the happily unmarried female dons at Oxford (who will make up Harriet's ebullient bridal party when she finally marries Wimsey) and the self-respecting women writers and artists of London.[27] Given her reluctance to marry, it is interesting that Harriet Vane's name was originally Marian,[28] suggesting she was perhaps inspired by Wilkie Collins's Marian Halcombe, that similarly strong and strangely alluring heroine who has been called "the most explicit exaltation of the old maid as a criticism of traditional wifehood" (Auerbach 142). Like Halcombe, Vane rejects traditional notions of wifehood, at least until she appears in "Talboys," a slight story written in 1942 but unpublished until 1972. Indeed, it seems likely that it was her heroine's alarming descent into conventional English housewifery that kept Sayers from publishing this story in her lifetime.[29] Even *Busman's Honeymoon* shows Harriet struggling against wifeliness (ch. 17). While it may not be true that Marian Halcombe was "fiction's first female detective" (Auerbach 138), she is one of the most striking examples of that type in a mainstream novel, the kind of book that Dorothy L. Sayers wanted to write. Certainly Marian Halcombe, with her superior intelligence, courage, and resourcefulness, must also be one of the greatest spinster-sleuths of all time.[30]

One of Sayers's great strengths as a novelist is her sensitive portrayal of the predicament of modern bourgeois women, a predicament which Ian Watt has ascribed to "the all but unendurable disparity between expectation and reality that faces sensitive women in modern society, and the difficulties that lie before anyone who is unwilling either to be used, or to use others, as a means" (225). In the character of Harriet Vane, Sayers explores the possibility of marriage and independence, or of love and work, coexisting in a woman's life, a possibility that exists only because Miss Climpson had first supported and defended Harriet's right to exist. A curious fact is that Harriet herself fails as a detective, perhaps because she has not made peace with her gender and sexuality as Miss

Climpson has. In *Gaudy Night*, Harriet's dreams reveal her sexual anxiety, and Wimsey, who is admittedly not disinterested in the matter, concludes that her temporary celibacy actually keeps her from solving the mystery (ch. 15).

Miss Climpson's brilliant maiden sleuthing is more analogous to the work of Lord Peter Wimsey and his precursor, Sherlock Holmes. Each delves into detection to find an object in life, to justify an otherwise meaningless existence. Miss Climpson is really Lord Peter's alter ego; both of them "great talkers upon little matters," her seemingly meaningless "twaddle" is as revealing as his "piffle."[31] She, too, seeks escape from the emptiness and ennui of modern life, utilizing the detective's essential rational, social, and psychological skills in a socially beneficial way.

Sayers's last completed novel was the 1937 *Busman's Honeymoon*, where Miss Climpson appears briefly as an ecstatic member of Harriet and Peter's wedding party, and we effectively bid adieu to this vibrant fictional world. But the novelist brought a few of her characters into the war years in "The Wimsey Papers," which were published in *The Spectator* from November 1939 until January 1940. Miss Climpson, who must have been one of her creator's favorites, is still gloriously alive in these witty letters, once again displaying Sayers's talent for characterization and the epistolary form. Here, the engaging spinster comments not only on the situation of women but on the world at large—the world at war. Like Wimsey, Miss Climpson is a detective who moves easily into even more demanding work for the Foreign Office. In a letter dated November 19, 1939, she writes to Lord Peter, who is "somewhere abroad" on a delicate diplomatic mission; it is interesting to note the similarities between Miss Climpson's language in this missive and the language Sayers used to introduce her in *Unnatural Death:* "I must tell you again how *proud* and *delighted* all the members of the 'Cattery' (to use your own humorous phrase!) are feeling to know that they are really being of *use* to their country in this terrible time of *emergency*. Especially the older ones—because it is so *humiliating and depressing* when one comes to a certain age, to feel that one is NOT WANTED" (*The Spectator*, December 1, 1939: 770). To be of use; to find suitable work; to discover meaning in one's existence—these are the imperatives of any human being's life, and the work of the spinster-sleuth is one means of accomplishing them.

There is another, perhaps more surprising voice heard in back of all Sayers's talk about unmarried women: "All the employees [of the Cattery] were women—mostly elderly . . . all . . . of the class unkindly known as 'superfluous.' There were spinsters with small fixed incomes, or no income at all; widows without family; women deserted by peripatetic husbands and living on restricted alimony, who, previous to their engagement by Miss Climpson, had *had no resources but bridge and boardinghouse gossip*" (*Strong Poison*, ch. 5, emphasis added). With this echo of Jane Austen's Mrs. Bates—that "harmless old lady" who was "past everything but tea and quadrille" after years as a distressed gentlewoman—Sayers acknowledges unabashedly "the economic basis of society" that is brought home to these women each day.[32] All are defined by their marriage status. As fully responsible human beings, each faces the bald reality stated by Miss Climpson in a letter to Lord Peter, a reality Dorothy Sayers had learned in the difficult years between going down from Oxford and finding success as a novelist: at least for those who do not marry or inherit wealth, finding work is not a luxury, for "you can't have money unless you *make* it" (*The Spectator*, December 1, 1939: 770). Although women had, by Sayers's time, acquired some of the means and opportunity for earning money of their own, the cruel fact was that society was still not ready to accommodate many of them with suitable work.

As Harriet Vane struggles with the question of whether she should marry, she observes the miserable women waiting around a dance floor in some vulgar watering hole in the south of England and thinks, "Did one come to this, then, if one did not marry? Making a public scorn of one's self before the waiters? She glanced again at the woman, who was rising to leave the lounge. She wore a wedding-ring. Marriage did not save one, apparently. Single, married, widowed, divorced, one came to the same end" (*Have His Carcase*, ch. 3). Since she is younger and better educated, Harriet is freer than Miss Climpson, but her life is consequently more complicated also. The history of Vane's choice, which is the focus of the novels in which she appears, calls to mind the pattern of both *Pride and Prejudice* and *Jane Eyre*, a book to which Harriet refers as she talks to Wimsey.[33] Like each of these great novels, the Vane-Wimsey books ask if it is possible for a strong, intelligent, independent woman to marry and retain her identity, her self-respect; if men and women can ever meet as equals in society's most basic institution. This connection, as well as Sayers's sensitive portrayal of the marriage question as a central preoccupation of a woman's life, suggests that she had indeed accomplished her original goal of "writing a mystery story that was more like a conventional novel"[34] and less like the standard detective story of her day.

In "Are Women Human?," which was written after the completion of her last novel, Sayers asserted the disarmingly simple truth that, as human beings, women want the same things as men: "interesting occupation, reasonable freedom for their pleasures, and a sufficient emotional outlet" (*Unpopular Opinions* 114). In her novels, she explores the possibility of fulfilling these basic human needs both inside and outside of marriage. Her creation of Miss Climpson, the first and, arguably, the best spinster-sleuth in modern detective fiction, is one answer to this complex problem of how women are to live as fully realized human beings in a changing world. Long before P. D. James's Cordelia Gray, Miss Climpson demonstrated that detection could indeed be a most suitable job for a woman, especially for an excellent woman like herself. A representative figure from the late nineteenth and early twentieth centuries, she stands as a sympathetic portrait of female experience in the transition period between the domestic security of the past and the full-fledged independence of our time.

NOTES

1. See Dorothy L. Sayers, "Gaudy Night," *Titles to Fame*, ed. D. K. Roberts (London: Thomas Nelson, 1937), and "The Present Status of the Mystery Story," *London Mercury*, 23.133 (1930): 47–52.

2. See "Present Status" and Sayers's reviews in *The Sunday Times* (London), June 25, 1933–August 18, 1935.

3. For laudatory views of Sayers, see Winks; Mann; and Haycraft. For an indictment of her work, see Symons. Even those who do not like her acknowledge her importance by the level of their antipathy.

4. See the manuscript of this novel in the Wade Center of Wheaton College, Wheaton, Illinois.

5. The other important unmarried women would include Clara Whittaker and Vera Findlater.

6. Lord Peter is here, but he is assisted greatly by Miss Climpson.

7. This is shown as a quote from Gilbert Frankau, source unknown.

8. See Dorothy L. Sayers, *The Mind of the Maker* (London: Methuen, 1941), and "Are Women Human?" *Unpopular Opinions* (London: Gollancz, 1946).

9. *Unnatural Death*, ch. 16; cf. Barbara Pym's "excellent women" who maintain this function.

10. In *Unnatural Death*, Climpson is described as "middle-aged" (ch. 3), but a short four years later in *Strong Poison*, she is introduced in chapter 1 as elderly, which suits her better.

11. I do not mean to suggest Sayers was using fiction as propaganda; rather, her novels were serious reflections on her world, as good fiction

traditionally is. Her later social criticism appeared in such essays as "Are Women Human?," *Begin Here* (London: Gollancz, 1940), *The Mind of the Maker*, and the collections *Unpopular Opinions* and *Creed or Chaos?* (London: Methuen, 1947).

12. It is possible, of course, to stretch the meaning of the term and consider Emma Woodhouse and Jane Eyre "detectives," but such blurring of the genre would seem to obscure as much as it illumines.

13. There is much evidence of this, including the manuscripts and notebooks in the Wade Center, as well as the allusions to mystery and detection that fill even Sayers's early novels.

14. "Introduction" to Wilkie Collins, *The Moonstone*, ed. Dorothy L. Sayers (London: J. M. Dent, 1944) viii. The positive use of the word "feminist" here is especially intriguing, because Sayers often went to great lengths—as in "Are Women Human?"—to dissociate herself from feminism.

15. Miss Climpson also predates the less appealing and more unrealistic spinster created by Patricia Wentworth, Miss Maud Silver, who appears in books filled with sexual and cultural clichés.

16. See "Present Status" on these two strains in the history of detection.

17. She will penetrate Lord Peter's consciousness after *The Documents in the Case*, when he is rendered vulnerable by his love for Harriet Vane.

18. This question is raised again in *The Documents in the Case* and *The Nine Tailors*.

19. Cf. Miss Hillyard of *Gaudy Night* and Miss Twitterton of *Busman's Honeymoon*.

20. The early female detectives who were married tended to serve family responsibilities even in their detection, often trying to exonerate a husband or brother. Today, a character like Amanda Cross's Kate Fansler is consciously revising the definition of female experience, especially as it relates to marriage. See Cross's *The Question of Max* or *Death in a Tenured Position*.

21. True of Dupin, Holmes, Poirot, and the early Wimsey, and of Nero Wolfe.

22. She is, therefore, much like the displaced aristocrat, Lord Peter Wimsey, who is looking for work and a place in this world.

23. *Unnatural Death*, ch. 23. The somewhat confusing relationships among characters in this novel demonstrate Sayers's interest in genealogy. Simply put, Clara Whittaker and Agatha Dawson were spinsters; two of their siblings married and the grandchild of these two people, Mary Whittaker, eventually murdered Agatha Dawson to insure her inheritance.

24. See Miss Meteyard of *Murder Must Advertise*, as well as the discussions of this subject in *Gaudy Night*, *The Zeal of Thy House* (London: Gollancz, 1937), and "Are Women Human?"

25. Most of her villains pervert work in some way, for example, the corrupt physicians in *Whose Body?* (1923) and *The Unpleasantness at the Bellona Club* (1928).

26. See ch. 17 and 18 of *Strong Poison*, where the notion of women's intuition is parodied in a seance.

27. See especially *Strong Poison, The Unpleasantness at the Bellona Club,* and *Murder Must Advertise* for the two kinds of unmarried women Sayers depicts.

28. See the manuscript of the novel in the Wade Center.

29. This story was published posthumously in the 2d. ed. of *Lord Peter,* an anthology of all the Wimsey stories (New York: Avon Books, 1972).

30. Marian Halcombe is a character in Collins's *The Woman in White.*

31. Cf. Jane Austen's *Emma,* ch. 3; *Strong Poison,* ch. 11; and *Unnatural Death,* ch. 8.

32. See *Emma,* ch. 3, for the prototypical incessant chatterer. Given the possible relationship between such talking habits and sexual frustration, it is curious that Wimsey's mother notices how profoundly still he becomes after his engagement to Harriet Vane (*Busman's Honeymoon,* "Prothalamion"). I am also quoting from W. H. Auden's famous lines on Jane Austen in his "Letter to Lord Byron," from *Collected Longer Poems.*

33. *Busman's Honeymoon,* "Prothalamion."

34. See the essay "Gaudy Night" 75.

WORKS CITED

References to novels by Sayers and others are given chapter, not page, citations so that readers may refer to any available edition. The following are the secondary sources cited.

Auerbach, Nina. *Woman and the Demon: The Life of a Victorian Myth.* Cambridge: Harvard University Press, 1982.

Brabazon, James. *Dorothy L. Sayers.* New York: Scribner's, 1981.

Craig, Patricia, and Mary Cadogan. *The Lady Investigates: Women Detectives and Spies in Fiction.* New York: St. Martin's, 1981.

Haycraft, Howard. *Murder for Pleasure: The Life and Times of the Detective Story.* New York: D. Appleton Century, 1941.

Mann, Jessica. *Deadlier than the Male: An Investigation into Feminine Crime Writing.* London: David and Charles, 1981.

Symons, Julian. *The Detective Story in Britain.* London: Longman's Green, 1969.

Watt, Ian. *The Rise of the Novel.* Berkeley: University of California Press, 1952.

Winks, Robin. *Detective Fiction: A Collection of Critical Essays.* Englewood Cliffs, N.J.: Prentice-Hall, 1980.

Laura L. Doan

Pym's Singular Interest: The Self as Spinster

In the spring of 1938, the twenty-four-year-old Barbara Pym made a curious, even bizarre, declaration in a joint letter addressed to her closest friends.[1] Writing in an uncharacteristic, stream-of-consciousness style and rendering herself the subject by using the detached third person, Pym proclaims herself a spinster: "And Miss Pym is looking out of the window—and you will be asking now who is this Miss Pym, and I will tell you that she is a spinster lady *who was thought to have been disappointed in love,* and so now you know who is this Miss Pym" (*A Very Private Eye* 67, emphasis added). The disparity between what is actually written ("who was *thought* to have been disappointed in love") and what might have been written (a more open, unequivocal statement of fact— "who *was* or *was not* disappointed in love") is telling. The choice of the former, more ambiguous expression points to the chasm between public perception and individual experience. The letter, an exercise in ambiguity, teases by gesturing toward disclosure only to draw back playfully. The promise of revelation is illusory: "This spinster, this Barbara Mary Crampton Pym, she will be smiling to herself—ha-ha she will be saying inside. *But I have that within which passeth show*—maybe she will be saying that, but she is a queer old horse, this old brown spinster, so I cannot forecast exactly what she will be saying" (68–69). Closing with a mock invitation to speculate on the reason for her happiness, the elusive text refuses to supply the answer: "you will never know now, because this Miss Pym, this old brown horse spinster, is all shut up like oyster, or like clam" (71).

Pym's recognition of the difficulty of a life on the margins of the social order resonates in this early letter, and we find a microcosm of Pym's problem within its various and conflicting views of a spinster. Among such scattered self-referential epithets as "dull" or "old brown" spinster, we find a seemingly contradictory reference to the "prudent, sensible spinster" (69). Pym readily asserts that she is "not . . . by any means one of your old fashioned spinsters," but instead of explaining what she is—what sort of different spinster she has become—the writer maintains silence (68). Could it be that

Pym "clams up," so to speak, because she has arrived at a knowledge of self at once liberating and frightening? The independence and autonomy of a life without the conventional (heterosexual) attachment is so socially problematic, indeed so deviant, that Pym's greatest difficulty as a writer is to summon the willingness to communicate her life-choice. In a very real sense, then, this letter works as the declaration of independence of a twenty-four-year-old woman. It is an extraordinarily young age, we might think, to embrace spinsterhood for life, though three years earlier Pym entered in her commonplace book the following passage from Virginia Woolf's *To the Lighthouse*: "it had flashed upon her that she . . . need never marry anybody, and she had felt an enormous exultation" (Malloy 195). Moreover, in 1934 (at age twenty), Pym confides in her diary that "sometime in July I began writing a story about Hilary [Pym's sister] and me as spinsters of fiftyish" (*A Very Private Eye* 44).

Just as Pym's letters and diary entries of the 1930s would seem to confirm spinsterhood as a deliberate choice—sometimes equating marriage with death—her early attempts at fiction explore the question of what sort of writer she would become, how to find a place for her (single) self in the text, and how to present the single state to the reader as a positive choice. After experimenting with various styles and subjects, by 1940 Pym settled into writing what she would often refer to as "her type of novel"; that is, the sort which invariably included spinsters, middle- or upper-middle-class English gentlewomen, living quiet, private lives in unfashionable London suburbs or obscure country villages. Even when publishers began rejecting her manuscripts in the 1960s, often arguing that the readership for her "type of novel" had disappeared, Pym made few substantive concessions in shifting to subjects purportedly more congruent with contemporary tastes.

Such a reluctance to relinquish an interest in an "old-fashioned" topic suggests the depth of Pym's emotional investment, especially in light of her willingness to appropriate its unpopularity, as a 1972 diary entry reveals: "the position of the unmarried woman—unless, of course, she is somebody's mistress, is of no interest whatsoever to the readers of modern fiction. The beginning of a novel?" (*A Very Private Eye* 269). Pym reintroduces the issue, albeit in a version slightly modified and curiously disengaged, in the opening of *Quartet in Autumn*, where Letty complains that "if she hoped to find [a novel] which reflected her own sort of life she had come to realise that the position of an unmarried, unattached, ageing woman is of no interest whatever to the *writer* of modern fiction" (3, emphasis added). Shifting the disinterest from the reader to the writer is significant because, in this last novel written before her "rediscovery," Pym displaces her private fear that the single woman might be uninteresting to an actual reader: the fictional spinster now questions why an actual reader neglects her experience.

In anticipation of the reader's objections to the preoccupation with spinsters, Pym exposes the gap between experience and the novel so that her subsequent work fills the fictional lacuna. The tactic gives the appearance of writing against her own text but, in fact, constitutes the means to justify and legitimize the larger project of locating a space for her (writing) self. For Pym, the act of writing and the process of self-definition are inextricably connected. As Judith Kegan Gardiner argues, "The woman writer uses her text, particularly one centering on a female hero, as part of a continuing process involving her own self-definition and her emphatic identification with her character" (357). Pym's determination to put the single woman at the center of her narrative suggests that writing becomes the process to facilitate her own personal reconciliation with the unmarried state and to resolve her ambivalence toward marriage and sexuality.

Crampton Hodnet (an early novel written in the late 1930s but published only posthumously and therefore untouched by any revisions Pym might have made for publication) offers an unusually transparent view of Pym's first strategy: to disrupt the spinster stereotype. In the opening, Pym's description of Miss Jessie Morrow borders on the pathetic: Miss Morrow, "a thin, used-up looking woman in her middle thirties," sits alone in a gloomy North Oxford sitting room on a rainy afternoon (2). Here her physical features are fully in keeping with the reader's expectations of the spinster stereotype. In the short span of a few lines, however, Pym abruptly contradicts this initial impression by informing the reader that Miss Morrow's appearance is "misleading" because she possesses a "definite personality." Yet the narrator then returns to Miss Morrow's "thin neck . . . small, undistinguished features, her faded blond hair done in a severe knot" (3). By deftly fluctuating between Miss Morrow's relative unattractiveness and her more admirable personal qualities, Pym throws the reliability of superficial impressions into question and posits the existence of a discrepancy between appearance and reality. If Miss Morrow's inner strength enables her to survey the outside world with an amused and self-assured eye, then appearance is of dubious relevance.

After measuring Miss Morrow against the physical stereotype, Pym establishes a further point of reference by comparing Miss Morrow to her employer, the aging spinster Miss Doggett, who specializes in interfering in the business of others. The generational difference between the two women suggests a continuum, the inadequacy of an exhausted stereotype and the possibility of a new image—one which the reader must patiently wait for Pym to create. Miss Doggett's incessant abuse of Miss Morrow merely amplifies the potential to assert a negative as positive: "'Miss Morrow,' said Miss Doggett in a warning tone, 'you are not a woman of the world'" (54). Miss Morrow lowers her head in silence, but the narrator tells us, "The last thing [Miss Morrow] would ever claim to be was a woman of the world" (54). By seditiously questioning the logic of a privileged attribute, the idea of a worldly woman, Pym neutralizes and ultimately dismisses the negative potential of unworldliness. Miss Doggett's admonitions—on appearance or character—are carefully undermined to establish the groundwork for a more positive characterization of the spinster.

If, as I have argued, the rupture of the spinster stereotype depends on labeling physical appearance as problematic and misleading, Pym must succeed in conveying an impression of the spinster that lies beneath the surface. By investing Miss Morrow with brutal self-honesty and self-acceptance, the same qualities that separate Pym's new spinster from the Miss Doggetts of the world, Pym gives the spinster an integrity that preempts the negative image and thus disarms it. Miss Morrow "did not pretend to be anything more than a woman past her first youth, resigned to the fact that her life was probably never going to be more exciting than it was now" (3). Her secondary status as a paid companion in a household is similar to that of a governess, and she freely admits to a laughing vicar that "a companion is looked upon as a piece of furniture . . . hardly a person at all" (17). This statement may register as hard and blunt, but the bold terms are Miss Morrow's own, uttered without bitterness.

Throughout the narrative, Pym repeatedly posits the equivalence of a paid companion and a piece of furniture and, surprisingly, even claims it is a virtue: "If [the new curate] had time to analyze his feelings," he would probably think of Miss Morrow as a "comfortable chair by the fire" (31). With remarkable economy, she transposes the analogy ("piece of furniture" to "comfortable chair by the fire") to imply that men are unthinking and, more important, that a spinster of Miss Morrow's caliber, like comfort itself, is hardly unwelcome. With a matter-of-fact acceptance rather than anxiety, Miss Morrow reflects that "inanimate objects were often so much nicer than people" (31).

The introduction of a male inhabitant into the household (a typical tactic in Pym's later novels) is the catalyst to demonstrate that Miss Morrow is not a spinster because she is unmarriageable. Stephen Latimer, an eligible bachelor, finds Miss Morrow quite pleasant to look at, sensible, and "safe." In other words, she "wasn't likely to throw her arms around his neck" (27). Latimer's intrusion into the all-female environment invites speculation about Miss Morrow's experience with men and with life in general. Miss Morrow does make a bit of a fool of herself in fumbling with makeup before Latimer's arrival, but the triumph of appearance over character is short-lived. Miss Morrow never repeats the momentary lapse of the makeup incident, and, in fact, Pym takes care to stress that Miss Morrow is beyond becoming infatuated with a man. Midway through the narrative, the tone shifts significantly as Pym becomes increasingly brazen about the inadequacies of the opposite sex. Latimer's little attentions—received as compliments rather than as signals to set about scheming on how best to trap a man—impel Miss Morrow to recall male shortcomings and to extol female virtues: "Men *are* feeble, inefficient sorts of creatures . . . women are used to bearing burdens and taking blame" (40).

In Latimer's proposal to Miss Morrow, Pym situates her most explicit and radical statement in favor of spinsterhood, denying that spinsters are spinsters because they cannot find husbands. Pym cleverly demonstrates how the prospect of marriage elicits different, and unanticipated, responses. In Latimer's case, the offer is a desperate and vaguely despicable act stemming from his own restlessness and a fundamental dissatisfaction with his career. Miss Morrow enjoys his attentions and finds his proposal flattering, but, because she perceives that his offer stems not from love but from a need to escape a dull life, she must reject him. A marriage for the sake of marriage (that is, without love) is out of the question. By casting Miss Morrow's rejection as a courageous endorsement of her values and her dignity, Pym distracts the reader's attention to preclude a negative interpretation and to demonstrate that Miss Morrow's motives are laudable. Pym's diversionary tactic leaves little room for the reader to realize that marriage would afford Miss Morrow the opportunity to escape her *own* dull life, not to mention the tyranny of Miss Doggett. Through this episode in which Miss Morrow accepts a life alone rather than compromise her ideals, Pym asserts that high standards, more than anything else, force spinsters to refuse marriage proposals. (Later we will see that "high standards" can cloak a more complex response to the idea of marriage.) The point here is that *she* makes the choice to marry or to remain single, and, as Joanne Frye notes, "choice becomes a part of the overall defining quality of . . . character and self. . . . To choose is itself an action and to be able to choose is the decisive characteristic of selfhood" (69–70). With the power that choice engenders, the possibility of being left on the shelf is not the most frightening prospect to Pym's spinsters.

Upon Latimer's holiday departure, Miss Morrow enjoys her newly restored sense of freedom—a liberation symbolically marked by the transformation of the monkey-puzzle tree. In the opening of the novel, the branches of the tree outside the sitting-room window obliterate the sunlight, forcing Miss Morrow to sit in dark isolation. When Latimer eventually takes his leave, the monkey-puzzle tree, once an emblem of loneliness, now becomes the focus for a celebration of life: "Even the monkey-puzzle was bathed in sunshine . . . one realized that it was a living thing too and had beauty, as most living things have in some form or another. Dear monkey-puzzle, thought Miss Morrow, impulsively clasping her arms round the trunk" (156). The incident constitutes one of the few occasions when Miss Morrow acts impulsively. Freely accepting spinsterhood so emboldens her that, when Miss Doggett pronounces her ridiculous for embracing a tree, the normally silent Miss Morrow "unexpectedly" challenges the censure: "'Only God can make a tree'" (156). Identifying with the tree itself, Miss Morrow perceives a natural place for women like herself in the vast plan of life. While continuing to think of herself as a "neutral thing, without form or sex," she is certain of her value as a living being and confident of her right to a bit of happiness (160). In this, Miss Morrow is successful, and, feeling no sentimentality over Latimer's leaving, she strips his bedsheets and thinks herself lucky to have escaped.

Depicting the psychological journey from complacent resignation to a joyful embrace of the single life, Pym ends the narrative with an account of a failed marriage, inviting the reader to decide who is really better off. The narrator juxtaposes Miss Morrow's contentment with Mrs. Cleveland's distress over her husband's affair. In an ironic twist, the wife, who realizes that the strange woman sitting beside her in a restaurant is probably not married, contemplates the spinster's enviable position: "She was a comfortable spinster with nobody but herself to consider. Living in a tidy house not far from London, making nice little supper dishes for one, a place for everything and everything in its place, no husband hanging resentfully round the sitting-room . . . Mrs. Cleveland sighed a sigh of envy. No husband" (172). Here the endorsement of spinsterhood resonates from the realizations of a wife trapped in a dreary, unsatisfying marriage—not from the rationalizations of a disgruntled spinster trapped in bitter isolation. Married women cannot escape.

As Pym's voice breaks through the text and rejects any attempt to negate women like herself, mere self-acceptance gives way to a more radical and subversive strategy designed to question the very validity of marriage. The life of a spinster only *seems* dreary to those on the outside; Pym demonstrates that, for those with a properly informed disposition, the life-style is a viable option and often preferable. When a young undergraduate named Barbara Bird flees her affair with Mr. Cleveland at the end of the novel, she also feels as if she has escaped. Young Barbara, a character Hazel Holt suggests is Pym herself, reflects, "She was sure she would never marry now, and there came into her mind the comforting picture of herself, a beautiful, cultured woman with sad eyes" (190). This romantic, if somewhat tragic, representation of the single woman is a far cry from that of the lonely, pathetic spinster.

In the introductory note to *Crampton Hodnet,* Hazel Holt speculates that, rather than find a publisher, Pym moved on to other projects because the manuscript "seemed to her to be too dated to be publishable" (vi). Given the power of her uncompromising attitude toward single women and marriage, it is equally plausible that Pym could not yet so blatantly present such an intensely personal view. Pym's own consciousness of marginality inhibits her temptation to denounce openly the constraints imposed by a rigid social order. In a sense then *Crampton Hodnet,* with its nascent, experimental narrative strategy, functions as a blueprint for Pym's other novels, which are in many ways variations on its theme. Pym's own conflicting attitudes toward the single life are slowly and cautiously plotted out because she believes her socially unacceptable life-style requires a modified or disguised voice rather than one ringing and explicit. Pym thus shares in the strategy that Elizabeth Meese claims for Mary Wilkins Freeman, a woman writer who elects to "display the shadows of her own doubt" (26). Pym can and does rebel against the edict that marriage is the only valid alternative, but her unorthodoxy culminates in a complex and indirect paradigm emblematic of her uncertainty: rebellion and retreat.

Pym resorts to multifarious means to achieve resolution, including the retention of the stereotype. In reiterating conventional notions of the spinster with the detached voice of an outsider, Pym gradually corrects the false impression that spinsters are helpless victims resigned to living vicariously: "'What do women *do* if they don't marry. . . . ' 'Oh, they stay at home with an aged parent and do the flowers, or they used to, but now perhaps they have jobs and careers and live in bed-sitting-rooms or hostels. And then of course they become indispensable in the parish and some of them even go into religious communities'" (*Excellent Women* 120–21). With the character of Jessie Morrow as an exemplum, Pym steals the thunder from her readers by embracing the caricature, only to turn around and undermine it by revealing its limitations. Sensing the power of language and naming, Pym introduces a phrase to accommodate her new concept: an "excellent woman." Whenever possible Pym supplants the preconceived notion of the spinster with this more daring, one might even say liberated, vision of the unmarried woman, whose persona is strong enough to reject the side effects associated with marginalization. If appearance and behavior play crucial roles in stereotyping, innovation and change are effected only through reinterpretation, and the possibilities of comparison and contrast are endless: plain and dowdy/handsome and elegant, eccentric and inquisitive/educated and cultured, dull and fussy/ happy and amusing, useless and pathetic/indispensable and comfortable, unwanted and lonely/practical and assertive. As the embodiment of so many enviable qualities, the proud, excellent woman is rarely an object of pity or contempt.

As I have mentioned, Pym says very early that resolution depended on the ability of the text to demonstrate that a chasm existed between appearance and reality, between how society viewed spinsters and how they really were. Hence the inclusion of stereotypical spinsters (such as Belinda Bede in *Some Tame Gazelle* who feels "dowdy and insignificant, one of the many thousand respectable middle-aged spinsters" [176]) neutralizes the negative by penetrating the superficiality of such generalizations. Like Belinda, Pym's spinsters struggle to emphasize their individuality: "nobody wanted to be one of many, and she did not like this picture of herself, only one of a great crowd of dreary women" (213–14). But the metamorphosis from spinster to excellent woman cannot be achieved by proclaiming one's individuality alone, as Mildred Lathbury recognizes in *Excellent Women:* "We had neither of us married. That was it really. It was the ring on the left hand that people at the Old Girl's Reunion looked for" (99). The absence of the all-important wedding ring still symbolizes the social stigma associated with spinsterhood.

Pym's critique of the institution of marriage is integral to her reconceptualization of spinsterhood. In a two-pronged attack, Pym first depicts marriage as a less than desirable state and then proceeds to show that spinsters choose *not* to marry for any number of reasons. While it would be too simplistic to claim that spinsterhood wins out unequivocally, Pym never presents marriage as anything more than an option. Marriage can certainly be a very tiresome affair, and wives find themselves envying their unmarried friends, with their independent lives and freedom to do as they wish. Rowena Longridge in *A Glass of Blessings,* for instance, confides, "'Sometimes, you know, I envy really *wicked* women, or even despised spinsters—they at least have their dreams . . . the despised spinster still has the chance of meeting somebody. . . . At least she's *free!*'" (149). The implication that marriage signals a loss of freedom, tantamount to "being caught," compels the spinster to reject the marriage offer when it comes. In *Some Tame Gazelle,* Harriet Bede "began to see that there were many reasons why she should refuse [Mr. Mold's] offer when it came . . . who would change a comfortable life of spinsterhood in a country parish . . . for the unknown trials of matrimony?" (136). Independence takes precedence over marriage.

Ironically, to reclaim a powerful new identity for independent women, Pym appropriates an exhausted, outdated attitude toward sexuality and romance. Typically, Pym's spinsters are sexually naive or even asexual—the physical manifestations of love, when unavoidable, can be unpleasant and must simply be endured. The fact that many of them fall in love with men who are married, or otherwise unsuitable or unavailable, reinforces the spinster's idealized notion of love. (Pym herself, as Constance Malloy observes, "tended to fall in love 'safely': she usually fixed her romantic longings on men she didn't know, on men she loved unbeknownst to them, or on 'unsuitable' men who were unstable, much younger, bisexual or homosexual" [5].) Since men, according to the rules of romantic love, are more interesting and attractive from a distance, the first actual encounter transforms the more "noble . . . abstract passions" into "sordid intrigue" (*Crampton Hodnet* 132). Passion dissolves rapidly once contact is established. As Ann Snitow writes,

"In romanticized sexuality the pleasure lies in the distance itself. Waiting, anticipation, anxiety—these represent the high point of sexual experience" (136).

Pym acknowledges that the spinster pays a high price for her romantic ideals. Thus, in *Quartet in Autumn,* Letty reflects on how "no man had taken her away and immured her in some comfortable suburb. . . . Why had this not happened? Because she had thought that love was a necessary ingredient for marriage? Now, having looked around her for forty years, she was not so sure. All those years wasted, looking for love!" (66). In what is perhaps Pym's most bleak novel, Letty's unhappy circumstances are, in a sense, a punishment for her (impossible?) demands on marriage. Yet the notion that marriage must be rejected if love is absent becomes yet another means to convince the reader of the unmarried woman's integrity.

The most extreme manifestation of Pym's views on marriage appears in *Jane and Prudence,* the story of a young spinster at the crossroads, with just a few years left to make the choice of whether to marry or to remain single. In a fascinating role reversal, a married Jane Cleveland is dowdy and frumpish, while an unmarried Prudence Bates is elegant and chic. Socially inept Jane spends her time matchmaking and scheming, while cultured Prudence—extremely adept at entertaining men—sees life as an unending series of affairs and enjoys romance and passion, without any commitment to marriage. Such a state of affairs, so to speak, cannot continue indefinitely, and Prudence faces the dilemma of whether to become "the comfortable spinster or the contented or bored wife" (200). Pym delights in averting closure by perpetuating the dilemma beyond the confines of the narrative. Yet, in Prudence's postponement of any final decision and in her recognition that marriage is not necessarily the best solution, Pym tips the balance in favor of spinsterhood:

> Husbands took friends away, [Prudence] thought, though Jane had retained her independence more than most of her married friends. And yet even she seemed to have missed something in her life; her research, her studies of obscure seventeenth-century poets, had all come to nothing, and here she was, trying, though not very hard, to be an efficient clergyman's wife, and with only very moderate success. Compared with Jane's life, Prudence's seemed rich and full of promise. She had her work, her independence, her life in London and her love for Arthur Grampian. But tomorrow, if she wanted to, she could give it all up and fall in love with someone else. Lines of eligible and delightful men seemed to stretch before her. (83)

It would be absurd, Pym argues, for the spinster to relinquish so rewarding a life-style for the unknown territory of marriage, as Mildred emphatically affirms in *Excellent Women:* "I valued my independence very dearly . . . I thought, not for the first time, how pleasant it was to be living alone" (19–20). Pym's spinsters know that their autonomy will be threatened if they succumb to marriage and, ultimately, no man is worth such a sacrifice. Because Pym recognizes that the patriarchy values only the married woman, she strives to show that spinsterhood is not a temporary solution to an impossible situation but a permanent resolution. Mildred refuses to accept any devaluation of the spinster and insists that excellent women are "for being unmarried . . . and by that I mean a positive rather than a negative state" (176). The use of the "I" opens up what Frye calls "the possibility of self-definition, the capacity to reconceptualize both experience and interpretive framework, the claiming of self-defined action as a way of eluding some of the constraints of an oppressive social context" (70).

While the sorts of tactics surveyed thus far (calling the stereotype into question or launching a critique of marriage) are undeniably useful in contradicting and undermining the dominant ideology, the primary obstacle to a permanent resolution remains in the chasm that exists between the individual and social reality. Pym understands that without a newly conceived narrative structure, the process of self-definition stands in danger of achieving only minor revisions. Since fundamental change must occur at the level of narrative structure, Pym adopts a way of writing that allows for the insertion of critical commentaries into the text so that, in effect, two voices, articulating differing positions, resonate from a unitary text. The development of this strategy aligns Pym with a tradition of women writers who, as Sandra Gilbert and Susan Gubar explain, "managed the difficult task of achieving true female literary authority by simultaneously conforming to and subverting patriarchal literary standards" (73). Like Austen's and Brontë's fiction, Pym's narrative works on two levels, where the surface meaning disguises the "deeper, less accessible (and less socially acceptable)" meaning (Gilbert and Gubar 73).

Pym's characters, as I've argued elsewhere, are "continually engaged in [a] quiet, civilized struggle which pits their individual needs against the larger social expectations. It is a rare occasion indeed when a Pym character freely pursues personal needs or desires without guilt" (64). The spinster, a character most susceptible to heeding this voice of duty, rarely eludes acting responsibly because all actions are measured against an invisible public standard. To neglect selfishly and recklessly the proprieties of the social order is to risk personal guilt. In *An Unsuitable Attachment,* Ianthe Broom visits the elderly Miss Grimes both as an act of Christian charity and an overarching sense of obligation. By juxtaposing Ianthe's private thoughts and her actual conversation with Miss Grimes and by situating the obligation just at the moment Ianthe would least care to fulfill it, Pym ensures that the reader is aware of the full measure of this difficult duty. Ianthe has just received a bunch of violets from her coworker John as she leaves work, and the "cold fresh scent and passionate yet mourning purple roused in her a feeling she could not explain" (75). Ianthe would prefer to enjoy the strange new sensation the flowers inspire; however, "it was with a slight shock of coming back to reality that she remembered her resolution to visit Miss Grimes on her way home that evening, as part of her contribution to Christmas goodwill, a sort of 'good turn' done to somebody for whom one felt no affection. To love one's neighbour, she thought . . . must surely often be an effort of the will rather than a pleasurable upsurging of emotion" (75). Only women, and spinsters in particular, are capable of such unselfish acts (though clergymen can sometimes rise to the occasion) because they can repress their own desires for the good of others, including those "for whom one felt no affection." Ianthe thus appears incapable of expressing her reluctance about visiting Miss Grimes and remains silent when Miss Grimes mistakes Ianthe's Christmas gifts for her own. To speak up and inform Miss Grimes of her error would violate the behavior code imposed on women by the dutiful voice.

Pym rescues the spinster from a debilitating sense of guilt and facilitates a psychological release by overriding the voice of the dominant social order to insert a more subversive voice into the text. When personal desire collides with duty, the dual-voiced narrative mediates between the two through the juxtaposition of inner thoughts with conversations and actions. When Ianthe gives fleeting consideration, "in a rush of wild impractical nobility," to inviting Miss Grimes to her house for Christmas, the second voice thus intervenes: "*That* would be true Christian charity of a kind that very few can bring themselves to practise" (75). There are limits as to how far the obedient spinster will go. Upon taking leave of Miss Grimes, Ianthe begins to "feel a little sorry for herself . . . she found herself resenting the way [Miss Grimes] had taken the violets" (78). Overzealous behavior is discouraged because spinsterish self-sacrifice cannot appear ridiculous; Ianthe does not degenerate into a total martyr.

At times the spinster's repression of her personal needs, coupled with an obsequious self-effacement, does lead to victimization. Yet this does not prevent Pym from allowing the spinster to speak out indirectly, as in *Quartet in Autumn* when Letty's retirement plans are torn asunder by the Reverend David Lydell's arrival in her friend Marjorie's village. Although Letty immediately suspects that Marjorie's romantic interest in the vicar poses a substantial threat to her own future plans of sharing Marjorie's house, the spinster initially puts on a brave face. During a church service, Letty sits beside Marjorie and, rather than contemplate her own precarious situation and worry that something unpleasant might be brewing, a "generously indulgent" Letty suspends all personal considerations and thinks, "Nice for Marjorie to have an interesting new vicar" (39–40).

Later, when the trio goes off for a day's drive in the countryside, Letty "was not surprised to find herself squashed into the back of the car . . . David and Marjorie in front made conversation about village matters which Letty could not join in" (43). A subservient spinster, Letty takes a backseat in the car, a place that emblematizes her position in society; within the social hierarchy, her insignificant needs do not even register. The seating arrangement at the picnic is also paradigmatic of Letty's inferiority: "Marjorie produced two folding canvas chairs . . . [and] these were solemnly put up for herself and David, Letty having quickly assured them that she would just as soon sit on the rug—indeed, she preferred it. All the same, she could not help feeling in some way belittled or diminished, sitting on a lower level than the others" (43–44). Again duty and desire collide to reveal the spinster's vulnerability, even as Letty fights to repress her own indignation. The dual-voiced narrative enables Pym (and Letty) to observe respectfully the restraints imposed by the dominant social order, in this case taking a backseat, in order to attack it subversively. But Letty does not remain a victim, as the unexpected turn of events at the end of the narrative demonstrates. When Letty learns that Marjorie's engagement to David is called off, reversing the fortunes of both women, Letty feels "curiously elated, a feeling she tried to suppress but it would not go away" (207). Marjorie, a widow with minimal understanding of the spinster, "naturally" assumes that Letty will leap at the opportunity to return to the original plan (209). These new circumstances, however, permit Letty to control the outcome and make the choices:

"[Letty] experienced a most agreeable sensation, almost a feeling of power. . . . Letty now realised that Marjorie . . . would be waiting to know what *she* had decided to do . . . life still held infinite possibilities for change" (217–18). The situation signals a more positive outcome for Letty, who now views her impending retirement with a sense of hope.

The dual-voiced narrative is also effective in allowing two attitudes toward the single woman to emerge simultaneously from the text: the voice of the patriarchy and the voice challenging that authority. In *Jane and Prudence*, Jane often functions as a mouthpiece for the social order, regarding her friend Prudence as an oddity and, occasionally, as an object of pity: "It was odd, really, that [Prudence] should not yet have married . . . poor Prudence" (9). Yet Prudence, weary of the misunderstanding of outsiders, reflects with impatience, and perhaps a hint of resentment, that "one's married friends were too apt to assume that one had absolutely nothing to do when not at the office. A flat with no husband didn't seem to count as a home" (73). The irony here, though, is that Prudence is in perfect control of her life—some of her relationships with men are unsuccessful, but on the whole she enjoys her freedom. As mentioned, in this novel Pym turns the tables on the situation of the married woman and the spinster. Jane's sort of marriage, a complacent cohabitation, is so unenviable that her observations on the plight of the spinster fail to convince even the most skeptical reader. Jane's assessment of the value of marriage—"Oh, but a husband was someone to tell one's silly jokes to, to carry suitcases and do the tipping at hotels"—is so ridiculous that it cannot detract from the attraction of autonomy (10–11).

In *Jane and Prudence*, Pym achieves the privileging of spinsterhood through a minor spinster character who seemingly embodies both voices. At the same time Eleanor Hitchens reassures Prudence that marriage would settle her unsettled life ("'You ought to get married,' said Eleanor sensibly" [200]), the underlying message is really "do as I do, not as I say." While Eleanor offers the sort of advice one might *expect* (in accordance with the social order) and even perpetuates an outmoded attitude, she calmly pinpoints her own disheveled appearance as the reason for her remaining single ("'I suppose I'll never get a man if I don't take more trouble with myself'" [200]). Just as these words are uttered aloud in Prudence's sitting room, Pym inserts a lengthy description of Eleanor's private thoughts: "she spoke comfortably and without regret, thinking of her flat in Westminster, so convenient for the Ministry, her weekend golf, concerts and theatres with women friends, in the best seats and with a good supper afterwards. Prue could have this kind of life if she wanted it" (200). On one level Pym suggests that Prudence has the option of marriage, but Eleanor's inner dialogue leaves little doubt in the reader's mind as to what the sensible woman would select. Eleanor personifies the new woman and serves as a reminder that the image of the reluctant, pathetic spinster is a creature of the past. The careful juxtaposition of two radically opposed positions demonstrates the inadequacy of Eleanor's spoken account of her spinsterhood. Pym once again reminds the reader of the disparities between perception and reality, between surface and depth.

Barbara Pym's novels become an opportunity to undermine traditional notions of the spinster and to create a positive self-identity. Pym presents spinsterhood as the embodiment or synthesis of all the better things life has to offer. So has Pym, in effect, created a third sex? To be sure, the spinsters' very exemption from the rules of the game grants them a different sort of power: they have the choice to play or not to, and from this choice their uniqueness springs. Spinsterhood, then, is an alternative life-style which offers women an active role in society and allows them the opportunity to examine others critically. As *active* "observers of life," the new excellent women claim singleness as "a positive rather than a negative state" (*Excellent Women* 67, 176). Like an uncertain lesbian writer who uses the text to justify her sexuality, Pym's experience of difference culminates in a text of persuasion, compelling an identification with the heroine and convincing the reader of the validity of her life-choice. By achieving this, she exemplifies another narrative strategy used by twentieth-century women writers: transform the negative and thereby reclaim an old identity. Her subversion, her process of interjecting herself into the text, enables her to argue the case for the spinster—a remarkable strategy in compliance with Hélène Cixous's imperative: "Woman must write her self. . . . Woman must put herself into the text—as into the world and into history—by her own movement" (245).

NOTE

1. In addition to her friend Robert Liddell, Pym addresses the letter to Henry Harvey and his new wife Elsie. Although the precise nature of Pym's relationship with Harvey is unclear, she did at one time hope to marry him.

WORKS CITED

Cixous, Hélène. "The Laugh of the Medusa." *New French Feminisms*. Ed. Elaine Marks and Isabelle de Courtivron. New York: Schocken, 1981.

Doan, Laura L. "Text and the Single Man: The Bachelor in Pym's Dual-Voiced Narrative." *Independent Women: The Function of Gender in the Novels of Barbara Pym*. Ed. Janice Rossen. New York: St. Martin's, 1988.

Frye, Joanne S. *Living Stories, Telling Lives: Women and the Novel in Contemporary Experience*. Ann Arbor: University of Michigan Press, 1986.

Gardiner, Judith Kegan. "On Female Identity and Writing by Women." *Critical Inquiry* 8 (1981): 347–61.

Gilbert, Sandra M., and Susan Gubar. *The Madwoman in the Attic: The Woman Writer and the Nineteenth-Century Imagination*. New Haven: Yale University Press, 1979.

Malloy, Constance. "The Quest for a Career." *The Life and Work of Barbara Pym*. Ed. Dale Salwak. Iowa City: University of Iowa Press, 1987.

Meese, Elizabeth A. *Crossing the Double-Cross: The Practice of Feminist Criticism*. Chapel Hill: University of North Carolina Press, 1986.

Pym, Barbara. *Crampton Hodnet*. New York: Dutton, 1985.

———. *Excellent Women*. 1952. Harmondsworth: Penguin, 1980.

———. *A Glass of Blessings*. 1958. New York: Perennial, 1980.

———. *Jane and Prudence*. 1953. New York: Perennial, 1982.

———. *Quartet in Autumn*. 1977. New York: Perennial, 1980.

———. *Some Tame Gazelle*. 1950. London: Granada, 1982.

———. *An Unsuitable Attachment*. 1982. New York: Perennial, 1983.

———. *A Very Private Eye: An Autobiography in Diaries and Letters*. Ed. Hazel Holt and Hilary Pym. New York: Dutton, 1984.

Snitow, Ann Barr. "Mass Market Romance: Pornography for Women Is Different." *Feminist Literary Theory: A Reader*. Ed. Mary Eagleton. New York: Blackwell, 1986.

VALERIE MINER

Spinning Friends: May Sarton's Literary Spinsters

> In the mirror she recognized her *self,* her life companion, for better or worse. She looked at this self with compassion this morning, unmercifully prodded and driven as she had been for just under seventy years.
>
> —May Sarton, *Mrs. Stevens Hears the Mermaids Singing*

> She who has chosen her Self, who defines her Self, by choice, neither in relation to children nor to men, who is Self-identified, is a Spinster. . . .
>
> —Mary Daly, *Gyn/Ecology*

Spinning a web of literary friendship, May Sarton gives renewed grace and power to single women. "With a hundred threads binding their lives to hers," as she says of one character in *The Magnificent Spinster,* Sarton expands and interweaves the definitions of the words "spinster" and "friend." May Sarton's spinsters are vital, often romantic women engaged in the world as teachers, writers, mentors, colleagues, and social activists.

Cam Arnold devotes herself to writing a biographical novel about Jane Reid as an act of friendship and commemoration in *The Magnificent Spinster.* Hilary Stevens befriends a troubled young man in *Mrs. Stevens Hears the Mermaids Singing.* Caro Spencer risks her own safety to protect another resident of her dreary nursing home in *As We Are Now.* These characters, like Sarton herself, are old women who have used their lives productively, indeed exuberantly. Although some might assume a tension between their friendship and autonomy, it is precisely the self-sufficiency of Sarton and her protagonists that locates their deep and lasting friendships as the source and expression of their best selves. Being spinsters has allowed them to give to their neighbors with time and spirit unavailable to many of their contemporaries who have chosen to reproduce and live in cloistered families.

The identity of the sisterly spinster is enacted in Sarton's own friendship with her characters. Their stories raise provocative notions: spinsterhood as a vocation of social responsibility; companionship as an alternative to motherhood; lesbian bonding as an alternative to marriage; friendship as an alternative to any sexual partnership; and writing as an act of friendship.

In this essay, I explore the uneasy borders between fiction and memoir by observing reflections between the characters in Sarton's novels, *The Magnificent Spinster, As We Are Now,* and *Mrs. Stevens Hears the Mermaids Singing,* and the spinster self-portraits in her journals, *At Seventy, Journal of a Solitude,* and *I Knew a Phoenix.* In particular, I am interested in Sarton's representation of the lesbian spinster and the literary spinster.

Friendship between Author and Character

May Sarton manages to create a special familiarity among writer, protagonist, and reader because of the way she balances her work on the boundaries of autobiography and fiction. "I think of myself as a maker of bridges—between the heterosexual and the homosexual world, between the old and the young," Sarton tells Karen Saum in an interview for the *Paris Review* (Saum 86). The flexible forms of Sarton's fiction allow unique access to all involved. Each of the three novels under discussion engages the audience in questions about purpose, process, and style of writing.

The Magnificent Spinster is a novel about Cam, a retired history professor, writing a novel about the life of her teacher Jane Reid. Here we learn not only about Cam and Jane but about the intricacies of conveying the qualities of a long friendship in fiction. Sarton is at her best shaping the distinctive temperaments of these friends—balancing Cam's rash enthusiasm and Jane's measured graciousness—revealing how the women complement and confound each other. *Mrs. Stevens Hears the Mermaids Singing* is an account of an extended interview with Hilary Stevens, an acclaimed old poet, in which the skeleton of her biography is constructed by the questions and answers, while the rest of her story is fleshed out by her own dramatic internal flashbacks. During the interview, Hilary Stevens reflects on past friendships while developing an incipient friendship with the interviewer Jenny Hare. *As We Are Now* is a novel written as a journal to be published after Caro Spencer dies. Of these three protagonists, Caro most closely resembles the stereotype of the spinster as an isolated, single, old woman, but the greatest drama of the book takes place within the friendships of her last months and in the fire she sets, destroying her grim nursing home and herself. Caro's final legacy—the journal—is a celebration of those precious relationships as well as a customary gift to those who might follow her into rest homes.

It is easy to find the seeds of these novels in Sarton's life. Jane Reid in *The Magnificent Spinster* is consciously modeled on Sarton's old friend and teacher Anne Longfellow Thorp. Thorp is lovingly described in *I Knew a Phoenix* and *Journal of a Solitude*. Sarton proceeds to discuss the difficult process of writing the novel about Thorp in *At Seventy*. Like the protagonist in *Mrs. Stevens*, Sarton lived for a time in England, where she found great artistic nourishment. She, too, had romances with both men and women and found women to be the sustaining muse for her poetry. The inspiration for Caro Spencer's decline in *As We Are Now* can be traced to a visit Sarton makes to a nursing home in *Journal of a Solitude*. Indeed, she has Caro's friend repeat the same words as Sarton's friend Perley Cole from *Journal*: "'I never thought it would end like this'" (23). All these women share Sarton's white, middle-class, New England background.

Although Sarton's fiction is autobiographical in the sense of memory recalled, it is also autobiographical in the sense of premonition. She relates to the characters in her novels as friends and models for her own life. Mrs. Stevens, a poet verging on seventy, is finally receiving the acknowledgment Sarton desires for her own poetry. The novel, published when Sarton was fifty-three, allows the author to try on the kudos, to see how she would feel looking back at her life from the distance of seven decades. (The name of Hilary Stevens's protégé, Mar, is not so different from the name of his creator, May. Mar's name and personality signify the anger with which Sarton so closely identifies.) This book also permits Sarton to watch Hilary come out as a lesbian in her narrative, before she herself comes out in her journals. Once Sarton reaches her own seventies, she chooses the character Cam, a seventy-year-old woman, to write a novel about Jane, to teach her how to write the novel she herself wants to write about Anne Longfellow Thorp. One step further into old age, Sarton creates *As We Are Now*, an unflinching study of rest-home existence. In *At Seventy*, she writes about putting a deposit on a modern, flexible retirement community, no doubt partially in response to her experience struggling with Caro's limited choices. It is useful to remember that the Sarton portrayed in the journals is also a persona shaped by the author. Just as her fiction is autobiographical, her autobiography is a creation of imagination. No doubt the May Sartons who emerge in the work of those who dare to write biographies of this formidable woman will be different characters altogether.

Sarton, then, develops a unique intimacy with her characters, between her characters, between the characters and readers, and between herself and readers. All her prose—fiction and journal—is rendered in a straightforward, yet elegant style. Although some may regard her commitment to realism as old-fashioned, I see it as yet another gesture of friendship because she makes her ideas accessible to a broad range of readers.

Social Vocations

May Sarton's spinsters forgo marriage for a wider province. Like Louisa May Alcott, they believe that the pursuit of good work and public service is "a better husband than love" (Cook 5). These middle-class women are friends rather than wives—friends over the backfence and in the public arena. Sarton, whose work seems more Edwardian than contemporary, grew up in an era of strong single women, both literary figures and political activists. In Britain as well as the United States, single women were among the most visible early twentieth-century feminists—working in settlement houses, living in single-sex communities, and campaigning for female suffrage.[1] Sarton, whose mother was English and whose father was Belgian, comes from a bourgeois European background noted for championing eccentricity. Given her girlhood acquaintance with genteel, socially concerned women in Cambridge, Massachusetts, it is not surprising to find her stories focus on the contributions of publicly generous, personally modest women. In addition, her place as an only child probably helped cultivate an affinity for spinsterly solitude. In Sarton's recollections about her youth, one detects a pleasure in her own company and an aptitude for independence which prepared her for spinsterly success.

Her characters are solitary figures only when narrowly viewed. They are deeply engaged in serving others through education, social activism, and the arts. In *The Magnificent Spinster,* Cam challenges sexism among her contemporaries and fights against fascism in the Spanish Civil War. Both she and the subject of her novel, Jane, are dedicated teachers. Jane works with French orphans after World War I and helps Germans reconstruct their lives after World War II. Later Jane confronts Boston racism—and her own bigotry—through her growing friendship with Ellen, the African-American director of the Cambridge Community Center.

Sarton's spinsters are often understated about their social contributions. Not all her spinsters are as comfortable with singleness as Jane is. For instance, Hilary Stevens describes her spinsterhood as deviance in her interview with the young writers Jenny and Peter: "'For the aberrant woman art is health, the only health! It is,' she waved aside Peter's attempt to interrupt, 'as I see it, the constant attempt to rejoin something broken off or lost, to make whole again'" (190). Earlier in the novel, Hilary reassures herself that life is not as bad as it might be, that she did not turn out like Aunt Ida, an artist who was institutionalized because she was suicidal: "Nevertheless, young Hilary reminded old Hilary, you have not done too badly, old thing. You did not break down like Aunt Ida; you kept going; you have worked hard, and you have made a garden, which would have pleased your mother; and once in a while you have been able to be of some use to another human being—Mar for instance" (71). Despite her self-effacing presentation, Hilary has had a very successful writing career and is a stimulating, encouraging friend to numerous people, especially Mar, the defensive young artist. She also inspires her interviewer Jenny: "'For some odd reason you've given me courage,' she [Jenny] said, 'courage to be myself, to do what I want to do!'" (197).

In *As We Are Now,* Caro Spencer questions the value of her own life after she is put out to pasture:

> Did they always hate me, my family I mean, because I was different, because I never married. . . . A high-school teacher in a small town is (or was in the years when I taught math) not exactly suspect, but set apart. Only in the very last years when I was established as a dear old eccentric did I ever dare have a drink in public! And even among my colleagues, mostly good simple-minded fellows, I did not quite fit in. They had their own club and went off fishing together and on an occasional spree to New York, but of course they didn't want an old maid tagging along. . . . (20)

Caro's tightly corseted self-image conceals the cosmopolitan attitudes she has developed in her wise travels and forty years of teaching. Precisely because of her reserved nature, her expressions of loyalty—such as defending a colleague facing dismissal for his homosexuality—are acts of courage. Once in the nursing home, she becomes friends with Standish Flint, another resident. His mistreatment makes her strength flare. "Yet, Caro, remember that anger is the wicked side of fire—you had fire and that fire made you a good teacher and a brave fighter sometimes. Fire can be purifying"

(43–44). It is this sacred fire which fuels the keeping of her diary and allows her to leave the world of her own accord.

In the journals, Sarton portrays *herself* as someone for whom solitude is a respite for nurturing social contribution—whether this is her art; her philanthropy to adopted families and needy friends; her support for HOME, a progressive housing project in Orland, Maine; or her advice to young writers. In *I Knew a Phoenix,* she honors spinsters who have influenced her life, including her teachers at Shady Hill School and the actor Eva Le Gallienne, who inspired her to give up college and join the theater. Like Sarton, these spinsters may be suspect in the outside world but only because their participation in that world is veiled by stereotype.

Alternatives to Traditional Motherhood

Because these women are unmarried, their class and generation dictate that they also be childless. For some, this state is a failure; for some a relief; for some an opportunity to "mother" in unique ways. The identity "childless" has taken on various meanings during their long lives. Sarton and her fictional spinsters grew up within an ethic which defined nonmothers as unnatural or barren. They have survived both world wars, experiencing the absence of men on the home front as well as the baby booms following the soldiers' return. They lived through eras when feminists questioned the maternal imperative and celebrated selfhood. More recently, some have found themselves in a period where women—including single heterosexuals and lesbians—are having a renewed romance with biological motherhood. Since Sarton and her characters are all WASPish women, under no pressure to compensate for the genocide of their culture, many would observe that their first contribution is the decision not to add to an already overpopulated world. Perhaps these women don't suffer the impulse to reproduce biologically because they have found other venues for self-creation.

In *Journal of Solitude,* Sarton describes Anne Longfellow Thorp:

> For her, life itself has been the creation, but not in the usual mode as wife, mother and grandmother. Had Anne married she would have led a different life and no doubt a rich one, but she would not have been able to give what she does here and in the way she does. . . . Here is a personal largess, a largess of giving to life in every possible way, that makes her presence itself a present. . . . Perhaps the key is in her capacity to make herself available on any day, at any time, to whatever human joy or grief longs to be fulfilled or assuaged by shar-

> ing . . . [or] longs to pour itself out and to be understood. So a teddy bear will materialize as if by magic for a one-year-old who has stubbed a toe; so a young woman who cannot decide whom to marry can have a long talk in perfect peace; so a very old lady can discuss with gusto the coming presidential election and feel a fire to match her own rise up in Anne's blue eyes. The participation is never passive, shot through with a sudden gust of laughter as it often is, always vivid and original. (172–73)

In contrast, Hilary Stevens is painfully conscious of her abnormality:

> "No, the crucial question seems to me to be this: what is the *source* of creativity in the woman who wants to be an artist? After all, admit it, a woman is meant to create children not works of art—that's what she has been engined to do, so to speak. A man with a talent does what is expected of him, makes his way, constructs, is an engineer, a composer, a builder of bridges. It's the natural order of things that he construct objects outside himself and his family. The woman who does so is aberrant." (190)

Near the end of the book, Hilary says to Mar, "'No, I think I would have liked to be a woman, simple and fruitful, a woman with many children, a great husband, . . . and no talent!'" (219, Sarton's ellipsis).

But Sarton's portrayal of the spinster or lesbian as perverted softens with the years. *Mrs. Stevens* is the earliest of the three novels discussed here. By the time readers meet Caro and especially Cam and Jane, the portrait of the spinster as an estimable figure of solitary strength is less qualified. If one accepts the threads connecting these books, one detects three distinct moods—anxiety in *Mrs. Stevens,* fury in *As We Are Now,* and tranquillity in *The Magnificent Spinster*—revealing a marked emotional moment. Perhaps the self-criticism so raw in *Mrs. Stevens* is due to the fact that this was Sarton's "coming-out" novel, and the writing process was filled with special conflict. Perhaps, too, she came to a greater peace about her own identity as spinster and lesbian in the years between this novel and the other two.

In *As We Are Now,* spinsterhood is portrayed both as freedom and loneliness. Caro doesn't think much about children, but, from her attitudes regarding marriage, readers gather that her independence from men and children comes from the same instinct for self-containment. When Anna asks Caro why she never married, Caro pauses, "It was a hard question to answer. How could I tell her, perhaps that I am a failure, couldn't take what it would have cost to give up an authentic being, myself, to take in the stranger? That I failed because I was afraid of losing myself when in fact I might have grown through sharing an equality with another human being. And yet . . . do I really regret not marrying? No, to be quite hontest, *no*" (95, Sarton's ellipsis).

Similarly, in *The Magnificent Spinster,* Cam describes Jane's spinsterhood in terms of potential: "she did not resemble anyone's idea of a spinster, dried up, afraid of life, locked away. On the contrary it may have been her riches as a personality, her openness, the depth of her feelings that made her what she was, not quite the marrying kind . . . a free spirit" (60, Sarton's ellipsis). And, like Caro and Hilary, Jane serves many different people with her "extra" time. Long after she quits teaching, Jane makes a point of inviting children to her family's country retreat.

Sarton's journals also reflect an active relationship with younger people. One of the most touching parts of *At Seventy* is Sarton's description of a visit by "little Sarton," a girl named after her by parents who fell in love while reading her poetry. She also discusses the satisfactions of her friendship with a young scholar named Georgia:

> What is wonderful for me is to be with someone whose vision of life is so like mine, who reads avidly and with discrimination, who goes deeply into whatever is happening to her and her family and can talk about it freely, so it feels a little like a piece of music in which we are playing different instruments that weave a theme in and out, in almost perfect accord. I had this experience always with my mother when I came home and we could talk. And I feel so happy that perhaps I can be that kind of mother for Georgia. (145)

The spinsters in these books are parents in the sense of being mentors and confidantes. While they lack some maternal satisfactions, such as the pleasure derived from physical resemblance between oneself and one's own offspring, they are freed from certain kinds of maternal guilt and legal responsibilities. In *The Magnificent Spinster,* Jane gently directs Cam. Both Hilary Stevens and Caro Spencer can look back to spinster aunts as inspirational yet admonitory examples. In her journals Sarton emerges as a wise, generous persona, a model for her readers.

In addition to the gratification of reproducing, mothers often look forward to being cosseted by their children in old age. What does a spinster do? Sarton offers various possibilities, from Jane, who is surrounded by loving friends until the end, to Caro, who creates her own end and arranges her own cremation. Caro's death is admirable, tragic, and—in keeping with Mary Daly's glorious self-definition of spinsterhood—transcendent. "Spinsters, too, learn to be at home on the road. Our ability to make our spirits our moving shelters will enable us to dispense with patriarchal shelters, the various homes that house the domesticated, the sick, the 'mentally ill,' the destitute" (Daly 395).

For each of these characters—Hilary, Caro, Cam, and the Sarton of the journals—the absence of one's own children is a blessing and a loss. Each in her own way expresses ambivalence and conflict about this aspect of being a *single* woman. The childlessness is one more instance of her autonomy from the family, if not from the society.

The Lesbian Spinster

Lesbian friendship is a sanctuary and a stigma for Sarton's spinsters. One conventional definition of spinster is a "woman who has rejected or who has been rejected by marriage." Today, however, marriage is so broadly rejected in favor of live-in, unmarried partnerships between women and men that the definition is outdated. If one reads "male-linked" for marriage, one has a clearer sense of the current popular definition. All lesbians, whether coupled or not, might claim to be spinsters. By choosing women, they have remained "unmarried" to, and unprotected by, male identity. (While many heterosexual feminists have fought for autonomy within their individual partnerships, they do have privileges unavailable to women who forgo such bonding with males.) Spinsters have historically been identified by what they are *not* (married) just as contemporary lesbians are ostracized for what they are not (male-linked). This "identity by lack" leaves room for the cultural imagination to conjure new labels. People often seem more threatened by dismissal of patriarchy than by antagonism to it and thus turn the sin of omission into a sin of commission, transforming the medieval spinster into a witch (consorting with the devil is more easily imaginable than not consorting with males at all) and the contemporary lesbian into a pervert. Witch-hunting spirals into gay-bashing. While few of today's lesbian spinsters are burned at the stake, they suffer enormous discrimination in employment, housing, and healthcare. To be a lesbian in the United States is to be "illegitimate," to be substantially without civil rights. Lesbians are declared unsuitable as teachers in certain areas and unfit to immigrate to this country. When lesbians aren't attacked, they, like other spinsters, are often ignored. Individually, some heterosexuals find lesbian bonding so threatening that they refuse to see it, and in an ironic twist on my theme, they interpret the intimacy between longtime partners as a tamer "friendship." Such women, particularly the older ones, are identified in their jobs and neighborhoods as "spinsters."

These novels reveal a multiplicity of lesbians, from Cam, who has a long-term relationship with Ruth in *The Magnificent Spinster,* to Caro, whose last great love is Anna ("I myself am on the brink of understanding things about love I have never understood before" [98]), to Hilary, who struggles with her aberration. Writing *Mrs. Stevens* was a profound psychological and professional risk for Sarton, as she explains in *Journal of a Solitude*:

> On the surface my work has not looked radical, but perhaps it will be seen eventually that in a "nice, quiet, noisy way" I have been trying to say radical things gently so that they may penetrate without shock. The fear of homosexuality is so great that it took courage to write *Mrs. Stevens,* to write a novel about a woman who is not a sex maniac, a drunkard, a drug-taker, or in any way repulsive; to portray a homosexual who is neither pitiable nor disgusting, without sentimentality. . . . But I am well aware that I probably could not have "leveled" as I did in that book had I had any family (my parents were dead when I wrote it), and perhaps not if I had had a regular job. I have a great responsibility because I can afford to be honest. The danger is that if you are placed in a sexual context people will read your work from a distorting angle of vision. I did not write *Mrs. Stevens* until I had written several novels concerned with marriage and family life. (90–91)

In fact, Sarton did lose teaching engagements as a result of the book's publication. Her poetry has been censored from school texts, not because of explicit sexual references but simply because she is now widely known as lesbian.

On the other hand, this visibility has brought many lesbian readers. The revelation also has freed her to write more openly about her own relationships in the journals. In *Journal of a Solitude* and *At Seventy,* she looks back on her primary partnership with Judith Matlock, an English professor. Matlock, lover, friend, and Friend (a committed Quaker) lived with Sarton for fifteen years.

Sarton, however, is not doctrinaire. The lesbian connections are honored without any of the throat-clearing fanfare of more didactic lesbian novels. Moreover, just as she poses lesbianism as an alternative to marriage, she poses nonsexual friendship as an alternative to sexual partnership. Comrades and companions are often valued over lovers. Sexual relationships are often set in the past or in the background of a story. The strongest relationship in *The Magnificent Spinster* is between Cam and Jane—a friendship of cherished mutual development. In *As We Are Now,* Caro's current friendship with Standish, Reverend Thornhill, and Lisa are more important than any sexual partnership. *Mrs. Stevens* ends as it began, showing Hilary cajoling young Mar. The last scene is filled with affection, hope, and a provocative sexual energy: "For a second they confronted each other, the bold blue eyes of Mar and the hooded gray eyes of Hilary. Then at the same instant, each reached for a pebble and threw it down. The two pebbles struck the water about two feet apart, and they watched avidly as the two great widening ripples intersected" (219).

In Sarton's journals, the sexual partnerships are also masked (as in the reference to "X" in *Journal of a Solitude*) or set in the past. Sarton is at her most vital when greeting friends in her house in Nelson, Massachusetts, or York, Maine. She frequently complains about her voluminous correspondence with people she has met through her books, but, of course, the descriptions of such correspondence are what prompt so many fans to write.

Writing as an Art of Friendship

Like spinning wool or silk or webs, Sarton's writing is a process of *conserving* the essential while transforming it into something useful for herself and others. Sarton spins her stories with intelligence and craft. Much as early spinsters turned their wheels, she uses her hands and wit to recycle raw experience.

Cam describes her impulse to write about Jane:

> What then has driven me so late in life to write a novel? Quite simply the unequivocal need to celebrate an extraordinary woman whom I had the good fortune to know for more than fifty years until her death a year ago. . . .
>
> I realized that in a few years everyone who knew Jane would be dead. Who would remember her? In fifty years who would know she had existed? She never married. There would be no children and grandchildren to keep her memory alive. She was already vanishing like sand in the ocean. . . . Then, almost without thinking, I went into my study, forgetting all about lunch, and began to write. (13, 14, third ellipsis Sarton's)

In *As We Are Now*, the most meaningful and candid connection Caro has is with readers—of her letters, her imaginary letters, and the journal which she intends to be read after her death. The journal is an epistle from hell. Her last act of friendship before setting fire to the rest home is to hide the journal in a refrigerator where it will not burn, where it will be preserved for others.

For Sarton, literary friendship is an *exchange* involving various levels of interaction with members of her audience as well as with her characters. She is neither puppeteer nor omniscient benefactor. She needs her readers. Sarton's most popular work is her journals, which resemble long letters addressed to a broad-based audience of friends. Indeed, many pages contain fragments of letters she has received from her readers or descriptions of feelings these letters have evoked. The personal connections become even more direct. Sarton reclaims storytelling as an oral form in offering readings all over the country to standing-room-only crowds. She does booksignings where people wait two hours to exchange a word and get an autograph. She describes one of these events in *At Seventy*:

> At three the next afternoon she drove me to a very different part of the city, a slum that is being rehabilitated, and there I found myself among "my people" at the Crazy Ladies—a subway crush of young and old but mostly young in blue jeans and sweaters, crowding around to get *Journal of a Solitude* signed (that is one for the young) and of course *Anger*. Some had brought a great pile of my books from home. Many had things to say to me, but it was rather a rush as the line was long and the time short. At the end of two hours when I had not stopped making my mark, it looked as though the bookstore may have been saved (they are having a hard time), and everyone was happy. And on the way back to the Regency and Heidi, two women from the cooperative told me they thought they had sold $1,500 worth. Once more I felt lifted up on all the delightful caring of these people who read me.
>
> It cannot be denied that it is these days a very good life for an old raccoon of seventy. (210)

Such encounters buffer Sarton against the pain and fury about what she considers the unfair treatment—not just negative evaluation—of her work by the reviewing establishment. She describes two more personal exchanges earlier in *At Seventy:*

> When Webster was here last winter he asked me shyly whether I would be willing to give him a signed copy of *A Reckoning* in exchange for the work done. I told him he was getting the lean end of the bargain, but he insisted the book would do it.

In the same order of good happenings, Bob Johnson at the florist's left a round planter filled with spring plants, a hyacinth, two yellow primroses, and some lilies on the terrace, this time with a note to say how he felt about *Recovering*. What do critics matter when workmen and florists are moved to respond with their gifts to mine?

I sometimes imagine I am the luckiest person in the world. For what does a poet truly want but to be able to give her gifts and find that they are accepted? Deprived people have never found their gifts or feel their true gifts are not acceptable. This has happened to me more than once in a love relationship and that is my definition of hell. (45)

May Sarton's spinsters are friendly women. Being spinsters allows them time to attend to numerous and often unlikely people. Like that legendary spinster Charlotte, who rescues her friend by spinning magical words, May Sarton's spinsters tend to their friends *in* their writing and *through* their lives.[2] We may hope the future of this tradition will be as luminous as its past, which extends at least as far back as Sappho, who wrote:

Tell everyone
Now, today, I shall
sing beautifully for
my friends' pleasure

NOTES

1. For an excellent study of single women, see Vicinus.

2. This reference was inspired by Daly. Generally, I found Daly's work to be very provocative in the writing of this essay.

WORKS CITED

Cook, Blanche Wiesen. "Incomplete Lives?" *Women's Review of Books* 3 (1985): 5.

Daly, Mary. *Gyn/Ecology: The Metaethics of Radical Feminism*. Boston: Beacon, 1978.

Sappho. "Tell Everyone." *Sappho: A New Translation*. Ed. Mary Barnard. Berkeley: University of California Press, 1958.

Sarton, May. *As We Are Now*. New York: Norton, 1973.

———. *At Seventy*. New York: Norton, 1984.

———. *I Knew a Phoenix*. New York: Norton, 1959.

———. *Journal of a Solitude*. New York: Norton, 1973.

———. *The Magnificent Spinster*. New York: Norton, 1985.

———. *Mrs. Stevens Hears the Mermaids Singing*. New York: Norton, 1965.

Saum, Karen. "The Art of Poetry XXXII, May Sarton." *Paris Review* 25 (1983): 80–117.

Vicinus, Martha, *Independent Women: Work and Community for Single Women, 1850–1920*. Chicago: University of Chicago Press, 1985.

Gayle Greene

An "Old Story": Gail Godwin's *The Odd Woman*

> Yes, that is the story we still love most. . . . How some woman went to work and got her man. Even "emancipated women" . . . love to hear the old, old story one more time.
>
> —Gail Godwin, *The Odd Woman*

Gail Godwin's *The Odd Woman* (1974) is one of several novels published in the early seventies that concern a woman's attempt to define herself against the cultural and literary tradition that has formed her.[1] Godwin's protagonist Jane Clifford looks to literary tradition for answers about the present, "ransacks novels for answers about life," and seeks an ending of her own that differs from the marriage or death provided by that tradition.[2] Jane is especially concerned with the relevance of George Gissing's *Odd Women* to her own situation as an "odd woman." *The Odd Woman* is—as its title suggests—a self-consciously literary novel that defines itself against earlier texts and assesses the relation of older forms to contemporary experience. Godwin's protagonist—like the protagonists of Doris Lessing, Margaret Drabble, Erica Jong, and Margaret Laurence—contemplates "images of women" and cultural stereotypes at the same time the first feminist critics were addressing these issues (Kate Millett's *Sexual Politics*, Carolyn Heilbrun's *Toward a Recognition of Androgyny*, and Annette Kolodny's *Lay of the Land* were published between 1973 and 1975).

The problem Godwin faces is a problem confronted by other contemporary women novelists: how to adapt essentially conservative narrative conventions to a new and unconventional view of woman. Roland Barthes and others have explained the conservative tendencies of realist narrative: since realism produces meaning by evoking and combining cultural codes that are the received ideas of the culture, appearing "realistic" because it draws on familiar systems that reaffirm our sense of the familiar, it "does the work of ideology" in masking contradictions and containing tendencies toward change.[3] One way women writers address such questions is to make them the subject of metafictional speculation. Lessing, Drabble, Laurence, and Jong make their protagonists writers who themselves ask such questions.[4] Lessing, who describes *The Golden Notebook* as "express-[ing] her sense of despair about writing a conventional novel,"[5] makes her protagonist Anna Wulf a novelist who is also dissatisfied with conventional form. Anna Wulf's search for new forms in her life is the correlative of a search for new forms in her writing, a search which takes her through breakdown and breakthrough to "something new."[6] Similarly, in *The Waterfall,* Drabble has Jane Gray write herself through and beyond the conventional romance.[7] *The Waterfall* and *The Golden Notebook* are (in Barthes's terms) *scriptible* texts which draw attention to their processes of production from the available discourses, reveal the contradictions involved in those processes, and disturb the ideological complicity of conventional form by inviting the reader to be part of that production.[8]

Jane Clifford is not a writer, but she is someone who believes in words, thinks about words, whose "profession" is words: "Her profession was words and she believed in them deeply. The articulation, interpretation, appreciation, and preservation of good words. She believed in their power. If you truly named something, you had that degree of control over it. Words could incite, soothe, destroy, exorcise, redeem. Putting a nebulous 'something' into precise words often made it so—or not so. The right word or the wrong word could change a person's life, the course of the world. If you called things by their name, you had more control of your life, and she liked to be in control" (9). But though she sees language as power, her reading has actually conditioned her in traditional—even anachronistic—ways. "Novel-reader" and "starry-eyed romantic" (379), she assumes her life will follow the forms of fiction—it will be shaped by a man and "end" in marriage. Jane is not only an odd woman but a woman at odds with herself—"in transit between the old values . . . and the new values, which she must hack out for herself" (140). Her deepest emotions are, like Anna Wulf's, "still fitted for a kind of society that no longer exists" (*Golden Notebook* 314). In the beginning of the novel, she has attained the end for which other contemporary protagonists strive—"Her impetus, her goal, had been, for so long, to become her own woman, and she had followed it to its end, just as other women feel the impetus toward marriage or motherhood and follow it to its end"—but she does not know what use to make of it: "Only now she could not see . . . what use, what joyful use, she could possibly make of this freedom" (149).

Besides, Jane's nineteenth-century yearnings keep coming up against twentieth-century realities. She seeks "eternal love" (175), a love "that exists in a permanent, eternal way" (286), only to find impermanence. She seeks "clear answers" (26), "the end of uncertainty, of joyless struggle without assurance of a happy award" (151), only to find that experience is "booby-trapped with uncertainties"—that "nothing in this world is certain" (120). Her lover Gabriel is a middle-aged, married man who shows every sign of remaining married and who offers Jane, not redemption, but the occasional weekend. His life's work—contained in eleven shoeboxes of notecards categorizing types of love in pre-Raphaelite paintings—makes Jane think uneasily of George Eliot's Casaubon. With her longing for certainty, she must accept uncertainty; with her longing for product, she must accept process. With her longing for a happy ending, Jane must accept being "odd," but she must re-envision "oddity" to mean "singularity" and "strength" rather than "peculiarity" or "strangeness"; she must make the transition from "spinster" to "excellent woman." She faces "the hard task of self-change," as George Eliot says of Gwendolen Harleth,[9] who is the only heroine Eliot does not kill or marry off at the end of *Daniel Deronda*, one of the novels Jane speculates about (151, 426).

Godwin suggests Jane's yearning for clear answers and firm shapes is nostalgic: "As the world spun faster, maddeningly, toward the year 2000 . . . wasn't it a cowardly retreat for her to expect clear answers, articulate standards . . . firm shapes? Wasn't the challenge—always in human progress—with the unformed rather than the solidly formed, the set, the congealed? But she was not a reformer. Damage distressed her too much. She liked to work with the materials of excellence, undamaged, ready to be worked into something marvelous" (26–27). Though Godwin criticizes this retreat, *The Odd Woman* is itself solidly formed in a way that affirms nostalgia rather than a "hacking out" of "new values" (140). The narrative is "an old story" in its adherence to the Aristotelian principles Godwin defines as "a good plot," which "goes from possibility to probability to necessity" (151), for notions of probability and possibility are themselves ideologically complicit.[10] Like Jane, Godwin is no reformer. Progress, as she rightly suspects, requires damage ("break-down" or "crack-up" in Anna Wulf's terms). Instead of hacking new forms from the unformed, Godwin retreats to the set and congealed. As the possibility that Gabriel will leave his wife narrows to the probability that he will not, Jane is stripped of her illusions as inexorably as any Jane Austen or George Eliot heroine. Godwin is, like Jane, at odds with herself, for though she tries to teach Jane to accept uncertainty and an unconventional end, her plot proceeds conventionally, its movement a narrowing, a constriction, which works against the open-ended process she means to suggest and precludes a sense of what Grace Paley calls the "open destiny of life."[11] Though Godwin's depiction of the single woman challenges the stereotype of the spinster as pitiful victim and suggests that options for single women are broader today than they were in the past, she also demonstrates—inadvertently—that the representation of the single woman is still constrained by narrative conventions and a conventional ideology of the single woman.

Jane's relationship to novels is complicated, for though she is a starry-eyed romantic whose reading has left her with sentimental notions, she is also a teacher and critic who is aware of the relation of "forms" to "the times." Whereas Gissing's message is simple—"If every novelist could be strangled and thrown into the sea we should have some chance of reforming women"—Godwin's is more complex.[12]

Though Jane feels the lure of the old story—"'I love a love story; you know me'" (196)—she can also critique it. She knows that the romantic fiction her mother Kitty wrote is the old story at its most reductive and formulaic, "the same old plot again and again; the plot of a girl . . . who threw everything out the window to get her man" (192)—terms which suggest repetition, repetition without revision, always to the same end. She is aware that even the best nineteenth-century novels offer variations on this theme. "*Jane Eyre* is great soap opera" (59); Jane Austen "dealt with marriages and the making of marriages" (28). George Eliot "forbade her characters" the "success in her profession and ecstasy with her married lover" which she herself found; the most one could hope from her novels was to "marry a nice man at the end and lead a useful life helping him" (28). When she tries to imagine herself in a Jane Austen or George Eliot novel, she realizes that their worlds are so far from hers that their messages no longer apply; she knows that history changes consciousness. Of even less value is the unhappy ending, which she terms "the 'Emma Bovary' syndrome," the "theme of literally dozens of 19th century novels": "Literature's graveyard positively choked with women who chose—rather, let themselves be chosen by—this syndrome; also with their 'cousins,' who 'get in trouble' (commit adultery, have sex without marriage; think of committing adultery, or having sex without marriage) and thus, according to the literary convention of the time, must die" (302).

Jane's analysis of the literary convention of the time anticipates feminist critics' analyses of the constraints of the ending. As Rachel Blau DuPlessis demonstrates, love in nineteenth-century fiction is a woman's quest and vocation, absorbing all possible *Bildung*, defining her success or failure and her transition to adulthood. Marriage symbolizes a woman's integration into society, and death, which results when a woman fails to negotiate entrance into the teleological love relationship, symbolizes punishment for female sexuality or aspiration.[13] Even George Eliot, whose own life was unconventional, subjected her heroines to conventional endings in her fiction. Jane's observation that Eliot forbade her characters the success she herself attained recalls Jane Gray's remarks (in Drabble's *The Waterfall*) about Zola, who, in spite of his punishing sexual morality, could be seen enjoying the company of his mistress and babes in the Tuileries and certainly was "more charitable to the flesh in his life than in his art."[14] Though nineteenth-century literary endings to some extent reflected nineteenth-century social practices, narrative convention is in ways even more constraining than social convention, which suggests that novels reflect ideology as much as actuality.

What Jane has learned from novels is essentially what she has learned from her grandmother Edith—"you had your choice: a disastrous ending with a Villain; a satisfactory ending with a Good Man. The message was simple" (29). Edith's simple message—that a woman's end, goal, telos, is a man—has been corroborated, in one way or another, by the women in Jane's family: Edith taught it by exhortation; Edith's sister Cleva, who met a bad end with a villain, taught it by example; and even Jane's mother, Kitty, who rebelled against Edith, illustrated the power of the romantic resolution by her elopement, her sacrifice of career to family, and the romantic fiction she wrote.

More relevant to Jane's situation are those nineteenth-century novels that do not end with marriage or death but leave their protagonists alive and alone. But besides being few and far between, these, too, are unsatisfactory.[15] Ellen Glasgow's novels require her women to live without love (61, 276); *Daniel Deronda*, Jane says, "poses some questions I can't even answer yet" (426). Gissing's *Odd Women* is more relevant in its investigation of the problems of women alone, but these women also meet "horrible ends" (61) and make adjustments that Jane finds unacceptable: "ESCAPE THROUGH

DRINK—PARTIAL REHABILITATION TO 'A USEFUL MEMBER OF SOCIETY'"; "STARTING ALL OVER AGAIN IN A CHILD. RETRENCHMENT"; "FINDING 'FULFILLMENT THROUGH OTHERS'"; "SUBLIMATION OF PERSONAL DESIRES AND FURIES INTO A 'CAUSE'" (301–2). Jane's reaction to this novel is a tangle of contradictions. She finds herself circling the outcry of Rhoda Nunn, "the young spinster career woman with whom she most identified": "'Love—love—love— . . . What is more vulgar than the ideal of novelists? They won't represent the actual world. . . . In real life how many men and women *fall in love?*'" (119). Jane wonders, "Was Rhoda right? Was 'love—love—love' never to be found outside the ideals of novelists?" (119). But she also chides her for "playing this feminist power game" and wishes she would "do more interesting things than destroy your love with ideologies" (119). She finds unacceptable the renunciations Gissing requires: "Well, who the hell" would "want to live without love of any kind?" (119). Though Gissing's novel is unconventional in subject and sympathies, the alternatives he allows his characters—either sexuality or autonomy—reaffirm conventional wisdom and so offer another version of the old story.[16]

Even in the most unconventional of nineteenth-century novels, lives have shape and significance, loose ends are tied up, products are assured—as Jane's neat summaries of Gissing's characters suggest. This is one reason Jane is drawn to literature. As her friend Gerda suggests, people in novels are safe, completed: "'Real people are sloppy and unpredictable and often boring. You like to have . . . a guarantee that everything is going to turn out in some coherent, aesthetic way'" (151). Jane's mother Kitty tells her, "'You're such a good little *student*. You've always been one to look up your life in books. . . . You're living in myths'"; but "'the trouble with myths . . . is that they leave out so much. They leave out all the loose ends, all those messy, practical details that make living less than idyllic'" (176–77). Jane finds Sheldon, her "good student," reassuring because he seems to confirm that "if only she kept on reading the right books, doing research on the things she did not understand, the mystery of her life would come clear" (25). She defines "her real profession" as "researching her salvation" (425). This also accounts for her attraction to Jungian archetypes, which seem to hold out the possibility of a "formula," the "solution to her life" (though Jung always "eluded her," "the message which had seemed so certain . . . dissolved in front of her eyes. It was only print, a lot of words about old things" [330]). She seeks "the Word" behind words, as though by naming her insomnia she can control it; "everything for her is measured in words" (266). Though her tendency to search for eternal forms is criticized by nearly everybody—her mother, her best friend, even herself—it is characteristic of the artist: Yeats's Byzantium poet longs for a form that conquers time, for an eternal artifact that transcends "the fury and mire of human veins";[17] Drabble's Jane Gray longs to write "a poem as round and hard as a stone" (69). Jane Clifford imagines "Art" as "the great exemptor. Like Death, it excused you from the annoyances and limitations of time" (152). But these terms also suggest the problem with this ideal: such exemption can occur only with death.

Given this longing for eternal forms, Jane is comfortable with the definition of literature as the expression of "universals," "things we all experience, which tug at all of us, however different we are" (23). She enlists Matthew Arnold's description of literature as "the best that has been known and thought—and felt—in the world," and she tells her student Howard (her "bad student") that "'literature is the collection of the best expressions of these universal emotions and thoughts. By "best," we mean the ones which have a special, extra power to tug at us. The ones which have endured because of a richness of language, an amazing distillation of many, many connected things, arranged in such a way that we see connections we hadn't seen before'" (23). Howard's criticism—"'I have this feeling you're just repeating things some teacher repeated to you'" (23)—is astute, because Jane is parroting the new critical dicta that she would have learned in graduate schools in the sixties. The conversation takes an interesting turn as Jane goes on to contradict herself (though she does not seem to notice that she has). Howard, who believes that language is something that "'gets in the way,'" appeals to direct experience, assuring her "'we would have felt the same thing'" about "'this fabulous full moon the other night,'" and Jane replies, "'I'm not so sure. You would experience, God knows, some sort of Zen moon, and I—what would I see?'" reaching for Coleridge to explain what she might have seen (24). If something as concrete as the moon is mediated by reading and language, appearing different when perceived by different people—and these two people inhabit the same culture at the same time—how much less universal is something as complex as a literary text, especially when interpreted by people of different cultures at different times? Jane thus calls into question the very notion of universals, though neither she nor Godwin seems to see this.

Besides, if literature expresses universals, Jane ought to be able to translate herself to a Jane Austen or a George Eliot novel; but she realizes she cannot because these works express their times. Godwin is clear about her own characters' relations to their times and delineates each woman in Jane's family in relation to her generation: Edith, Jane's grandmother, was "always in style" (62) with her white gloves and impeccable appearance, in harmony with her *Zeitgeist;* Emily, Jane's younger sister, is in harmony with hers, in her pragmatic, unromantic ordering of her life; Jane and her mother Kitty have both fallen "'in the interstices of the *Zeitgeists*'" (178), as Jane says when they come across Edith's white gloves while sorting through her possessions. Kitty tells Jane that she felt torn between her ambition to write and her love for her babies, that she was "born too late or too early," with "one foot in one era and the other foot in the next" (178). Jane, like her mother, is in transit and confused about what she wants. But Godwin does not see the contradiction between her view of people and literary works as the products of their times (as Kitty says, "We are products, we are prisoners of our times" [178]) and the ideal (which she seems to share with Jane) that literature expresses universal thoughts and emotions.

Jane says something that suggests a sense of this problem when she asserts that "the real thing" is knowable "after fifty years": "There was the real thing, and there was the approximation, the imitation, and the barefaced hoax. She became increasingly convinced, more so since she had read a collection of nineteenth-century reviews praising as masterpieces novels no one now remembered and explaining why people like Hardy and Emily Brontë were flashes in the pan, that the world could not tell the difference till at least fifty years had elapsed" (153). But neither she nor Godwin confronts the question of why fifty years should provide the "true" perspective or what it means when a hundred years later that masterpiece falls out of fashion again and the same work that moves one generation to tears moves the next generation to laughter. The 1905 melodrama *The Fatal Wedding,* "an old play" (331) which moves us to laughter, moved Great-aunt Cleva to defy family and convention—or to defy one sort of convention to fall into another. Jane has a moment of uneasiness when she senses that she may be no different from Cleva—"a Southern girl, raised on a farm, a little in arrears of her *Zeitgeist*"—and she wonders what a great grandniece of hers "some seventy years in the future" will be able to see about her (337). Jane imagines this grandniece thinking, "*What was wrong with her? Couldn't she see that it's all a matter of . . .*" (337, Godwin's ellipis). It follows that those qualities that have special "power to tug at us," those criteria by which we define the masterpiece, will seem as quaint as Edith's white gloves, for in our judgments we are as time-bound, as imprisoned in our *Zeitgeists,* as stage-struck Cleva was. If Edith's decisions were "written out of some etiquette book, copyrighted about 1890" (48), then the question follows, what book writes our lives, what ideology are we part of—a question Godwin raises but does not confront. Instead of following through on this analysis of the ideology of forms, pushing it to an inquiry that might produce new forms, Godwin retreats to the assumptions of her time.[18]

Godwin brilliantly renders a sense of reality as process, as subject to the shaping power of imagination and language and written according to the needs of the moment. Her depiction of Jane's thought processes demonstrates that our reality—past and present, our own selves and others, the significance we assign events—is a creation of the fictionalizing imagination. The meaning of things is in constant flux, subject to Jane's interpretation and reinterpretation, taking shape from the voices and words that invade her mind. Zimmer voices and Gerda voices, "naysayers" who provide "a running cynical commentary on her life" (264), gnaw at her ideals and illusions; "phantoms" haunt "the present moment" (249).

The past, like the present, is a creation of the stories we tell ourselves and others. As Morag Gunn, protagonist of Margaret Laurence's *The Diviners,* says, "A popular misconception is that we can't change the past—everyone is constantly changing their own past, recalling it, revising it."[19] Jane has always been intrigued by her family's "mythmaking" (as Gerda calls it [62]), especially by Edith's use of Cleva as a cautionary tale, and she realizes that she herself is "mythmaking" when she transforms Edith into "the perfect Southern lady" for the benefit of Sonia (62). She is also aware of how we reconstruct the more immediate past and realizes that she and Kitty will remake their conversation, "do it over in [their] memories" (89) according to what they need to believe about their relationship.

Jane is fascinated by how many of our efforts are devoted to self-creation, what she calls the "terrible task of personality" (279). She is "amazed" at Gerda's "continued ability to re-create herself" (42) and impressed by Sonia's willingness to "revise herself" (58). Her sense of the "undefined, unresolved self" is so acute that she wonders if the very concept of self may be "only a bygone literary convention" (27). She sees that the self is a creation of time and circumstance, tailored to occasion and audience, and understands the importance of appearance in this process—which is why she so often checks her image in mirrors, trying to see herself as others see her, as though she might understand herself if she could only see herself clearly. So dependent is she on such reflections that when she is alone, dissolution threatens. She experiences herself as "a sort of liquid state" held together by a "thin web of sanity" which, if slit, would "start running out of me and seek its natural source, some kind of Source Sea which contains elements of everybody, all kinds of habits and attitudes and characteristics of future people"—"If this should happen, I know I will cease to be" (69, 72). When she is alone, she has a sense of herself as existing only as an image in the minds of others and imagines "that's what it was like to be dead" (74). She is therefore consoled, the morning after Edith's death, that Edith's story exists in someone else's mind, that Gerda "knows [her family's] stories" (40).

Jane also sees that we create others by our ideas of them and that our ideas are determined by needs and desires. This is particularly apparent in men's views of women, which are so obviously self-interested: *"You are the most ——— woman I have ever met because that's what I want you to be, by God"* (375). Such images are persuasive: Jane realizes that her family's image of her exerts a powerful hold and is the "most compelling weave of all" the nets they cast at her (89). Knowing another person is a matter of choosing a version of that person to believe, as Kitty does of her other daughter, Emily (97). A relationship is a kind of reciprocal creation that works as long as one person's image of the other squares with that person's self-image but stops working when the balance shifts. Jane initially sees Gabriel as her savior, and as long as she needs to be saved, she puts up with anything he asks of her, but when her needs change, so does the relationship. Her decision to leave Gabriel is a repudiation of his image of her, though she tells Gerda that "'if I ever found one who saw me as large as I'd like to be, I might ask him to stick around'" (412). She sees also that people bring out different potentials in one another, that "one partner could actually derive strength from the weakness of the other" (79, 198).

Jane understands the ways words shape reality: "One had to be careful about triggering things by finding the right words for them. . . . Sometimes you could set things in motion purely to watch the actions imitate a group of emotionally satisfying words: 'I'm leaving you'" (191). She "creates" Gabriel with words—"words contained magic, all right"; she "looked him up in a book . . . and took his name and his words home, where . . . she carefully dreamed him"; "Yes, if you believed in words, if you lived by words, *you had better be careful which words you say and how you say them*" (305–6); "I dreamed him and them summoned him with words" (371). She feels that his words also "summon" her, and, indeed, his delicate distinction between "irrevocable" and "irredeemable" (he tells her that choices in his life have "hardened into the irrevocable" but not the "irredeemable" [261]) is "a bit of etymological foreplay"; this "lady of letters" is "wooed by his wordplay" (265).

Consistent with this is her awareness of the influence of literary forms on our lives: "'we are always in some play or other. . . . What I am interested in is: do we create the roles, or do they create us?'" (358). Cleva's story illustrates a point made by Jane's colleague, Sonia, that women pattern their lives after soap opera (59, 337). Jane wonders at the end if she enjoyed "watching herself play the abused mistress" (342). No sooner has she written the farewell note to Gabriel than she finds herself "rehearsing" the incident "for a future scene" (371); and as she is leaving him, she has to hold firmly to her resolve to make the scene "her scene," to shape it according to her own emotional necessities rather than allow it to conform to a prefabricated pattern.

Given Godwin's sense of reality as process—structured by imagination and language and shifting with the needs of the moment—it is no wonder that Jane's search for an "eternal constant" (14) is doomed to failure. Early in the novel, the morning after Edith's death, Jane has an important "insight about stories" or, rather, about the limitations of stories: "Stories were all right, as long as you read them as what they were: single visions, one person's way of interpreting something. You could learn from stories, be warned by stories. But stories, by their very nature, were Procrustean. Even the longest of them had to end somewhere. If a living human being tried to squeeze himself into a particular story, he might find vital parts of himself lopped off. Even worse, he might find himself unable to get out again" (49). In thinking about "'mistress' stories," Jane realizes that "the word 'mistress' itself was a story," "as was 'career woman,' or 'spinster,' or 'professor of English,' or 'intellectual,' or 'Romantic.' I am all of these . . . but all of them are only parts of me" (50). She concludes, "You remained indestructible by eluding for dear life the hundreds and thousands of already written, already completed stories. . . . You reminded yourself that . . . you had to write yourself as you went along, that your story could not and should not possibly be completed until *you* were: i.e., dead. . . . *She* was not dead yet. Nothing was finished, nothing at all . . . she had not written herself into any premature endings . . . there was, she felt, still time, still hope to do, be anything . . ." (50). As long as she is alive, "THIS IS NOT THE FINAL DRAFT" (241); she will be completed only when she is dead. The problem Jane faces is like that of Lessing's Anna Wulf—to find a form for her life which does not surrender to conventional form or to formlessness; the problem Godwin faces is like that of Doris Lessing—to forge a narrative correlative to the form her protagonist makes for her life, a form that expresses open-ended process, writing yourself as you went along.

What is disappointing is that, having so skillfully suggested this sense of uncertainty and flux, Godwin's narrative rigidifies to so sure and fixed a form. Though Jane expresses exhilaration that "this is not the final draft," Godwin's novel is very much a final draft—finished, completed, congealed. Though Jane is being true to herself in putting an end to the affair with Gabriel, the sequence of events leading to the end of the affair moves her inexorably from the possible to the probable to the necessary, according to the Aristotelian principles that Godwin has described as "a good plot."

At the beginning of the novel, the possibility has already narrowed to the probability that Gabriel will not leave his wife. Jane is beginning to outgrow Gabriel's image of her, and necessity is asserting itself in the form of her own needs. Nevertheless, she keeps trying, the day she spends in New York killing time while waiting for Gabriel, to tailor herself to the requirements of this relationship.

She tries to remake herself in Gabriel's image by attempting to make herself as he likes her (i.e., patient) and to make herself like him. Gabriel is the silent type, and Jane's attempt to renounce "word-knowledge" and know him "wordlessly" is an extreme effort of self-renunciation. She tries "to empty herself of a lifetime of preconceptions in order to approach what she could not figure out in words about this man": "Never had she so completely doubted every form of reason; never had she doubted herself, all that she had based her life on, so completely"; "She struggled against the mode of thinking that had been her life" (294–95). But she cannot relinquish reason, language, or her "conscious," "recording" ego (297–98). Whether Gabriel cares about any of this is unclear, but Jane does. The standard evoked (though Godwin does not say so) recalls D. H. Lawrence's view of women as caught within an imprisoning ego and rationality, a compelling cultural stereotype and one to which Jane, as an avid reader who is timid about her sexuality, would be particularly vulnerable. (As Erica Jong's Isadore Wing testifies, Lawrence's versions of female sexuality have made other women readers feel inadequate.)[20]

Neither can Jane remake herself according to the standard represented by Saks Fifth Avenue department store. Though she tries to "refurbish her image" in the mirrors at Saks (309, 316), she realizes that it is too late to remake herself as a beautiful object; years spent in the library have decided that. The scene in the department store fitting room, when she panics at losing herself among the dresses, is a high point of comedy in the novel and one of those scenes in contemporary women's fiction that women readers remember as crystallizing some essential aspect of their experience (the construction-worker scene in Lessing's *Summer before the Dark* is another). But the dresses on the racks at Saks do not fit Jane any more than other peoples' stories do—"She would not look in any more mirrors for awhile" (318)—and she hardly cares when she loses the dress she has just bought, leaving it on the seat of the cab, since it was never really hers in the first place.

Her next destination, the library, reveals more of who she is. At the library she decides to track down the truth of Great-aunt Cleva, enlisting the tools she has developed as scholar and critic and bringing them to bear on her past. What she finds in researching the old play—that "the villain" of Cleva's life was the hero of the play, the incongruously named Edwin Merchant, rather than (as in Edith's moralization) the stage villain played by Von Vorst—is further uncertainty, "one more 'illusion'" (420). The story thus takes on another meaning for Jane, how difficult it is to get "to the bottom of anything in her life" (420)—though this ambiguity suggests less that people and events are radically unknowable, as Godwin seems to intend, than that there has been a misunderstanding.

Gabriel's postponement of their meeting stretches Jane's patience and makes her departure more "probable." But though she packs her suitcase, she does not take it with her as she sets off to visit Von Vorst because she has not yet "felt . . . the necessity of leaving" (348). Sorry that she is not more "sensational," she nevertheless insists on making the scene "my scene," on "play[ing] it as I see fit . . . honor[ing] it with the consistencies on which, so far, the drama has been constructed" (348). What provides the necessity is Gabriel's further postponement, which strains her patience to the breaking point. But even in the cab on the way to the airport she asks herself, "Do you really want to be here? . . . What is this drama? Did you choose it? Or are you letting some facile director . . . force you into this premature dénouement?" (372). To this question she can at last formulate an answer; necessity asserts itself, finally, as an affirmation of something she wants: "Oh God, I don't want to be *patient* in somebody's eyes, I want to be *first!*" (373).

Jane Clifford is not redeemed by passion (as Jane Gray is), however much she would like to be; she learns, rather, to relinquish illusions, accept herself, and depend on her own efforts. When Jane returns home and receives Sonia's note promising an interesting bit of news, her heart leaps at the possibility that Sonia has found the perfect man for her—someone who will combine the attractions of a Knightley and a Heathcliff; instead, Sonia's news concerns a job opportunity. When the phone rings, Jane anticipates hearing Gabriel's voice at the other end; instead, it is a student—someone who requires, rather than offers, rescue. Though Godwin makes gestures toward open-endedness—we don't know if Gabriel will get the Guggenheim or if he will ask Jane to accompany him to England—probabilities are strongly suggested. Jane is left alone with herself, depending on her own efforts, attaining the self-awareness and self-reliance that make it impossible for her to pick up and follow Gabriel to England, or anywhere else.

In the final scene of the novel, as in the opening scene, Jane is in bed with insomnia, imagining herself addressing the "enema bandit." But the advice she imagines herself offering him—"'turn your oddities inside out like a sock and find your own best life by making them work for you instead of being driven by them'" (429)—indicates a new self-acceptance. Having learned that she does not fit Gabriel's image or the dresses in Saks or anyone else's story, she can accept oddities of her own and make them work for her; this is her own best life. This return to the beginning provides a measure of distance traveled and change.

But occurring at the end of a movement that represents a narrowing of possibilities, the circular structure creates a sense of constriction, a sense reinforced by the careful symmetry, the contrasts and parallels, on which the novel is structured.[21] Each woman in Jane's family is shown in relation to her generation; Jane's voice opposes Gerda's; Gabriel's opposes Zimmer's; Sheldon the good student opposes Howard the bad; Sonia, the colleague who has it all—success, marriage, children—contrasts with Marsha, the graduate student Jane meets as she travels to Edith's funeral, who flounders professionally and personally: winner against loser, "how to" against "how not to." Coincidence obtrudes when Von Vorst just happens to be interested in the same questions Jane is thinking about—the relation of literature to life—and when Jane just happens to encounter "a sort of alternate fate" (405) in the story of Nan Frampton, a young woman who has managed to win her lover from his wife. At such points one feels the strong hand of the author.

Godwin is her own best critic on this. In a fascinating essay, "Becoming a Writer," she describes precisely this problem: "I think the most serious danger to my writing is my predilection for shapeliness. How I love 'that nice circular Greek' shape . . . a nice, neat conclusion with all the edges tucked under. And this sometimes leads me to 'wrap up' things, to force dramatic revelations at the expense of allowing the truth to reveal itself in slow, shy, and often problematical glimpses."[22] Even as *The Odd Woman* gestures toward open-endedness, its nice circular shape works against open-endedness to wrap things up. Even as Godwin gestures toward an unconventional ending, she (like Great-aunt Cleva) resists one kind of convention to succumb to another: her predilection for shapeliness wins out in the end. The novel is conventional in this adherence to narrative conventions that recuperate the very ideology being challenged. Jane is, as Kitty calls her, "'such a good little student'" (177); Jane's failure is Godwin's. Neither of them challenges the world or the forms that express that world; neither hacks out new values or new forms to express those values.

When as a child Jane asked Kitty, "'Why don't you write a story about a woman who teaches school at the college and writes love stories on the weekend and has a little girl like me?'" Kitty answered, "'It wouldn't sell, that's why'" (32–33). Godwin extends this discussion in the essay "Becoming a Writer," where she describes the formula of the romantic fiction her own mother wrote for a living: "GIRL MEETS MAN. MUTUAL ATTRACTION. THINGS DEVELOP. A PROBLEM ARISES. CONFLICT AND DOUBT. RESOLUTION OF CONFLICT. FINAL EMBRACE. The formula was unvarying. All the stories . . . were imprisoned in that plot," on that "romantic treadmill . . . the mutual attraction, the developing passion, the necessary conflict, the happy ending" (234).[23] Godwin wonders whether her mother had "moments when she was tempted to rip out the 'happily-ever-after' lie she was perpetuating . . . and tell her own story": "It would have been much more interesting. But who would have bought it?" "When you write for the market, you lock yourself willingly into the prison of your times" (234–35). Since novels imitate ideology as much as actuality, "a story about people like us" "won't sell": Kitty "could only sell stories about girls who could throw everything out the window when the man came along" (331).

In "Becoming a Writer," Godwin speculates about "what parts of their stories" writers "still feel obliged to suppress": "[Today's] fictional terrains support . . . divorced mothers, unmarried mothers, even well-to-do suburban wives who may or may not 'keep' that unplanned-for last child. And I think of the writers of these stories, safely within the ideologies of their *zeitgeist*, and I wonder what parts of their own stories they still feel obliged to suppress, what dark blossomings of their imaginations still lie outside the realm of the current 'market'? Yes, even in these 'liberated' times" (234). She adds that "it is the dark blossomings, the suppressed (or veiled) truths that I court. Not always successfully. Like my mother, I, too, am the child of my times" (234).

Godwin is right to be uneasy about being a child of her times, safely within the ideology of her *zeitgeist*, for though it may once have been unconventional to show a protagonist leaving the doll's house of a confining relationship, this ending itself became conventional in the early 1970s in novels like Barbara Raskin's *Loose Ends*, Erica Jong's *Fear of Flying*, and Dorothy Bryant's *Ella Price's Journal*, all published within a year of *The Odd Woman*. As Jean Kennard points out, "By 1977 when Marilyn French published *The Women's Room*, she talked of this convention as 'an old rule,' 'a convention of the women's novel' which she intended to break."[24] Long before this, in the early fifties, Lessing's Martha Quest reflected, "There's something so damned *vieux jeu* . . . in leaving like Nora, to live differently! . . . [as though] rushing off to earn one's living as a typist is going to make any difference. One is bound to fall in love with the junior partner and the whole thing will begin again."[25]

We may understand some of the suppressed or veiled truths that elude Godwin by comparing her to contemporary women writers who do probe these truths. Other protagonists take greater risks and work out more unconventional forms in their lives. Anna Wulf descends into madness; Morag Gunn becomes single parent to a dark-skinned child in a racist society; Jane Gray finds salvation in an adulterous and slightly incestuous affair with her cousin's husband. It is significant that these characters are writers, for "the power of the pen" (to use Sandra Gilbert and Susan Gubar's phrase[26]) gives them an authority Jane lacks and enables them to forge new forms in order to "write themselves." Jane Clifford takes no such chances; in fact, Godwin elsewhere mocks the excesses of her contemporaries, targeting especially Margaret Atwood's *Surfacing*.[27]

In a revealing passage, Jane describes her education as an education in pleasing men—"She had connived to win her degrees . . . partially through the charms of her sex"—and compares the way she trimmed and tailored her mind to the way other women shape their bodies—"the college term papers, carefully researched, accurately footnoted . . . then shaped and tinted (as other women shaped their figures with foundation garments, tinted their skins with make-up) with a delicate wit, an irresistible . . . turn of phrase" (149).[28] There is all the difference between this careful shaping of self to fit male approval and Jane Gray's abandon and abandonment to the sticky mysteries of sex and birth. Jane Clifford's fear of letting Gabriel hear the sounds of her bodily functions, so extreme that she returns home constipated after spending a weekend with him, is particularly revealing by contrast with Drabble's and Laurence's use of "shit" and "muck" to suggest qualities their protagonists must accept: in Laurence's *The Diviners,* Morag learns to accept "muck," symbol of the toughness and complexity represented by her stepfather Christie, the town scavenger; in Drabble's *The Middle Ground,* Kate learns to "turn shit to gold." Gerda tells Jane that "'until you can let him hear you shit, there is going to be *no* free dialogue'" (134); perhaps this is the symbolism of the "enema bandit," the mysterious figure with whom Jane has imaginary late-night conversations.

There is all the difference between the neat, symmetrical shape of this novel and Drabble's "writing the body." Jane's caution and conventionality are related to a certain fastidiousness about sexuality which actually reaffirms, in a way, the stereotype of the spinster. Jane fears "the menacing relationship between blood and impurity and a dead aunt . . . who was done in by her womanhood" and would like "to have it over with, to be respectable and old" (246–47). Her asceticism is also apparent in her fond memories of the winter she spent writing her dissertation, which she cherishes for its qualities of frozen stillness: "Outside and inside her, all was cold, white, pure" (222).[29] Though Jane's development may be seen as epitomizing the evolution of the spinster from a lonely, powerless figure to the newly independent woman who discovers, if not her own voice, at least her own feelings, she is no radical, transgressive figure who threatens existing structures.

In both *The Waterfall* and *The Odd Woman,* fastidiousness is associated with the longing for perfect form. As Jane Gray immerses herself in the sticky processes of birth and sex, she relinquishes the desire to write "a poem as round and hard as a stone," realizing that "a poem so round and smooth would say nothing" (69). The form Drabble creates to express these mysteries is as unconventional as the form Jane works out in her life, encompassing—as her protagonist's life does—struggle and mess. *The Waterfall* is an open-ended, unfinished tale of unpunished passion that draws its metaphors from birth, sex, and death—"complexities of mire or blood" (in Yeats's words, *Byzantium* [1.24]); its ending allows for ongoing process, "all the conflicts, all the bitterness, all the compromise, that is yet to be endured" (247). But Godwin does not risk the messiness and damage she rightly senses are necessary to make something new.

In *The Golden Notebook,* Anna Wulf descends to "the place . . . where words, patterns, order, dissolve" (634), risking a confrontation with formlessness which leads to a new understanding of form and forging "out of the chaos, a new kind of strength" (467). Confronting chaos, she breaks her own form and enters experiences beyond her own. Though she ends by accepting the forms that enable her to endure—getting a job, moving into a smaller flat, pulling herself together for the sake of a child—such forms are accepted within full ironic recognition of their limits and only after her explorations have broadened the idea of "form" itself. Godwin's forms, however, are not expanded or redefined in this way but are simply anachronistically reasserted.

Lessing and Drabble create new form by risking formlessness and resisting the impulse to perfection. They suggest a sense like Yeats's that the eternal artifact, the golden bird, is part of "the fury and mire" of mortality—that product is involved with process, dancer with dance, and "the artifice of eternity" arrived at by immersion in time, in "what is past, or passing, or to come" (Yeats's words in "Among School Children," "Sailing to Byzantium," and "Byzantium"). But Godwin opts for an eternal artifact, for product over process. The image with which the novel concludes—"the barely audible tinkle of a soul at the piano, trying to organize the loneliness and the weather and the long night into something of abiding shape and beauty"—is haunting and lovely, but it nevertheless affirms this impulse to order.

I can't help feeling this failure is related to another of the novel's problems: the caricature of Gerda and the dismissal of feminism. Godwin initially seems to allow Gerda a voice to critique Jane's illusions, making her a kind of double who represents some of the anger and vitality Jane herself lacks, though she has also suppressed the "inner life" to throw herself into fad after fad, the most recent of which is the women's movement. But Godwin does not sustain this tension, for Gerda emerges as silly and trendy and is finally dismissed. Rather than allow her a voice that would make for genuine tension or complexity, Godwin resolves all into a single, unified perspective. Moreover, Gerda's feminism, far from being presented as a viable alternative, is reduced to that deadliest of stereotypes, man-hating, as she and her cronies try to enlist Jane's assistance in compiling a list of "One Hundred and One Ways He Uses You Every Day" (373).

The world of this novel lends itself to analysis in feminist terms. There is Jane, stuck in one-year teaching appointments, marginalized professionally, unable to take herself seriously or challenge her situation; there is Gabriel, secure in a tenured job and marriage, with a mistress on the side (though to be fair, the portrayal of Gabriel is good; he is not stereotyped as men often are in feminist fiction but is presented as a complex, sympathetic human being who has problems of his own). Surely these are related phenomena, but Godwin does not relate them. When Jane arrives home at the end of the novel, she finds: "Nothing new on national news. A few shots of a war, in a place where snow never fell, a war she had been watching, in its perfunctory snippets and shots of continual coverage, for years. A politician's angry face appeared briefly, denouncing an opponent. Nothing new" (415). She shows no awareness that this war has anything to do with her. Even Sylvia Plath, with her weirdly dissociated sensibility, manages to suggest that the Rosenbergs have something to do with Esther's nervous breakdown and suicide attempt, that the repressive political climate which killed them nearly kills her. But Godwin shows no sense that Jane's problems have a political dimension—that the war may not be irrelevant to Jane but may be part of the same power structure creating her unhappiness and dictating the shape of the literary marketplace Godwin herself serves. Whereas Lessing in *The Golden Notebook* relates Anna's writer's block to her problems with men and relates these to the horrors of the time and these horrors to the literary marketplace—the personal is political is aesthetic—Godwin makes none of these connections; she accepts the world she inherits in a way that assures her imprisonment in it.

There is a powerful moment in the novel, when Jane stumbles out of Saks, panicked, seized by a vision of the end that makes all other destinations irrelevant (328), of New York reduced to rubble and her own flesh as returning to dust; she imagines a time after the end, after centuries, when "a curious visitor from another planet, with archaeological interests," comes across a fragment of

Jane (325–27). This apocalyptic vision resembles Mrs. Dalloway's specter of London in Virginia Woolf's novel and moments in Lessing's *Four-Gated City.* Jane is panicked by time, panicked that her biological clock is ticking away her childbearing years and that "tempus fugit" (the name she gives her alarm clock). But her response—and Godwin's—is nostalgic and looking backward toward fixed, solid forms, reactionary rather than revolutionary. As good as Godwin is at articulating the relation of literary to social convention and contrasting nineteenth-century forms to twentieth-century complexities, her protagonist's longing for order and clarity is finally her own. No reformer and no re-former, she fails to conceive of alternatives to the structures of the past. Thus *The Odd Woman* not only analyzes the difficulties involved in women's efforts to forge new forms but itself illustrates these difficulties. By understanding the limitations of this novel, we can appreciate how hard it is even for a writer as aware as Godwin is to escape "the times" that produce and imprison us and to say "something new."

NOTES

1. Erica Jong's *Fear of Flying,* Lisa Alther's *Kinflicks,* Margaret Atwood's *Surfacing,* Margaret Laurence's *The Diviners,* Margaret Drabble's *Realms of Gold,* Doris Lessing's *Summer before the Dark,* Toni Morrison's *Sula,* and Dorothy Bryant's *Ella Price's Journal* were also published between 1972 and 1975. Prior to these were Lessing's major works—*The Children of Violence* (1952–69) and *The Golden Notebook* (1962)—and Drabble's *The Waterfall* (1969).

2. Gail Godwin, *The Odd Woman* (New York: Warner Books, 1974) 29.

3. Barthes discusses "the constraints of the discourse" (*S/Z* [New York: Hill and Wang, 1974] 135 and passim). In her discussion of the post-Saussurean position represented by Barthes, Catherine Belsey refers to realism as "the accomplice of ideology" (*Critical Practice* [London: Methuen, 1980] 73). She contends, "It is intelligible as 'realist' precisely because it reproduces what we already seem to know" (47); "to this extent it is a predominantly conservative form" (51; see also 46, 52). Stephen Heath described realist narrative as "aimed at containment" (quoted in Rosalind Coward and John Ellis, *Language and Materialism: Developments in Semiology and the Theory of the Subject* [London: Routledge and Kegan Paul, 1977] 49).

4. Jean E. Kennard suggests that "woman's search for her own story, which ends in its creation, is a response to the absence of that story in literary history" ("Convention Coverage or How to Read Your Own Life," *New Literary History* 13 [1981]: 84). Elizabeth Abel discusses the "complex interplay between self-discovery and writing" in women's writing ("(E)Merging Identities: The Dynamics of Female Friendship in Contemporary Fiction by Women," *Signs* 6 [1981]: 444). Carol P. Christ refers to the

"key role of language in articulating and shaping women's experiences of new being" (*Diving Deep and Surfacing: Women Writers on Spiritual Quest* [Boston: Beacon, 1980] 81).

5. Florence Howe, "A Talk with Doris Lessing," *Nation* 204 (March 6, 1976); rpt. in *A Small Personal Voice: Doris Lessing, Essays, Reviews, Interviews*, ed. Paul Schleuter (New York: Vintage, 1975) 81.

6. Anna seeks "something new," and the expression recurs throughout *The Golden Notebook* (New York: Bantam, 1973) 61, 353, 472–3, 479; it occurs also throughout the Children of Violence series (*Martha Quest* 53, 141, 216; *Landlocked* 117 [New York: New American Library, 1964, 1966]), where it symbolizes the object of Martha Quest's quest.

7. See Joanne S. Frye's discussion of *The Waterfall* (*Living Stories, Telling Lives: Women and the Novel in Contemporary Experience* [Ann Arbor: University of Michigan Press, 1986] 147–63) and my reading of it ("New System, New Morality," *Novel: A Forum on Fiction* 22 [1988]: 45–65).

8. Barthes makes a distinction between the *"scriptible"* text (as "process" which is open to being "written," "produced") and the *"lisible"* text (as "product" which "can only be read"): whereas the *"lisible"* text—which is the mode of nineteenth-century realism—is an object for "consumption" that makes the reader a passive consumer, the *"scriptible"* text "make[s] the reader no longer a consumer, but a producer, of the text" (*S/Z* 4–5). Barthes's terms are elucidated by Belsey 139–40, and Coward and Ellis 45–47.

9. *Daniel Deronda* (Harmondsworth: Penguin, 1976) 842.

10. Nancy K. Miller discusses Gerard Genette's ideas of "plausibility" and "probability," *"vraisemblance"* and *"bienseance"* ("Vraisemblance et motivation," *Figures II* [Paris: Sueil, 1969] 74); she refers to the laws of probability and possibility that govern realist fiction as a kind of "contract" between writer and reader ("Emphasis Added: Plots and Plausibilities in Women's Fiction," *PMLA* 96 [1981]: 36). See also Pierre Macherey, *A Theory of Literary Production*, trans. Geoffrey Wall (London: Routledge and Kegan Paul, 1978) 48–49. Frye suggests that "the traditional plotting that moves from possibility to probability to necessity through the selection and structuring of events is closely tied to the available paradigms for reading women's lives" (39).

11. The phrase occurs in "A Conversation with My Father": "'I would like you to write a simple story . . . ' he says. . . . he means the kind that begins: 'There was a woman . . . ' followed by plot, the absolute line between two points which I've always despised. Not for literary reasons, but because it takes all hope away. Everyone, real or invented, deserves the open destiny of life" (*Enormous Changes at the Last Minute* [New York: Farrar-Straus-Giroux, 1974] 161–62).

12. George Gissing, *The Odd Women* (New York: Norton, 1971) 58. I disagree with Susan E. Lorsch's reading of *The Odd Women* as simply an "indictment of literature and the harmful effects it can have on its readers" ("Gail Godwin's *The Odd Women:* Literature and the Retreat from Life," *Critique* 22. 2 [1978]: 31).

13. Rachel Blau DuPlessis, *Writing beyond the Ending: Narrative Strategies of Twentieth-Century Women Writers* (Bloomington: Indiana University Press, 1985), ch. 1. Nancy K. Miller distinguishes between the "euphoric text," which ends with the heroine's integration into society, and the "dysphoric text," which "ends instead with the heroine's death" (*The Heroine's Text: Readings in the French and English Novel, 1722–1728* [New York: Columbia University Press, 1980] xi). See also Carol Pearson and Katherine Pope, *The Female Hero in American and British Literature* (New York: Bowker, 1981) 11, 34; Annis Pratt, *Archetypal Patterns in Women's Fiction* (Bloomington: University of Indiana Press, 1980) 78; and Frye 40–41, 111.

14. *The Waterfall* (New York: Fawcett Popular Library, 1976) 138.

15. They are not, however, as few and far between as we tend to think. Pratt's chapter "Singleness and Solitude" draws attention to the existence of a surprising number of novels, from the early nineteenth century to the present, on the subject of women alone: "Judging from the popularity of fiction concerning her, the self-sufficient, autonomous woman who chooses not to be married, who happens to remain unmarried, or who finds herself out of the marriage market . . . fascinates the reading audience" (114). But that most of these novels did not make it into the literary canon makes the interesting point that novels which affirm prevailing ideology have a better chance of being "canonized" than those which do not.

16. This is the main question confronted by Frye's book: "why is it so difficult for women writers to create female protagonists who are both autonomous and affirmatively female?" (15).

17. W. B. Yeats, "Byzantium," 1.8, *The Collected Poems* (New York: Macmillan, 1964).

18. Godwin describes herself as "a feminist" in her response to the responses to her review of Sandra M. Gilbert's and Susan Gubar's *Norton Anthology of Literature by Women* (*New York Times Book Review,* April 28, 1985); but, as this exchange and her review indicate, she is quite traditional in her assumptions about literature. She refers to "the achievement of the individual artist" as though it were a universal that transcends gender; and (as Carolyn Heilbrun, Nina Auerbach, Myra Jehlen, Nancy K. Miller, and Catharine R. Stimpson point out in their responses) she implies that "anthologies from the canon are 'universal,' unideological, while any reformation of the canon is the work of ideologues."

19. Margaret Laurence, *The Diviners* (New York: Bantam, 1975) 60.

20. "So I learned about women from men. I saw them through the eyes of male writers. . . . Naturally I trusted everything they said, even when it implied my own inferiority. I learned what an orgasm was from D. H. Lawrence, disguised as Lady Chatterley. I learned from him that all women worship 'the Phallos'" (Erica Jong, *Fear of Flying* [New York: New American Library, 1973] 154).

21. The over-patterning of *The Odd Woman* has been commented on. Anne Z. Mickelson (*Reaching Out: Sensitivity and Order in Recent American*

Fiction by Women [Metuchen, N.J.: Scarecrow Press, 1979]) notes "the symmetrical form of the novel, the careful plotting of characters as either parallel or antithetical to one another" (76) and suggests it "gives the novel a constricting quality of a *fait accompli* which prevents it from moving toward a more expansive experience. The reader has a feeling of being caged in the author's constrictions" (79).

22. "Becoming a Writer," *The Writer on Her Work*, ed. Janet Sternburg (New York: Norton, 1980) 253. Godwin elsewhere expresses a sense of this problem. In *The Finishing School* (New York: Avon, 1984), Ursula De Vane tells Justin, "There are two kinds of people. . . . One kind, you can tell just by looking at them at what point they congealed into their final selves. . . . Whereas the other kind keep moving, changing. . . . In my opinion, they are the only people who are still alive. You must be constantly on your guard . . . against congealing" (4–5). The melodramatic resolution of this novel, however, is an instance of conventionality that verges on cliché—"the pistol shot in the last act," as it was termed by Chekov. In *A Southern Family* (New York: Avon, 1987), Theo, the brother whose suicide everyone is attempting to understand, issues a last challenge before his death to his novelist sister: "'Why don't you write a book about something that can *never* be wrapped up?'" (44).

23. This represents an interesting reversal of the feminist *Kunstlerroman* pattern described by DuPlessis (ch. 6) where the daughter becomes a writer in order to extend her mother's insights in more permanent form. Here, it is the mother who is the writer, but beneath this apparent difference is a deeper similarity: since Kitty writes pulp fiction rather than "serious" fiction, the mother still represents principles the daughter must move beyond.

24. Kennard 72. Kennard is quoting French, "Breaking the Conventions of the Women's Novel," *Boston Globe*, November 28, 1977, 15.

25. Doris Lessing, *A Proper Marriage* (New York: New American Library, 1962) 271. Godwin describes her first novel (unpublished) as ending with "a modern Nora fleeing her doll's house in her own compact car" ("Becoming a Writer" 245).

26. Sandra M. Gilbert and Susan Gubar, *The Madwoman in the Attic: The Woman Writer and the Nineteenth-Century Literary Imagination* (New Haven: Yale University Press, 1979), especially ch. 1.

27. In Godwin's *A Mother and Two Daughters* (New York: Viking, 1982), Cate is reading a book which "had been highly recommended by several colleagues. It was about a young woman who flees modern technology to rediscover her basic instincts in the honesty of the deep woods. In the past year, Cate had read at least three novels about women fleeing into the honesty of the woods. In the first book, the woman fell in love with a bear; in the second, the woman discovered latent artistic impulses; in this book, the woman was, at the moment, down on all fours naked in the forest, rooting and snuffling around, trying to get back to her basic instincts and wonder-

ing if she could grow hair over her whole body" (442). She adds, "But at least these writers are trying to . . . envision new ways to live" and asking "what have we done wrong, and how can we do better next time? I don't knock these writers; how can I? I'm stuck in the same place—between re-assessment and what comes next—but I allow myself the right to be impatient with them, all the same. Why can't they come up with something marvelous to solve my life?" (443).

28. It is unclear, in connection with this, how we are to take Jane's advice to her student Marsha on how to choose a major field of study: "Think of it like one of those 'Test Yourself for Grooming'" (76). Is Jane suiting her terms to her audience or is her mind so permeated by the clichés of popular culture that she used these terms?

29. As Lorsch suggests, "Godwin links Jane's interest in fictions with the wish to avoid sexuality, to ignore or de-emphasize the physical world in favor of the world of the imagination" (22).

PART FOUR

Radical Spinsters

Barbara Brothers

Flying the Nets at Forty: *Lolly Willowes* as Female Bildungsroman

Unmarried women, until post–World War II fiction, had been allotted the spare room in the houses built by social and fictional conventions. They were visitors, onlookers at life's drama, "redundant" or "superfluous" women (as the British had so explicitly labeled them). How impertinent Sylvia Townsend Warner must have seemed in 1926 when she chose such a woman for the heroine of her novel *Lolly Willowes or the Loving Huntsman.* Tradition prescribes that Lolly be "absorbed into the household of one brother or the other" (6) upon the death of her widowed father, given the "small spare-room . . . the handiest . . . for ordinary visitors" (2) in that household, and made semi-useful doing needle work and escorting nieces to dancing lessons. Warner depicts her heroine as literally and figuratively bound by this convention until Lolly decides at age forty-seven to escape from the Victorian household of her brother to a room of her own choosing, a room in which she brews herb teas, listens to stories about the people of the secluded village to which she has moved, and creates her own imaginative understandings of her life and their lives. Lolly transforms herself in the novel "from powerless other to self-empowering subject" (Doan, intro. 15).

Lolly's age and her spinsterhood make her an unusual heroine, especially for a bildungsroman. Yet *Lolly Willowes* is revolutionary and subversive in more than its portrayal of an old maiden aunt who casts off the role society has created for her and rejects other middle-class values that define what is good and proper. Warner also mocks both social and literary conventions when she transmutes her seemingly innocent and comically realistic bildungsroman into a satiric fantasy, flouting literary conventions by combining the two types of fiction. In Part 1 of the novel, the narrator realistically details Lolly's life at Apsley Terrace, the London home of Lolly's brother, and relates in a flashback the details of the Willowes family history and the first twenty-eight years of Lolly's extended youth in Somerset. In the next two parts of the novel, she combines realism and fantasy; Lolly achieves womanhood by making a pact with the devil and becoming a witch.

Warner realizes that a radical re-visioning of Western culture and the literary tradition that expresses and imparts Western values is necessary if women are to come to know themselves and create their own stories. Anticipating Virginia Woolf's call in *A Room of One's Own* (1929), *Lolly Willowes* retells social and literary history from the perspective of a woman who refuses to cast herself as Eve. For a woman to achieve adulthood, in Warner's view, she must use her independent income to claim more than a room of her own. She must, like Lolly, challenge what Adrienne Rich has called the male prerogative of naming. The numerous literary and biblical allusions, particularly to Milton's *Paradise Lost* and the story of the fall, call attention to the fact that women, married or unmarried, have been confined not only within men's rooms but even more restrictively within man's prison house of language. Warner questions the naming and the stories of not just Milton but those before and after him in literature, in government, and in the church. To escape from the powerful scripts of the patriarchy, a woman must reinterpret what is "natural" and retell the myths of the past. Through Lolly's observations in the last two parts of the novel, Warner rewrites Milton's characterization of Adam, Eve, and Satan and his interpretation of the fall and of good and evil. In the conclusion of the novel, Lolly reaches maturity by redefining what is good and what is natural through revealing a new Satan and creating a new understanding of witchhood.

The novel opens with Lolly's being cast out of her garden, Lady Place, the name of her family home embodying her innocence and virginity. At twenty-eight, Laura—her name at Lady Place—moves to her elder brother Henry's home in the city because of the death of her father. There, she loses her independence, the social and intellectual freedom she knew as a girl whom her father looked upon as a "pretty young vixen" (13), represented in her middle name Erminia. In London, she is spiritually imprisoned for twenty years in Henry's home and family. Laura becomes "Lolly" and "Miss Willowes," both a child and a spinster; "a sort of extra wheel, [she] soon found herself part of the mechanism, and, interworking with the other wheels, went round as busily as they" (46–47). Her being is forced "underground," becoming a mere "murmuring brook" (64), and she learns the nature of the male patriarchal society, literally and metaphorically epitomized and embodied in the city and its institutions.

London is an orderly though hypocritical world: "There were the shops, processions of the Royal Family and of the unemployed, the gold tunnel at Whiteley's, and the brilliance of the streets by night" (4). Through Warner's use of satiric understatement, those in want are reduced to one more exotic sight, like the goods in the shops or the coaches of the queen. If the patriarchy is unfeeling in its view of the poor, it is both hypocritical and dehumanizing in its labeling of the women who walk the streets at night. The city is depicted as fundamentally unnatural through the imagery of the novel, though Warner is no romantic Rousseau who believes in the natural goodness of man or woman. Like Henry's Apsley Terrace family of which Lolly becomes another cog, the city and the civilization it represents are a power-driven machine.

Lady Place, of course, could not be Lolly's. What else can she do but accept the place where her family has decided she will live, even though she dislikes the move from the country to the city, which produces chilblains, chapped hands, and the dullness of spirit that comes with meaningless and unnatural activities such as embroidery: "Each time that a strand of silk rasped against her fingers she shuddered inwardly" (46). Lolly is by nature no spinster, a title once applied to any woman, married or unmarried, who performed such typical domestic duties. She becomes an "inmate" of Apsley Terrace, a domestic pet in the imagery of the novel:

> Divested of her easily-worn honours as mistress of the household, shorn of her long meandering country days, sleeping in a smart brass bedstead instead of her old and rather pompous four-poster, wearing unaccustomed clothes and performing unaccustomed duties, she seemed to herself to have become a different person. Or rather she had become two persons, each different. One was Aunt Lolly, a middle-aging lady, light-footed upon stairs, and indispensable for Christmas Eve and birthday preparations. The other Miss Willowes, "my sister-in-law Miss Willowes," whom Caroline would introduce, and abandon to a feeling of being neither light-footed nor indispensable. But Laura was put away. (62)

Yet she does again become Laura. Given the determinism of the plot in which women are cast by fiction and society, the wonder, as the novel makes clear, is that a woman grows up at all, not that it takes her nearly fifty years to do so.

More than a witty fantasy about witches, the novel presents a psychologically realistic portrait of a woman and the attitudes of the society in which she lives. What Lolly, what any British woman in Warner's view, must struggle against to grow up is the very language of her culture. Names, both proper and common, impart the values of a culture, for they carry with them the stories and practices of past generations. Warner in *Lolly Willowes* shows that the names by which Western women know and interpret themselves and their place within the scheme of things have made adulthood unnatural for them.

British literature has always reflected British social attitudes in the treatment, or lack thereof, it accorded unmarried women. Though, as the narrator of the novel remarks, "in 1902 there were some forward spirits who wondered why that Miss Willowes, who was quite well off, and not likely to marry, did not make a home for herself and take up something artistic or emancipated" (6), the prevailing social attitudes toward women reflected a belief that women who did not marry were "odd," an exception to what God and natural laws had intended. (One might note the title, *The Odd Women,* that George Gissing selected for his novel about women who do not marry.) In the view of that society, Lolly is properly a figure of jest, antithetical to all the traditional values reflected in the conventions of literature. Who has ever heard of a sallow, "nut-crackerish" old maid (*Lolly* 59) being the heroine of a serious novel? Jane Austen might choose a "sallow" girl with "dark lank hair" who was an intellectually independent though naive reader and who enjoyed the outdoors and "boys' plays" for the heroine of her early nineteenth-century bildungsroman, *Northanger Abbey* (13), and Elizabeth Gaskell might make the everyday village life of genteel women, most of whom were unmarried or widows, the subject of her novel *Cranford,* but the typical heroine of the fictional and social plots in 1926 still remained the lovely, golden-haired girl who achieved fulfillment and adulthood through love. Even Virginia Woolf did not create a significant role for a spinster until she created Lily Briscoe in *To the Lighthouse* (1927), and even then Lily remains the observer rather than the observed.

Traditionally, spinsters have been both an embarrassment and a threat to society and literature. They have had no place in the social structure and no role in fictional plotting, except the role of attending to the family of man—the particular family, his wife or his children; or the generic, his church, his schools, or his hospitals. What after all were men to do with women to whom they had denied an education and the right to pursue a career? Until the twentieth century such women were clearly a burden on their families or on the church and community, especially after there were no longer convents, "convenient storage for . . . withered daughters," as Milton described the abode and the unmarried who abided there.

Marriage has been both the prescribed occupation for a woman and her rite of initiation into adulthood. This conception of what turns a girl into a woman continues to be reflected in both the real world and fictional depictions of it. Mothers and fathers still anxiously await the marriage that will transform their college-educated, career-oriented daughters into women, and even the heroines of contemporary feminist novelists—for example, Joan Foster of Margaret Atwood's *Lady Oracle*—most often have to pass through marriage before embarking on a self-determined life as an adult. Though society values creativity and independence in men, and fiction treats such males as heroes, neither fiction nor society is yet entirely comfortable with women striving for autonomy. As late as the beginning of this century, observes Elaine Showalter in *A Literature of Their Own,* women who chose to write the scripts for their own lives or to create nontraditional scripts for imaginary characters were considered "vain, publicity-seeking and self-assertive" (20). Ironically, in the eyes of some members of society, women become overgrown adolescents when they exhibit the traits of assertiveness, self-determination, and independence that society views as marks of the mature male. Fiction still provides few portraits, such as Warner's Lolly Willowes, of a girl becoming a woman by vowing to serve her own desires and not those of a man or the hierarchical society man has created.

More openly subversive than her predecessors, Warner does not make her heroine pay with her life for rejecting female subordination, as did George Eliot in *The Mill on the Floss,* Kate Chopin in *The Awakening,* and Virginia Woolf in *The Voyage Out.* Not does she have her heroine choose to make herself useful in what society might consider a worthwhile role or what might be justified as a "higher" cause. There were those in Victorian England who conceived of a heroic role for the "authentic old maid," as Nina Auerbach points out in *Woman and the Demon* (148). They were women who, like Florence Nightingale, saw marriage as Lolly did—an imprisonment of women's souls, forcing them into meaningless social activity and subjugating their minds and spirits as well as their bodies to a husband's will *(Cassandra).* But the self-apotheosis those few heroic spinsters achieved in fiction and society was accomplished in the name of an accepted social value for a woman—self-abnegation. While Nightingale was no meek lady of the lamp, as we now know, she did sell her soul to God when she chose not to marry, justifying her existence through living a life of Herculean or Amazonian service and commitment.

Warner, however, has Lolly reject the whole value system of the patriarchal society and decide that if God is on the side of female servility and propriety, male pomposity and tradition, and the institutionalism that is civilization, then her calling is to be a servant of the devil, a witch. Warner depicts the patriarchal value system as resulting in a meaningless busyness at best, a wanton destruction of lives at worst. The system rests on a false belief in the godliness of man, with the male as interpreter and spokesman of God. It encourages hypocritical conformity.

None of the critics of the female bildungsroman identify a spinster heroine, not those attempting to construct a theory—such as Elizabeth Abel, Marianne Hirsch, and Elizabeth Langland—or reconstruct a history—such as Charlotte Goodman.[1] That Lolly is forty-seven when she completes her journey to maturity certainly sets her apart from her male counterparts of the genre; however, as recent studies of the female bildungsroman have pointed out, heroines of such stories, though not as old as Lolly, usually do not achieve womanhood until past the age that society associates with the achievement of male adulthood (see Abel et al., intro). The late age at which female adolescents arrive at adulthood in fiction reflects what has been the case for many women outside of fiction. The educational and professional opportunities afforded girls and their family's and society's expectations of proper behavior have, at least in the past, made it difficult for them to achieve independence.

In their examination of fictions of female development, Abel, Hirsch, and Langland find that not only is the culmination of the heroine's journey delayed but also her story is likely to be nonlinear, interrupted by "periodic returns to the past" or "compressed into brief epiphanic moments" (12). Lolly's decision to leave the city of her surrogate father and return to the country, where she gradually sheds the cocoon of patriarchal social conventions that have enveloped her since the death of her father, is provoked by the sights and smells of her past that she encounters in a greengrocer's shop in London. Lolly had ignored the previous stirrings of her spirit evoked by her memories and dreams of life in the country. Each autumn when Lolly returns to London from vacation with the family, she experiences a deep disquiet, an anxiety that dissipates only with the setting in of winter. From September through the end of November, the moon, the earth, darkness, and visions of woods, marshes, and fens seems to speak to her soul. The "murmuring brook" of her being, however, bubbles to the surface as she looks at the homemade jellies and bottled fruits on the greengrocer's shelf, and she determines to re-create her life in the village of the Chilterns from which the condiments come.

That Lolly gains independence by moving from the city to the country reverses what Jerome Buckley finds to be the pattern for the male protagonists in the novels of development he examines in *Season of Youth* (he does not identify even one female bildungsroman in his history of the genre in England). Nor are the false gods that the city in Warner's novel proffers money and lust, those identified by Buckley in the novels he discusses. What the city tempts men and women to believe in, the false god in Warner's story, is the established social order that is embodied in and perpetuated through its institutions. For Warner, it is not just women who must leave the city to achieve selfhood. Men, too, must leave the city, the home of their bourgeois, patriarchal fathers, to stand outside the culture which teaches men that they are next to angels and that women are dependent on them and meant to serve them. It is a culture Warner wants reshaped and redirected. Lolly's Adam, for example—though she is not Eve—has come to live in the Chilterns to raise poultry rather than return to his bank job in the city following World War I. After a prolonged visit with Lolly in her chosen country village, her nephew Titus leaves not for the city but for the family home in the country with his about-to-be wife Pandora. For Laura, "the real match was made between Pandora and Lady Place" (227), a chance for the first man and a new woman (Pandora is a social worker) and their progeny to create a new myth out of the old.

Warner prepares her readers for Laura's metamorphosis by the circumstances the narrator supplies about Laura's life at Lady Place: "Laura grew up almost an only child" (14). Her two older brothers are rarely at home, having been sent to public schools. Admired and indulged by her father, she spends her days roaming the nearby fields and woods, her interest in "rural pharmacoepia" heightened by her reading, her visits to her father's brewery, and the herbal knowledge of the servant Nannie. She is essentially motherless: "Mrs. Willowes ma[kes] a poor recovery after Laura's birth" (16), becomes "more and more invalidish," and is reminded of her motherly duties to Laura only by the sporadic visits of the ladies of the neighborhood, who prod her about the shortness of Laura's skirts and the need for Laura to be sent to school to "have the companionship of girls her own age" (17). Certainly they would not have approved of the books Laura reads, "Locke on the Understanding or Glanvil on Witches" (24), for Laura is free to choose from the family library and never reads any of those books thought proper for a young lady.

Laura thus escapes the "restrictive education and intensive conditioning" (27) that Showalter points to as producing generation after generation of *ladies,* as if that were what women were innately intended to be. Her father encourages her to write about her interests in botany and brewing, paying for the publication of her little book, "Health by the Wayside." In spirit her upbringing is similar to the family life that Carolyn Heilbrun in *Reinventing Womanhood* cites as characteristic of women who succeed: little contact with other siblings and a father for a role model (107). Her father's books open a door to a world about which most women, brought up under the firm hands of their mothers charged with turning them into marriageable creatures, know nothing. After all, those mothers know there is nothing "so sexually displeasing as learning" (*Lolly* 25).

In her father's eyes, Laura is a lovely and natural creature. Even when her mother dies and she must become at sixteen a lady in her garb, he is content to leave her spirit free. She intends to keep it that way. His motives may be somewhat selfish, as the narrator remarks, for Laura's father has deluded himself with the idea that the ideal suitor to whose arms and home he would relinquish her has simply not yet appeared. But Laura knows she is not awaiting any Prince Charming.

Indeed, Laura repeatedly refuses to be tempted by the role of wife in the social plot. When her Aunt Emma tries to seduce Laura into leaving Lady Place by relating tales of the sights, sounds, and people of India, Laura reacts with the wariness of one who senses an emissary from the devil, the adversary of God. With God in his heaven, Laura in her garden has no use for the leader of the apostate angels yet. She knows that the visions of "parrots flying through the jungle, ayahs with rubies in their nostrils," are the "outer wrappings" (28), enticements meant to conceal the quest to make her conform and bind her to a husband. Laura does not intend to become an outcast from her garden like her Aunt Emma, who "picked up the windfall apples and ate them with the greed of an exile" (27). (Warner seems to suggest that Austen's Emma might better have served herself had she remained wedded to her vision of life as a single woman.) The scene is a comic reversal of the temptation of Eve. How innocent it is to eat apples. How natural it is for a woman to want to remain single. How unnatural and sinful are the imperialistic values of the English patriarchal society recalled by the reference to India. In the scene, Warner challenges what Milton and his progeny depict as the intended order of things.

The scene also evokes the stereotype of women who never marry—shriveled and sour, old before their time—and conveys Warner's scoffing at society's attitude that such women are dried-up human beings of no substance, windfall apples cluttering the ground. Through Lolly's observations, Warner reverses the designations: women who marry are transformed into mere shadows of themselves. Lolly "mourned" for her mother shrouded in trailing shawls and "skirts that reached the ground," her physically restrictive clothing symbolizing the "stays" by which her soul as a lady is bound (18). Lolly sees her sister-in-law Sibyl as having "exchanged her former look of a pretty ferret for [a] refined and waxen mask" that she wears at family gatherings: "Which, what, was the real Sibyl: the greedy, agile little ferret or this memorial urn?" (91). Lolly also associates her sister-in-law Caroline with images of death: "graveclothes . . . folded in the tomb," the very words Caroline uses to describe the "beautiful orderliness with which [her] body linen was arranged" in the mahogany wardrobe (52).

As a girl Lolly had thought "coming-out" an "odd term [which] meant, as far as she could see, and when once the champagne bottles were emptied and the flimsy ball-dress lifted off the thin shoulders, going-in" (19). In a witty, acerbic pun, the narrator of *Lolly Willowes,* whose perceptions are clearly at one with Lolly's, also connects marriage and death: the prospective husbands to whom Henry and Caroline introduce Lolly are referred to as "suitable and likely undertakers" (56). Lolly shocks everyone when she observes to one stuttering suitor that he may be a "werewolf." In her mind, she determines not to be the "lamb dangling from his mouth" (59). Certainly what Lolly has seen of marriage in her brother's home is enough to convince her, if she has not been convinced before, that the institution of marriage and the roles assigned to husband and wife have wreaked havoc on the personalities of both. The traditional role of a woman, as Woolf notes in *A Room of One's Own,* was to serve as a man's looking glass, "reflecting [his] figure . . . at twice its natural size" (35). Caroline's performance of that role has been so good, as Lolly observes, that Henry's character has taken a turn for the worse: "Caroline was a good woman and a good wife. She was slightly self-righteous, and fairly rightly so, but she yielded to Henry's judgment in every dispute, she bowed her good sense to his will and blinkered her wider views in obedience to his prejudices. Henry had a high opinion of her merits, but thinking her to be so admirable and finding her to be so acquiescent had encouraged him to have an even higher opinion of his own" (55). Henry has thus become pompously self-righteous and authoritarian.

To escape the living death that characterizes her life in London, Lolly, who has seen her niece Fancy break with the Willowes tradition by marrying someone her family considers beneath them and then going off to drive a motor lorry in France after he is killed in the war, decides to move to Great Mop. The name mimics the names of so many small villages in Britain and metaphorically expresses the sweeping-clean of Lolly's life while foreshadowing the homely witchcraft fantasy of the latter part of the novel. Laura sees Caroline's and Henry's lives as "carpeted with experience" (91). The "accumulations of prosperity, authority, daily experience . . . absorb and muffle the impact" of anything new or untoward that occurs (90–91).

Informing her family of her intended move is easier than shedding her culturally imposed identity as Aunt Lolly. Lolly's new life in the secluded village is marred for a time because she brings with her the "habit of useless activity" that had characterized her life in London (112). Like a tourist, she seeks to know the village through setting out to explore it by map and exertion, so much territory to be covered each day. She finally retires to her hearth to read the books lent her by her landlady, Mrs. Leak: "From *Enquire Within Upon Everything* she learned how gentlemen's hats if plunged in a bath of logwood will come out with a dash of respectability, and that ruins are best constructed of cork" (115). (Warner's droll wit is ever in evidence in the novel.) Expressing her appreciation for the homemade wines Mrs. Leak serves with her dinner, she established a friendship with Mrs. Leak, who introduces Lolly to the personages of the village by recounting tales in which she calls up her neighbors "to pass before Laura . . . in a dispassionate way, rather like the Witch of Endor calling up old Samuel" (127). The allusion links witchcraft with storytelling and the imagination. The stories are much more congenial to Lolly than social gatherings are. She is fascinated with people and their singular ways, but she cherishes her privacy. Her sense of people is that their true selves are not the "nice" ones they wear in public. She becomes content to sit and doze at the edge of the woods and throws her guidebooks down the well, symbolic of her casting off the socially institutionalized and literary traditions of her culture.

In Great Mop, Lolly rejects the role of child and spinster that her family had created for her and the whole set of patriarchal values and institutions that govern English society—work, so much purposeless busyness to Lolly; social pleasantries and the church, so much hypocrisy. She realizes through her inquiry within that she has been a victim not just of her family. The "tyrants" of her life include "Society, the Law, the Church, the History of Europe, the Old Testament, great-great-aunt Salome and her prayer-book, the Bank of England, Prostitution, the Architect of Apsley Terrace, and half a dozen other useful props of civilisation" (152). She intends to forgive none of them.

In Part 2 of the novel, Warner employs psychological realism to blend the modes of realism and fantasy. Great Mop and its denizens are described as Lolly perceives them, the narrator's voice conditioned by the idiosyncrasies of Lolly's perceptions as the anonymous omniscient narration, characteristic of Part 1, begins to give way to third-person limited omniscience. To Lolly, the inhabitants of the village seem not only to be somewhat unsociable but also to be hiding dark secrets and acting in mysterious ways. Indeed, in Lolly's view, the villagers have a forbidden and authoritative power, like the power attributed to witches and warlocks that the name of the village whimsically suggests—the witch's broom transformed into a mop. The presentation thus takes on overtones of fantasy. In Great Mop, after rebelling against the traditions that have informed her life, Lolly is learning to listen to the "secret country of her mind" (137). By achieving a measure of independence, she has earned the right to become the partial narrator of her own story.

But the inner peace she establishes through the quiet and solitary pursuit of her own ways and the acceptance of and respect for the gnarled creatures of Great Mop is threatened when her much-loved nephew Titus decides to live in Great Mop too. (Ironically, Titus comes to write a life of Fuseli, the painter-lover of Mary Wollstonecraft.) When Titus arrives, Lolly finds herself "dressed . . . in the old uniform," resuming "her old employment of being Aunt Lolly" (165). Love has been and is what many women have sold their souls for—if not as wife then as sister, aunt, or charity worker. Titus, as loved one, tests Lolly and her newfound independence, his arrival marking the beginning of Part 3 of the novel.

That the description of the characters in Part 2 is basically Lolly's imaginative perception of them is revealed in Part 3 by Titus's threatened transformation of the villagers and their environs into quaintness. When Lolly's beloved Titus decides to make Great Mop his home, he immediately makes friends. He joins the cricket club, gives readings at the institute, subscribes to the bowling-green fund, rings the bells and reads the lessons at church, and drinks at the Lamb and Flag (161). Whether the villagers are ordinary folk or members of a witch's coven is ambiguous, a matter of perspective. Even Lolly herself is unsure if what seems so extraordinary to her is not merely ordinary after all.

Warner dramatizes the fact that Titus represents a fundamental threat to Lolly. It is not merely a matter of cooking his meals, serving as his secretary, or having her time become his time. He would make his story her story as well. In Lolly's view, men love—but with a difference. Their love is "possessive," giving them dominion over that which they survey, "countryside" or "body." Titus, like a "usurping monarch," transforms her field, ridges, and valleys into a "pastoral landscape," a "place like any other place," and her dark and secret people into a sociable "village community" (160–65). Like Henry Tilney in *Northanger Abbey* lecturing to Catherine on the correct way to look at the landscape, Titus assumes the role of her guide—"commenting, pointing out, appreciating" (163). How else is Lolly to save herself except through a pact with the devil? How else is she to avoid accepting the values and meanings man has assigned to people and place? God is obviously on *his* side, or so say the patriarchs, and God and society have said that what *she* wants—to live without being a servant to others—is wrong.

Not to be cast out of her newly found garden, Lolly calls upon Satan. Certainly this is not the Miltonic version of the naming of things and the fall. Lolly recognizes she is not just being impertinent when she refuses to succumb to Titus's interpretations of the people and place and rejects her role as Aunt Lolly. Her decision to live a life based on her own independent interpretations is heretical. In her own eyes, Lolly has entered into a pact with Satan and has become a witch, like those women of the seventeenth century she has read about in the books in her father's library. Given Lolly's reading during her childhood, Warner makes it natural for Lolly, faced with the enormity of her actions, to find an explanation for her rebellion against society's codes in the dark and potent source of Satan and witchhood. Lolly's understanding also underscores the psychological trauma that one who defies society's prescriptions must experience. At the same time, Warner uses Lolly's perceptions to mock society's superstitious and anachronistic attitudes toward women. The novel is both a psychologically realistic bildungsroman and a satiric fantasy attacking those patriarchal values and attitudes that make a woman who doesn't marry and doesn't choose to serve her family a threat to society, a witch.

Masking the revolutionary spirit of her novel in a tone of whimsicality, Warner takes aim at the literary and religious heritage of Western society that is manifested in the epic, particularly *Paradise Lost*. (That other women writers have also had to wrestle with the mythology of Milton's epic to take their place in English literary history is the subject of Sandra Gilbert and Susan Gubar's study *The Madwoman in the Attic*.) Warner echoes and mocks the conventions of the epic by beginning *in medias res* and relating the exploits of the members of her heroine's family tree, which includes, among others, no less an illustrious warrior than Great-great-aunt Salome, who served up puff paste on a tray for George III, and Great-aunt Emma, who died quite young from a "decline" (9). Like the epic, Warner's novel is divided into parts instead of chapters. Lolly invokes a supernatural force, Satan, to aid her in ridding herself of Titus, who bears the name of the first identified member of the Willowes family and whom Lolly serves as an amanuensis, much like Milton's daughters, whose "sufferings" in writing "some one else's book" she thought must have been great (213). *Paradise Lost*, as Lolly recalls "with a shudder," is Milton's and the patriarchy's epic (213). It undergirds Western society's subjugation of women, the weaker vessel, and provides the justification for limiting women's access to education, restricting their voting privileges (only women over thirty who met certain educational and property qualifications could vote in England in 1926), and allowing them little control over their own personal, political, and economic lives.

Most important, however, *Paradise Lost* and the myths it perpetuates undergird our conception of what is and is not *natural*, innate and normal and therefore right.[2] *Lolly Willowes* expresses the vision of Milton's daughters. Lolly's observations on the character of Satan and the character of Adam Saunter—her "Adam" is an effeminate rejector of society—mock Milton's presentation of these characters. Laura thinks when she sees Mr. Saunter that he must be Adam; that is, for the first time, Laura understands "the saying that man is the noblest work of nature" (133), a saying that until now she has rejected. But though she learns from Saunter how to tend and care for chickens, she does not desire to be his helpmate, and he does not desire her to assume the role meted out to Eve in *Paradise Lost.* In addition to Mr. Saunter's being an accomplished "henwife," he darns his own stocking and makes Lolly a cup of tea. It is his self-sufficiency and gentleness she admires, but she needs him no more than she needs Caroline or her family. She is at peace with her surroundings in her independence, the same kind of independence that her Adam enjoys in challenging the gender codes and middle-class values of the patriarchy.

So, too, does Lolly's understanding of "witchhood" mock the meaning that men of the seventeenth century gave to the term. What makes the power of a witch so extraordinary is not its unnaturalness but its naturalness, the ability of a witch to be herself and not *woman* as defined by society. Lolly, in seeing herself as another in the long line of witches about which she has read, casts herself as one of those women who have chosen to exercise their own powers and are therefore society's outcasts: "One doesn't become a witch to run round being harmful, or to run round being helpful either, a district visitor on a broomstick. It's to escape all that—to have a life of one's own, not an existence doled out to you by others . . . " (243).

In *Lolly Willowes,* Warner plays with the popular conception of a witch in having Lolly reveal the true essence of witchhood. Even in the seventeenth century, there were men who recognized that being a witch was an imaginary state induced by women's lack of social power over their own lives. Antonia Fraser chooses for the epigraph to her chapter on witches in *The Weaker Vessel* a quotation from Arthur Wilson on the Chelmsford witches: "[I] could see nothing in the evidence which did persuade me to think them other than poor, melancholy, envious, mischievous, ill-disposed, ill-dieted, atrabilious constitutions." Lolly may be an old, somewhat unattractive, and unattached woman with a "hook nose" and a "sharp chin" (59). She even has a kitten named Vinegar, but the only plagues for which she holds herself and Vinegar responsible are the bedevilments of Titus: his milk curdles, his thumb festers from a cut in opening a tin can, hoards of flies collect in his room, bats come to feed on the flies, a mouse gnawing on his bedstead keeps him awake at night, and he steps into a nest of wasps. Lolly is like most women who, as Lolly tells Satan, are forced to become witches, given their "vivid imaginations" and the "dullness" of their "dependent" lives:

> When I think of witches, I seem to see all over England, all over Europe, women living and growing old, as common as blackberries, and as unregarded. I see them, wives and sisters of respectable men, chapel members, and blacksmiths, and small farmers, and Puritans. . . . Well, there they were, there they are, child-rearing, housekeeping, hanging washed dishcloths on currant bushes; and for diversion each other's silly conversation, and listening to men talking together in the way that men talk and women listen. Quite different to the way women talk, and men listen, if they listen at all. And all the time being thrust further down into dullness when the one thing all women hate is to be thought dull. (239)

Warner's Satan listens and faithfully attends to Lolly's words. His is not a masculine posture, as Warner's juxtaposition of Lolly's words and his attentiveness makes clear. Because Satan is someone Lolly addresses in long reveries, much like one talking to an alter ego or a psychologist, Warner makes Satan into what Lolly conceives him to be. What Milton had conceived him to be is merely another person's fantasy.

Satan's gender then should not trouble feminists. Like God, Satan has been genderized in men's imaginative depictions. Nor is he Lolly's spiritual guide and mentor, though she designates herself as one of his followers. Lolly's perceptions of Satan and her perceptions of the essence of witchhood challenge not only the literary and social conventions that have defined "witch" and "Satan" but also the designation of Satan as a masculine character.

In *Lolly Willowes,* Satan is, as the epithet of the title suggests, a "loving huntsman," a shepherd figure, a gardener, who listens to Lolly's discoveries rather than tempting, beguiling, and seducing her as Milton's Satan does Eve. Nor does he love possessively like other males and seek to transform her story into his. His maleness is an attribute ascribed by the myth Warner attacks rather than of the character she presents. In Lolly's view, Satan is "quite stupid" since he knows nothing more than what humans know (249). In fact, Lolly concludes that what makes him the "enemy of souls" (250) is that he has "an unforgetting and unchoosing mind" (249). He knows us as we are and therefore knows the discrepancies between our pretensions and our selves. Though Warner's Satan is a dark and potent power, he is not an adversarial predator. As a spirit, he encourages one not to perform unspeakable and unnatural acts but to seek the "dignity of natural behaviour and untrammelled self-fulfilment" (249). He is what one would see if one had the courage and independence to look within oneself and examine the world of the spirit, which is without gender and without perfection but which within the world wears the cloak of self-pretentiousness and sits in judgment of how the world should be for others.

Much of the imagery of the novel pits the natural world Laura loves and is associated with against what she sees as the unnatural and artificial world man has created. Man's misunderstandings have produced so much foolishness, like Maulgrave's Folly, a "byronic" but "perfectly respectable" (230–31) monument to Satan and death, where Lolly, in the concluding scene of the novel, pours out her observations to Satan after seeing Titus and Pandora to the train that carries them away from Great Mop. Death and evil did not enter the world when Eve fell victim to the tempting fruit of Satan. That is a myth made up by man and elaborated on by Milton. The shadows and silences, the dense wood of folly, are always there: "The Vatican and the Crystal Palace, and all the neat human nest-boxes in rows," none of the "monuments and tinkerings of man" can change or dispel what is (234–35). Men might have pretended that Satan was "the embodiment of all evil." They might have "a little later on [imagined] that he didn't exist" (250). But Satan and death, with which he is equated, are not the province of either witches or warlocks. Lolly's musings emphasize that Satan is a concept, defined in different ways at different times by males who have controlled the definitions of the labels circumscribing and delineating our lives.

Thus, in yet another reversal of the myth of the Garden of Eden, Warner depicts Lolly feeding the apple of knowledge to Satan (he is after all, as she has told us, "quite stupid"). Lolly does not find herself by joining a coven of witches, as Annis Pratt and Jane Marcus have stated. She dislikes the village late-night party on the hillside to which she is invited, and which she thinks must be a witches' Sabbath, as much as she disliked the dances and social gatherings to which she was summoned as a girl. She does not dance with the devil, for he is not there. Lolly turns away in disgust from a young author who disguised himself as the devil because he desired to be "the most important person at a party" (246), though she experiences a fleeting moment of sexual attraction while dancing with a red-haired young woman. Lolly takes on the patriarchal designation of "witch," a follower of Satan, but Warner has reversed the traditional connotations and challenged the depictions of evil covens. The sisterhood Lolly joins is one of the mind. It is the sisterhood of storytellers, women like Elizabeth Browning's Aurora Leigh—"a witch, a poet, scholar" (40).

For Lolly, to grow up has meant to cast off the view of the way things are according to the patriarchal scriptures—indeed, what it means for any girl to become a woman. The harmlessness of her fantasies about the village folk mocks the capricious but stern and unyielding attitudes of those scriptures, which assume women are inferior beings. Like several of her contemporaries, Dorothy Richardson and Virginia Woolf among them, Warner writes with a knowledge that the conventions of the realistic novel must be broken if that inner space over which women have achieved some dominion is to be shared with others and a rewriting of the conventions of society is to occur.

NOTES

1. Goodman discusses Emily Brontë's *Wuthering Heights,* George Eliot's *The Mill on the Floss,* and Willa Cather's *My Antonia.* Of the three heroines, only Maggie does not marry, but she can hardly be described as a spinster.

2. In an essay, "Man's Moral Law," Warner wittily proposes to investigate the pseudonatural phenomenon of her title, which "history and fable" have taught us is taboo, for "it is not good for us to know everything," or at least we have been schooled to think "an investigation into this aspect of the male of the human species" is a "fruit" not to be "plucked" (222). She chooses to investigate man's moral law by looking at certain idioms in which it is expressed—"we have learned from Freud what rich results may be gained from an examination of traditional idioms" (227). What her "scientific" research demonstrates is that man's moral law is based on his "primitive," fetishistic worship of himself (237) and reveals nothing more than the male penchant for artificial games with complicated rules. One might say, to borrow their idiom, how uncricket.

WORKS CITED

Abel, Elizabeth, Marianne Hirsch, and Elizabeth Langland, eds. *The Voyage In: Fictions of Female Development.* Hanover, N.H.: University Press of New England, 1983.

Auerbach, Nina. *Woman and the Demon: The Life of a Victorian Myth.* Cambridge: Harvard University Press, 1982.

Austen, Jane. *Northanger Abbey and Persuasion.* 1818. Oxford: Oxford University Press, 1972.

Browning, Elizabeth. *Aurora Leigh: A Poem.* 1864. Chicago: Academy Chicago Limited-Cassandra Edition, 1979.

Buckley, Jerome. *Season of Youth: The Bildungsroman from Dickens to Golding.* Cambridge: Harvard University Press, 1974.

Fraser, Antonia. *The Weaker Vessel.* New York: Knopf, 1984.

Gilbert, Sandra M., and Susan Gubar. *The Madwoman in the Attic: The Woman Writer and the Nineteenth-Century Literary Imagination*. New Haven: Yale University Press, 1979.

Goodman, Charlotte. "The Lost Brothers, the Twin: Women Novelists and the Male-Female Double *Bildungsroman*." *Novel* 17 (1983): 28–43.

Heilbrun, Carolyn. *Reinventing Womanhood*. New York: Norton, 1979.

Marcus, Jane. "A Wilderness of One's Own: Feminist Fantasy Novels of the Twenties, Rebecca West and Sylvia Townsend Warner." *Women Writers and the City*. Ed. Susan Merrill Squier. Knoxville: University of Tennessee Press, 1984.

Nightingale, Florence. *Cassandra*. Old Westbury: Feminist Press, 1979.

Pratt, Annis. *Archetypal Patterns in Women's Fiction*. Bloomington: Indiana University Press, 1981.

Rich, Adrienne. "When We Dead Awaken." *On Lies, Secrets and Silence*. London: Virago, 1980.

Showalter, Elaine. *A Literature of Their Own: Women Novelists from Brontë to Lessing*. Princeton: Princeton University Press, 1977.

Warner, Sylvia Townsend. *Lolly Willowes or the Loving Huntsman*. 1926. Chicago: Academy Chicago Limited, 1978.

———. "Man's Moral Law." *Man, Proud Man*. Ed. Mabel Ulrich. London: Hamish Hamilton, 1932.

Woolf, Virginia. *A Room of One's Own*. New York: Harcourt, Brace and World, 1929.

ANDREW M. LAKRITZ

Jane Bowles's Other World

Jane Bowles's 1943 novel *Two Serious Ladies* is a delightful, surprising, yet seldom-read excursion into the social worlds of two adventurers. At the same time, Bowles's novel uncovers the ideologies defining and confining women and ventures its own ideology of the place of the upper-class white woman in twentieth-century America. This essay explores the stories of Bowles's two female protagonists, Mrs. Frieda Copperfield and Miss Christina Goering, examining Mrs. Copperfield's ambivalent attachment to a marriage that strangles her and Miss Goering's decision to remain a single, independent woman, a decision that proves threatening to the people around her who wish to make her conform to the norms of "appropriate" behavior for single women. Bowles exposes not merely the content of exhausted stereotypes for women but also the powerful influence these habits of thought have on the content of her characters' visions, aspirations, and judgments. Bowles's spinster is a woman who defies spinsterdom. Christina Goering is one who makes that term "Miss" peculiarly outrageous because she ultimately never stands still long enough for others to assimilate her to their class- and gender-based notions of who she should be and how she should behave. She is a modern amoralist, detached from the social codes that seem to weaken her friend Mrs. Copperfield yet at the same time profoundly committed to a vision of experience she chases restlessly after, one that brings her into contact with people and life always on the cusp of change.

Two Serious Ladies is the story of Christina Goering's life, from childhood to adulthood, with a long detour through Panama and Mrs. Copperfield's adventures on vacation there. One might say that the Copperfield vacation is enveloped by Miss Goering's life in New York, except that, contrary to normal expectations, Miss Goering's life is far more adventuresome and astonishing than Mrs. Copperfield's experiences outside the United States. In fact, the metaphor of the envelope is useful in understanding several passages in the novel (Frieda Copperfield's dream, for instance, is enveloped by her swim in the sea with Pacifica, a Panamanian prostitute) and suggests both the idea of some content delivered or packaged for delivery and the unpacking of that content. According to this metaphor, the envelope—Miss Goering's life—ought to appear conventional, as the formal outside to the heart of the matter, Mrs. Copperfield's life. Indeed, given that she constantly refers to her search for salvation, we are invited to think, like her friend Lucy Gamelon, that Miss Goering might be that respectable, if dangerously unmarried, figure one calls the "single woman." In other words, the narrative confounds traditional dichotomies of inside/outside, form and content, envelope and letter, social surface and psychological interior to show how confining those binaries are, how they limit the possibilities for human experience. Miss Goering's life, with which we begin and to which we return at the end—in the form of a chiasmus—constantly surprises us in its incessant deviation from the concept which might (or ought to) envelop her: the spinster.

A spinster is a woman who works, a woman who needn't work but remains unmarried, a woman who is beyond marriage in some way, usually age, or, finally, a woman temperamentally unsuited, for whatever reasons (conventionally not good ones), for marriage. These definitions can be found in the dictionary of one's choice, but they occur more profoundly in the ideologies and ways of life and language of individuals. Christina Goering is a gentle woman by birth who, from the very beginning, appears to have chosen unconventional forms of expression for herself, even as she inhabits conventional forms.

Although she assumes the conventional role of head of household—"lady" of the house—Christina Goering soon subverts that position, abdicating the throne, as it were, first by selling her paternal estate and moving to a tiny, poorly heated house—living on one-tenth of her income—and then by taking solitary excursions into the wilderness of a working-class world. She takes a train into this world and encounters a solid-looking "bourgeois" woman (128); this scene demands attention, for it not only sets up her "fall" into the world of criminality but also suggests precisely what sort of values she denies as she falls into that other world. In fact, this scene sets up the following "recognition" crucial to understanding this perplexing novel: "'Why, people have been living here for years,' she said to herself. 'It is strange that I hadn't thought of this before. They're here naturally, with their family ties, their neighborhood stores, their sense of decency and morality, and they have certainly their organizations for fighting the criminals of the community.' She felt almost happy now that she had remembered all this" (130). Although it is unclear whether this is a recognition of something new to her or a memory of something she had lost, the terms "naturally," "decency," and "morality" indicate her recognition of the limits her excursion attempts to transgress.

Living with her odd assortment of friends in her run-down house and with no particular aims, save the nebulous, ill-defined "salvation," has obscured the image of upright, moral America she now sees in the landscape offered by the train. To see that "they're here naturally" is to see with more clarity that *she* is there unnaturally. In other words, the sight of the bourgeois woman helps Christina know the value of her trip. This value is also determined, however, by her decision to go it alone: "Her excursions would be more or less devoid of any moral value in her own eyes if they [her housemates] accompanied her, but she was so delighted that she convinced herself that perhaps she might allow it [them to come along with her] just this time" (162). Her trips have moral freight when and because she travels alone, and the moral freight she is interested in is sin: excursion as transgression. Unlike the bourgeois woman on the train, Christina travels to no place in particular and to no purpose in any concrete sense. Her movement is a repetition of Kant's aesthetic category: it has the look of purposiveness without in fact leading to any purpose. Or, to put it in terms Michel Foucault uses in an early essay of Georges Bataille, Christina's movement toward "salvation" takes place in the context of a world emptied of the sacred:

> Perhaps we could say that [sexuality] has become the only division possible in a world now emptied of objects, beings, and spaces to desecrate. Not that it proffers any new content for our age-old acts; rather, it permits a profanation without object, a profanation that is empty and turned inward upon itself and whose instruments are brought to bear on nothing but each other. Profanation in a world which no longer recognizes any positive meaning in the sacred—is this not more or less what we may call transgression? In that zone which our culture affords for our gestures and speech, transgression prescribes not only the sole manner of discovering the sacred in its unmediated substance, but also a way of recomposing its empty form, its absence, through which it becomes all the more scintillating. (30)

Christina Goering's project for salvation belongs within the horizon of Foucault's posthumanist articulation of transgression in that her sense of the profane has no more than a local reference; while her transgressions all take place out in the world, they nevertheless belong to the interiority of a subject void of authority, of positive being. Her transgressions are important, then, to the extent that they allow her to name more precisely the emptiness of the world she inhabits and to discover "the sacred in its unmediated substance."

The woman who motivates these thoughts for Christina Goering is a "middle-aged stout woman" who is holding in one hand what looks like a flyswatter (126). She occupies a seat on the train Miss Goering takes into the mainland and is the only other adult in the car. Miss Goering imagines that speaking to the woman might be the "natural" thing to do: "'After all, I suppose it's quite a natural thing for ladies to approach each other on a suburban train like this, particularly on such a small island'" (127). But their meeting does not prove propitious; the woman has no interest in speaking with Miss Goering, which the narrator speculates has something to do with her "red and exalted face and her outlandish clothes" (127). After several perfunctory responses to very simple questions (Where do you live? Where are you going?), Miss Goering takes offense: "'Why do you lie to me?' she asked, 'I assure you that I am a lady like yourself'" (128). The woman explodes with this, and she soon strikes Miss Goering on the ankles with her umbrella and runs off to complain to the conductor, who returns with her to give a wonderful impromptu speech on the prohibitions that attend travel by train:

> "You can't talk to anyone on these here trains," he said, "unless you know them." His voice sounded very mild to Miss Goering.
>
> Then he looked over his shoulder at the woman, who still seemed annoyed but more calm.
>
> "The next time," said the conductor, who really was at a loss for what to say, "the next time you're on this train, stay in your seat and don't molest anybody. If you want to know the time you can ask them without any to-do about it or you can just make a little signal with your hand and I'll be willing to answer all your questions." He straightened up and stood for a moment trying to think of something more to say. "Remember also," he added, "and tell this to your relatives and to your friends. Remember also that there are no dogs allowed on this train or people in masquerade costume unless they're all covered up with a big heavy coat; and no more hubbubs," he added, shaking a finger at her. He tipped his hat to the woman and went on his way. (129)

On one level, of course, Bowles is having fun with the working and middle classes by having the conductor do his best to make excursions error free, so to speak, for the middle classes. Immediately after this scene Miss Goering smiles to herself, a smile the reader ought to share. But the passage offers more than a humorous diversion for sophisticates. The enumeration of gratuitous prohibitions circumscribing excursions indicates a fundamental void at the heart of the social order. One might say that Christina's transgressive excursions reveal both a hollowness within contemporary culture—these railroad laws merely serve to keep up the appearance of order—and the value of always testing or recomposing those weakened limits. As Foucault explains, transgression makes possible (again) a vision of the sacred, even if it is a vision hollowed out, merely formal, in the context of a world no longer moved by the sacred itself.

For example, she takes up with Andrew McLane at one point in her travels to the mainland, an out-of-work slumlord who calls himself, self-deprecatingly, Citizen Skunk. She actually spends eight days living with Andy—"living in sin" in the phrase of that time—in his apartment until he begins to change his ideas about himself, a change that appears to have something to do with her being there in the first place. "For several days it has been quite clear to Miss Goering that Andy was no longer thinking of himself as a bum. This would have pleased her greatly had she been interested in reforming her friends, but unfortunately she was only interested in the course that she was following in order to attain her own salvation" (172). The moment he begins to think of himself as respectable, he is no longer attractive to her, given her spiritual purposes. The other reason she leaves him is that an "unfamiliar" man shows up at the bar she frequents with Andy, and this gangster type—Ben—begins to interest her a great deal. Only the experience of the profane can lead to salvation.

I will discuss below in more detail the meaning of the two different forms of resistance the novel's two characters articulate for us. Suffice it to say here that the spinster figure, Christina Goering, is unable to establish contact with other women in the narrative; the prohibitions against such contact are powerful. She finds it possible to resist bourgeois norms by subverting—using for her own purposes—the conventional narrative of the heterosexual encounter between strangers.

In a sense Bowles's novel gives us a new definition of radical spinster. She is a figure who eludes the dominant culture's definitions of gender roles by repeatedly shifting—on her own terms—the rules of the game. She is a powerful figure who takes power by always moving to a new position. In Ralph Waldo Emerson's terms, she achieves power in the "moment of transition from a past to a new state," in the "darting to an aim," and in doing so becomes a subject in transition confounding hegemonic discourse around her (40).

Two Serious Ladies presents two narratives, the first one in sections one and three and the second in section two. Christina Goering's narrative is interrupted by seventy-six pages devoted to her friend Mrs. Copperfield's adventures in Panama. In broad outline, we see Christina Goering move, in section one, from the protection of a privileged childhood, to her own home near New York, and finally to a "more tawdry place" (28). Along the way she keeps house with three people: Lucy Gamelon, an unimaginative companion, the sister of Goering's former governess who appears to be at the mercy of circumstances; Arnold, a real estate agent who would rather be in "the book line, or in the painting line" (20); and Arnold's father, who leaves his wife to be with Miss Goering. Suddenly, she leaves her run-down house and her surprised housemates and for eight days takes up with Andy and then leaves town with Ben. Mrs. Copperfield's adventures in the second part of the book occur in Panama, largely without her husband with whom she does not travel well. Eventually she leaves him and returns to New York with Pacifica. The two serious ladies have a brief reunion in the novel's final pages, but the meeting proves as inconclusive as the narrative's end. Christina Goering stands at the end of the novel alone, having participated in several inconclusive and wildly unmotivated events.

The metaphor of excursion—the many excursions as metaphors—appears to have an important role as frame in this novel, not only as narrative form but also as a repeated image of venturing out, from the mock-baptism in the woods of Christina's childhood to Frieda Copperfield's adventure in Central America to Christina's experience with New York gangsters at the end of the novel. The characters' understanding of or attitude toward excursion is fundamental to the novel. For example, early in the Central American section, we get a bit of Mrs. Copperfield's journal on tourism: "'Tourists, generally speaking, . . . are human beings so impressed with the importance and immutability of their own manner of living that they are capable of traveling through the most fantastic places without experiencing anything more than a visual reaction. The hardier tourists find that one place resembles another'" (45). Mrs. Copperfield devalues visual experience as superficial (or untrustworthy) compared with what she experiences: the sordid, complicated lives of the people who live in that other world. The passage implies that beyond the resemblances and simulacra is a more fundamental—and authentic—experience accessible only to those willing to give way to its influence. The hardier travelers, for whom Mrs. Copperfield has only contempt, have a merely factitious strength because they are not prepared to risk undergoing the changes that experience might produce.

Bowles represents another hardier tourist in her short story "A Guatemalan Idyll," originally a section of *Two Serious Ladies* Paul Bowles suggested be cut.[1] There she introduces a traveling American businessman who has just arrived at a pension in Guatemala. The opening of the story concerns a perceptual difficulty the man has as he walks out to look at the town. Through a "very large arch" the man sees in the distance what he takes to be "figures seated around a far-away fire" on a plain (321). He has difficulty with the vision because the wind blows and his eyes tear. Then he says to himself, "How dismal. . . . But never mind. Brace up. It's probably a group of boys and girls sitting around an open fire having a fine time together. The world is the world, after all is said and done, and a patch of grass in one place is green the way it is in any other" (321). In this curious passage Bowles leaves tantalizingly unclear what the man must have thought he saw out there on the plain, a vision sufficiently strange that it scares him into the banal tautological rationalization he utters about the world being the world and forces him back to his pension: "He was a little worried that he might not be able to recognize a door of his pension" (321). Like Mr. Copperfield in *Two Serious Ladies,* this American represents the typical philistine tourist: "It was terrible to have done something he was certain none of his friends had ever done before him, nor would do after him" (350). He has an experience in this Guatemalan pension that he is unable to match with any concept of experience he has brought with him to this land of Indians and jungles: "[The traveler's] behavior until now had never been without precedent, and he felt like a two-headed monster and as though he had somehow slipped from the real world into the other world, the world that he had always imagined as a little boy to be inhabited by assassins and orphans, and children whose mothers went to work" (349). The experience of the unprecedented is intolerable to this traveling businessman and reluctant tourist, and it leads him to project onto the scene the romanticized figures of adolescent fiction.

In *Women's Ways of Knowing: The Development of Self, Voice, and Mind,* Belenky, Clinchy, Goldberger, and Tarule argue that such projective ways of knowing the world are peculiarly common to men. They quote Peter Elbow, who speaks approvingly of such projection: "'It takes practice over time to learn not to "project" in the bad sense—not to see only your own preconceptions or preoccupations; and to learn to "project" more in the good sense—to see more of what's really there by getting more of the self into every bit of it'" (122).[2] The authors find this definition of projection to be similar to the definition of "empathy" in *The Oxford Universal Dictionary:* "'the power of projecting one's own personality into, and so fully understanding, the objective of contemplation'" (122). Both definitions seem to ignore the possibility of receptive openness to experience, just as Bowles's tourist is incapable or unwilling to be open to the experience of travel. This theme of gender-specific capacity or incapacity to receive the world openly informs much of Bowles's novel.[3] Warring with this impulse to risk herself by receiving the world openly, however, is an opposing conservative tendency: "Mrs. Copperfield hated to know what was around her, because it always turned out to be even stranger than she had feared" (59). Mrs. Copperfield, I would argue, is at an early stage of estrangement from her husband at this point in the novel and has not yet learned to open herself without anxiety to the influence and life of others.

The opposition between the venturesome and the timid can be set up in the following way. Mrs. Copperfield learns to be venturesome in Colon. She becomes personally involved with the life of the people there, specifically with Pacifica and Mrs. Quill, the owner of a run-down hotel that caters to sailors and other travelers in search of brief encounters with the local prostitutes. On her first day in Colon, in fact, she leaves her husband in the street to go "talk" to a black prostitute in her room, saying "'I love to be free'" (43). Mr. Copperfield, on the other hand, is timid, exuding the typical reserve of the bourgeois American tourist. Like Christina Goering, he prefers to move restlessly, but, unlike her, he never gets caught up in the life of the places he visits. His typical response to the exotic is visual; after a walk to the sea with Frieda in Panama City, he remarks to his wife, who he knows is thinking of other things, "'You must have enjoyed some of it, because we've seen such incredible things'" (62). For him, the exotic is a visual distraction to displace his troubled thoughts; what he is troubled about in the novel is his wife's lesbianism, a subject they never confront directly.

Mr. Copperfield's letter to his wife at the end of section two is marvelously indirect, vague, and pompous—not to say patriarchal—but the last sentence reaffirms his belief in detachment and independence, almost abstraction: "For God's sake, a ship leaving port is still a wonderful thing to see. J. C." (111). To the extent that he speculates about himself and his wife in this way—turning life into a fitting visual symbol, projecting the appropriate image in language—he, in fact, paradoxically confirms his own inability to go forward into the world itself, into experience itself. Mrs. Copperfield's physical deterioration from section one to section three underscores the material costs, the experiential costs, of her choice. She has risked far more ethically and socially than her husband can imagine because her choices are so profoundly antithetical to bourgeois morality.

Although her resistance is neither profound nor effective, the deterioration of her body is a sign of the powerful forces arrayed against her in her quest for the love and companionship of other women. In her controversial essay "Compulsory Heterosexuality and Lesbian Existence," Adrienne Rich argues that "a feminism of action, often, though not always, without a theory, has constantly reemerged in every culture and in every period" (195).[4] In fact, one might distinguish Mrs. Copperfield from Miss Goering precisely on these grounds: Copperfield has no theory that might guide her through her particular form of resistance, while Goering has theorized her course of action, using the unexpected terms of religion (she wants salvation). The reason why Mrs. Copperfield is not able to theorize her own subjectivity should be apparent. Rich quotes the playwright Lorraine Hansberry: "'A woman of strength and honesty may, if she chooses, sever her marriage and marry a new male mate and society will be upset that the divorce rate is rising so—but there are few places in the United States, in any event, where she will be anything remotely akin to an "outcast." Obviously this is not true for a woman who would end her marriage to take up life with another woman'" (197). As Rich points out in her essay, the very existence of the lesbian in Western culture is largely untheorized and unprepared for. Or, to be more precise, conventional theories of homosexuality have until recently been largely negative, defining the invert as ill. If Mrs. Copperfield has trouble defining the terms of her resistance and the course of her action, perhaps it is because she has not sufficient intellectual or communal resources to make coherent resistance a possibility. This lack is certainly not something related to her intelligence; rather, it has its origins in the intellectual poverty of her culture.

It is important, then, to understand both the resistance Mrs. Copperfield mounts against her husband and her timidity, a contradiction that goes very far in articulating a central contradiction of modern culture. What I am calling here contradiction, Rich calls "double-life." Mrs. Copperfield, unlike Miss Goering, experiences herself in terms of this contradiction. On the one hand, she has been taught by her culture to obey the strictures of the patriarchy and to receive real joy in the benefits of its goodwill. On the other hand, she has come to see an association with other women as liberating, and she is beginning, during the course of the novel, to explore that association. Because it is simply impossible to trade one frame of reference for another—these frames are too profound, too much a part of the deepest lessons of experience from infancy to adulthood—Mrs. Copperfield is a hodgepodge of timidity and strength, the two sides of her double-life that tear at her.

Rich puts the case in this way: "This *double-life*—this apparent acquiescence to an institution founded on male interest and prerogative—has been characteristic of female experience: in motherhood, and in many kinds of heterosexual behavior, including the rituals of courtship; the pretense of asexuality by the nineteenth-century wife; the simulation of orgasm by the prostitute, the courtesan, the twentieth-century 'sexually liberated' woman" (197). Rich's terms for this double-life, however, suggest that women who engage in it have a control and authority that Mrs. Copperfield simply does not express. The double-life she leads is debilitating, perhaps because she teeters on the brink of a new life, one that would not be double and therefore would be more dangerous. She is on the brink of giving up "apparent acquiescence" in favor of real rejection of male bourgeois norms. It is this rejection of norms that animates both Christina Goering's quest for salvation and Bowles's parallel quest for a new novel.

It should be clear at this point that what we see through the frame of these excursions, these repeated attempts to shove off into the world of criminality and vulgarity, is the same thing the man in "A Guatemalan Idyll" thinks he might have seen through the archway of the village: a scene of primitive abandon, the world of assassins, orphans, and abandoned children. Unlike the man in that story, however, Goering and Copperfield feel the necessity of that fall into the void or space of freedom, and they do not understand these terms with the same moral squeamishness. While neither imagines that freedom is necessarily possible, they both believe that excursions into that space are necessary.

At one point in her breakup with Andy, Christina Goering violates conventional morality by denouncing shame as a necessary moral and social category. Instead, as she tells Andy, "'I really have no sense of shame . . . and I think your own sense of shame is terribly exaggerated, besides being a terrific sap on your energies'" (188). By denouncing shame, she denounces any sense that the world defines her and limits her acts. The name "spinster" would mean nothing to her but an impertinence. Lucy Gamelon demands that she feel shame, but Christina believes it does not apply to her. One could say, then, that Bowles's narrative constitutes a play of transgressive desire, which is not presented as some more utopian moment or vision as opposed to Gamelon's domestic ideology. Instead, in Foucault's terms, transgression "is neither violence in a divided world (in an ethical world) nor a victory over limits (in a dialectical or revolutionary world)" (35). The narratives of Mrs. Copperfield and Christina Goering involve the testing of limits, the vulgar transgressing against the civilized, the low crossing the limit of the high, the shameful scandalizing propriety. By following her characters as they transgress the boundaries between worlds, Bowles articulates the struggle of these two women to reveal the prohibitions and limits of patriarchal culture for what they are: hollow. One way of articulating the value of this narrative, then, is to say that it marks off in its play of transgression the precise limits of modern culture; the reader can see with startling clarity the rule of laws that otherwise remain tacit.

Monstrosity is the moral opposite of shame, for to feel shame is to participate in a system of ethical limits to which the monster is insensitive. Andy's response to Miss Goering is telling: "'You're crazy. . . . You're crazy and monstrous—*really* Monstrous. You are committing a monstrous act'" (188). By abandoning Andy at the very moment when it looks like he might turn around and become a pillar of society, Miss Goering makes the choice of refusing to be prescribed as spinster.[5] Although she is a spinster in deciding to remain an independent woman, she does not accept the evaluative freight of that term. As she violates the code of compulsory heterosexuality and the nuclear family, she also violates or resists the name that conventional society gives to its deviants: "'Well,' said Miss Goering, 'perhaps my maneuvers do seem a little strange, but

I have thought for a long time now that often, so very often, heroes who believe themselves to be monsters because they are so far removed from other men turn around much later and see really monstrous acts being committed in the name of something mediocre'" (188). Miss Goering is much too subtle for Andy. She has twisted the meaning of the monstrous to suggest the hero, the one far removed from others, whereas Andy simply meant it to have a derogatory force. Heroes for Goering are alienated (removed—on excursions); to be normalized is to be mediocre, to risk mediocrity. Goering creates her own heroism by debunking the "normalcy" of her culture, by risking the names—from lunatic to spinster—because to change the definitions is to make possible a world in which sexual difference, in itself, might not be lunatic but heroic. She evades the cultural definition of her behavior, indeed the masculine effort to define her, by a process of self-definition—which can never end and can only repeat itself with thoroughgoing variation.

Another way to articulate this problem is to return to the various forms of projection that occur throughout the novel. Part of what makes Ben, the gangster, brutal is his habit, I would almost say a masculinist habit, of projecting onto others a concept in order to get things done with the least amount of thought. Lucy Gamelon also has this habit, which represents part of her own weakness. When Ben first meets Miss Goering, he asks her where she works, an absurd question to a woman who does not require such an activity as work. Ben, however, is "certain" that she does work, that she is a prostitute "working" the bar, despite all her protestations: "'You look like a prostitute, and that's what you are. I don't mean a real small-time prostitute. I mean a medium one'" (185). Ben is a real charmer with his flattery, of course, but he has made up his mind that women alone in bars look like one thing and one thing only; there can be no alternatives to this rule. By returning to the bar later to go with Ben to his home, she does not disappoint him.

Lucy Gamelon engages in this sort of thinking when she claims her certainty about the impossibility of sports having anything to do with sin, which is what Christina says sports "feel" like to her. Significantly, the sport at issue is golf, which Lucy says to Christina would "'straighten you out in a week'" (122). Golf is an appropriate example here, given its imagery of the straightaway, the driving range, and the well-manicured lawn, all images associated in one way or another with both business and afterlife (the Elysian Fields). Characteristically, Miss Goering subverts the imagery by focusing (changing the frame) on the fall: the arc of the ball, no doubt, or the hole to the underworld. But Miss Gamelon insists on her frame of reference and complains that one cannot "'sit down for more than five minutes [with Goering] without [her] introducing something weird into the conversation'" (123). The violence and arrogance of this strategy ought to be apparent. Unwilling to go with Miss Goering on her excursions, either physically or in her imagination, Miss Gamelon places a dislogistic covering (Kenneth Burke's term) on Miss Goering's ideas and behavior. What the novelist must try to do is skew that covering by pulling positive ideological content out from under the projection. This projection occurs most clearly in a later scene with Andy.

She has been talking with Andy, or trying to, and he has announced what sort of person he is: "'I have a habit of never paying attention to whoever I am talking to'" (145). This announcement does not bode well for her, even though it is precisely the sort of thing she would explore. The narrator explains her feeling of dis-ease: "Miss Goering did not feel very much more at ease now that he was talking to her than she had before he had sat down. He seemed to grow more intense and almost angry as he talked, and his way of attributing qualities to her which were not in any way true to her nature gave his conversation an eerie quality and at the same time made Miss Goering feel inconsequential" (145). I think she is astonished by the narcissism she encounters here and later with Ben, a kind of impermeable shell which allows him to hold tight to his own conceptual center and objectify others.

This sort of thinking permeates the novel in another form as well, the use of animal metaphors to belittle people: from the people of Panama described as "monkeys in the streets" (36), to Arnold as elephant (114), to the "nigger" as monkey (13), to Andy as gutter puppy (169), and many others. Theodor Adorno analyzes this sort of bigotry in *Minima Moralia* as relating to "pathic projection" (105), suggesting that those who lead the pogroms are precisely the ones who fail to recognize the human in the gaze of another because they wish to see, or can only see, their own image reflected there. Hence, in Nazi (as well as American) propaganda, the enemies (Jews, gypsies, and so on) are often represented as animal-like, dark, subhuman (105). Jane Bowles seems to be particularly sensitive to these issues, although she focuses on the position of independent women, with Jews, African Americans, and third-world peoples having a minor, but noticeable, presence. What she wants to imagine is the possibility of changing the frame of reference that we habitually turn to or that inevitably overtakes our vision out of laziness or conditioning.

Early in the novel, when Miss Goering decides to sell her estate and move into modest quarters, Miss Gamelon complains bitterly about the decision. She insultingly comments that "'it's a real crime against society that you have property in your hands. Property should be in the hands of people who like it'" (28). But as Miss Goering had explained to Mary (her sister's childhood friend) early in her life (and early in the novel), it is not for fun, not for the love of it, that she does what she does. She wants to "'work out my own little idea of salvation'" in a place that is far from her natal ground and rank of birth (28). Miss Gamelon claims that she might be saved right in her own home, "'during certain hours of the day without having to move everything'" (29). But that would not work, Miss Goering says; it "'would not be in accordance with the spirit of the age'" (29).

Bowles refers here to the restless expatriation that took place during the twenties and thirties. She started writing the book in 1938 and was already a serious traveler herself. Given the interest in travel in much of her fiction, it might also be true that Bowles has in mind the radically different sort of travel that had taken hold of the world during the thirties: the mass migrations from Spain, Germany, and Ethiopia as well as the internal movement in a country suffering from massive unemployment, drought, and the collapse of banking institutions. It might be argued that Mr. Copperfield represents the fashionable traveler of the twenties who, only a few years later, appears vulgar. Mrs. Copperfield is drawn to the sordid, poverty-stricken districts of Colon for her experience, which suggests at least Bowles's disaffection with the ethos of travel American writers inherited from the "Lost Generation."

In any case, Miss Goering's denial of property is consistent with her rejection of propriety, the proper, the middle ground that Americans hold on to with such avidity. Travel and property function in the novel as parallel elements. Both are metonymies for the privileges the monied classes hold on to. At a time many Americans are forced to give up their privileges, Christina Goering chooses to give up hers, to give up an entire way of life to achieve salvation. That means she must give up her property and travel more like an exile from spinsterhood than a fashionable single girl in search of *a* man. I think it is important to recognize that her goal in giving up these privileges is not to live an ascetic life for its own sake but rather to search out and write a new self-definition. That is, she wants a change in the ideology of who she is and who she can be as much as a change in her material circumstances. Travel then, for both Goering and Copperfield, belongs to an ideological project of social change for women, change that was indeed taking place during this period when the Western democracies were struggling to redefine their social organizations.

To fall off the middle ground, to lose one's grip, to fall into sin and degradation, these are the terms of the novel, and they have an honorific cast, which accounts for its power in reorienting the frame of reference and value for figures like the spinster. During her discussion with Dick and Bernice (Dick is a leftist, Bernice his girlfriend) in the bar, Miss Goering offers her assessment of what the Communist party in the United States (which Jane Bowles belonged to at one point) is in fact fighting. Dick gives the party line:

> "They have the power in their hands; they have the press and the means of production."
>
> Miss Goering put her hand over the boy's mouth. He jumped. "This is very true," she said, "but isn't it very obvious that there is something else too that you are fighting? You are fighting their present position on this earth, to which they are all grimly attached. Our race, as you know, is not torpid. They are grim because they still believe the earth is flat and that they are likely to fall off it at any minute. That is why they hold on so hard to the middle. That is, to all the ideals by which they have always lived. You cannot confront men who are still fighting the dark and all the dragons, with a new future." (143)

This is the same fear of falling expressed in Mrs. Copperfield's dream of falling down a hill covered with broken bottles and stones; but both Mrs. Copperfield and Miss Goering, in different registers, seek that fall. Whereas the Marxist, having abstracted a structural comprehension of political economy from Marx's historical analysis, would speak of the mode of production, Miss Goering would speak of ideas and ideals, attitudes and beliefs that chain men and women with more tenacity, she thinks, than mere material circumstances. Of course, she can afford to think this way, given her only recent renunciation of wealth. That is the form her transgression of limits takes, limits constricted by an ideology that has her in its grip too.

In the last pages of the novel, the two serious ladies—Miss Goering and Mrs. Copperfield—meet and discuss the events of the year. Or, at least, Mrs. Copperfield does. She explains how much she depends on Pacifica, whom she brought from Panama. Pacifica threatens to marry a "'blond boy'" with a "'weak character'" (197). Goering accuses Copperfield of having "'gone to pieces,'" a judgment with which Copperfield readily agrees. But Mrs. Copperfield adds, "'I know I am as guilty as I can be, but I have my happiness, which I guard like a wolf, and I have authority now and a certain amount of daring, which, if you remember correctly, I never had before'" (197). By leaving Mr. Copperfield for Pacifica, Mrs. Copperfield gains her own authority, shifting her frame of reference in the act of leaving behind a timidity schooled in a conventional marriage. Like Christina Goering's adventures with Andy and then with Ben, Mrs. Copperfield's experience with Pacifica demonstrates the power of transgressive desire: it brings them into contact with the sacred. Although Pacifica threatens to leave her, Mrs. Copperfield recognizes the power of her newfound authority. Although Ben leaves the restaurant without Goering, she too does not seem excessively moved by the event.

The ending, in fact, does not present an ending, a closure. Instead, Miss Goering stands at the curbside looking with mixed emotions into the New York street:

> She stood on the street and waited to be overcome with joy and relief. But soon she was aware of a new sadness within herself. Hope, she felt, had discarded a childish form forever.
>
> "Certainly I am nearer to becoming a saint," reflected Miss Goering, "but is it possible that a part of me hidden from my sight is piling sin upon sin as fast as Mrs. Copperfield?" This latter possibility Miss Goering thought to be of considerable interest but of no great importance. (201)

Miss Goering reflects on what remains hidden, on the possibility (or inevitability) that something must always escape her frame of reference. For her, this is not a cause of great consternation; it is very interesting but not crucial. She is neither the sort who would project onto the scene some construction that would make it more palatable to her nor the utter relativist who celebrates the death of God and the absence of all frames. According to Foucault, to transgress against God, against limitlessness, gives us neither a new world full of existential limits that might shape our lives nor a world of utter freedom: "The death of God does not restore us to a limited and positivistic world, but to a world exposed by the experience of its limits, made and unmade by that excess which transgresses it" (32). She does not engage in this either-or way of thinking, which allows her to negotiate necessary confusions and contradictions, perhaps with more success (though this is not the right word in view of its associations) than Mrs. Copperfield, who seems to suffer physically from her efforts. *Two Serious Ladies* is a novel which does not reduce experience to a higher closure, but instead holds that experience is incommensurate to any concept, that therein lies the possibility of negotiating differences, of accepting as human what appears different, whether it be gender or racial difference that is involved. The serious vision of these two serious ladies involves the continual making and unmaking of a world through the transgressions that both subvert and redefine bourgeois norms.

In 1936, Jane Bowles writes to Miriam Fligelman Levy that her excuse for not writing is "much bigger and deeper" than any trite excuse she might muster. Instead, Bowles confesses that she "finds herself staring at [her] writing materials from the couch as though they were 'Nazis'" (*Out in the World* 15). In the next paragraph, she claims, "I get nauseous at the thought of putting a pen to paper for any purpose, literary or otherwise. This incapability of mine to 'act' is spreading. I stare at my corset for hours now before I put it on" (15). I choose this passage, strange as it is, to end this essay because it represents for me the weird character writing itself seems to have had for Jane Bowles early in her career. In the same letter, she confesses, "I am perfectly serious and solemn about the whole thing" (15). That seriousness involves the writer's courage in doing ideological battle with the politics and morality of her readership, a battle that she in some senses loses, given what she perceived to be harsh reviews and the printing history of her novel.[6] She would later repudiate the novel, saying it wasn't really a novel in the first place, forgetting in her pain over those reviews that novels in their very substance and history defy definition, complicating and undoing the genre in their very structure—just as they complicate and undo the ideologies that support the genre.

One might argue, in fact, that Bowles's exploration of a new definition of the spinster is homologous to her project of writing a novel that defies generic expectations. That there should be only one novel by Jane Bowles, then, is itself an emblem of her refusal to conform to expectations for a series of novels by one author.[7] The problem would be how to write seriously without succumbing to the definition of the serious given to her by tradition. She recognizes this problem in a letter to Paul Bowles in 1947: "God knows it is difficult to write the way I do and yet think their way" (*Out in the World* 33). She speculates that Paul can manage it because he has a truer sort of isolation and independence, one that yields more authentic results: the results convince. Her own writing, she thinks, was not successful because her isolation was merely "accidental" (33). What could that mean except that independence is a natural attitude for men and a cultivated one for women? The opposition, by now, is a familiar one: independent men have the strength to oppose gods; independent women, on the other hand, do not enjoy a cultural context in which strength might mean something. They are spinsters—weird, troubling, their strength looking more like something monstrous than something positive.

Despite Bowles's resignation to forces that have succeeded to some extent in making her novel mute, we have a novel that attempts to find some avenue toward socially and politically integrating single and singular women into the world, into a community.[8] Each venture into the wild life of Panama or New York produces a speculative foray, a stepping over the line of genre. Those who depend on the enclosure and power of bourgeois norms will be unable to see that, for instance, Ben the gangster is wrong about the character of Christina. The irony that even a criminal like Ben clings helplessly to the value system that names single women in bars prostitutes—and Ben himself an outsider—should not be missed. For Ben, Miss Goering is a whore. For the reader who is open to the adventures of Goering and Copperfield, these excursions into crime and degradation should look more like spiritual tests, none of which can ever be conclusive, none of which lead her anywhere but to another test. In this sense, to name "Goering" is already a problem, a setting down of a law which the character is quite prepared to violate. Like the narrative itself, the name is calculated to raise certain expectations (and must have had a private irony for the descendant of German Jews, Jane Auer), given that Hermann Goering was, in his time, an infamous figure in the German Third Reich. But the very inability of that name to govern this character is precisely the point of the novel. Bowles shatters these expectations without ever substituting anything in their place. The novel invites the reader to explore a kind of pure, excessive play, but a play that destroys our ability to remain comfortable with the old names for things and people. We cannot get a fix on Christina. That is not an indictment of either the character or the novel but rather an index of the inability of our culture to understand, say, the word "spinster" (in connection with the thing, the person it names) with the same neutrality that we understand, say, the word "bachelor." Bowles, in any case, would not have us be neutral; rather, *Two Serious Ladies* asks us to muster all the commitment we have to our notions—of the normal, the gender "female," the single woman of independent means—and put them to the test of Christina Goering's travels into that other world.

NOTES

1. Millicent Dillon indicates that Paul suggested major cuts in the manuscript and argues that these cuts were salutary both for the novel and for Paul's own career as a writer, since the experience of working on Jane's novel inaugurated his own career. See note 8 for a discussion of what we lose in the edited version of the novel. I would like to express my thanks to professors Dale Bauer and Keith Tuma, who read and commented on an early version of this essay.

2. The model of learning that Elbow presents in his books is so thoroughly integrated into many writing programs across the country as a progressive, liberal agenda for student empowerment that is is hard to perceive the gender bias at the heart of the theory, a bias that militates against the progressive intent.

3. I am not interested here in making the claim that projection is a constituent aspect of maleness or that open receptivity belongs to some essential female being. Later in this essay, I draw on a similar critique of projection by the critical theorist Theodor Adorno, whose analysis belongs not under the rubric of gender—though significant passages from *Minima Moralia* are in fact feminist in orientation—but under that of race. Both kinds of analysis uncover not the essences of human character but the social constructions people adhere to in times of historical crisis as well as in everyday life.

4. Rich's essay would suggest that Copperfield, not Goering, is the more radical of the two "serious" ladies because, from within the confines of a traditional marriage, Copperfield attempts to break that bond while Goering, free by her wealth to do as she pleases, remains attached to brief sexual encounters with men. This is an important qualification for any reading of this novel, but no definitive judgment is possible until the actual text that Bowles composed can be reconstructed. My point here is to underscore the social and physical costs of the two separate but related rebellions: Goering becomes a pariah who stands alone at the novel's end, while Copperfield, likewise at a loss, becomes a physical and emotional wreck.

5. Another famous single woman illustrates how deeply these ideas are imbedded in our culture. Mary Magdalen is described in the New Testament as a woman of independent means, single, a traveler, and someone who walked erect. Nowhere in the New Testament does any writer claim that she is a prostitute. Yet the constellation of facts—single, independent, mobile, tall—all signal a threat to male hegemony that produces the need

for some form of retaliation. In this case the retaliation is ideological, which makes it all the more difficult to root out. I am indebted to Adalaide Kirby Morris, whose work on H. D.'s *Trilogy* informs my own thinking here, for a discussion in which she pointed out the lack of a textual ground for Mary's reputation.

6. The harshest review of the novel was written by Edith H. Walton in the *New York Times Book Review.* Walton begins her review: "While it is not often that one comes across a novel which makes as little sense as this one . . . " (14). It is interesting, however, that the language of her attack on this novel so uncannily mimics the language of the bourgeois values Bowles attacks: "Their world, in short, is an almost frighteningly fantastic one—the more so because its outward lineaments are so natural and so normal" (14). The supreme indictment comes in precisely the language that Bowles would undermine: Christina Goering is called a "wealthy spinster . . . who suffers from obsessions" (14). Other terms that pepper the review are equally telling: "bizarre aberrations," "easy virtue," "weird" (14). It is Millicent Dillon's judgment that reviews of the novel were "generally disheartening" to Bowles (Bowles, *Out in the World* 29), and this may accurately reflect Bowles's own feeling about the novel's reception. However, the Walton review is the only negative review I was able to discover in my library's holdings; I found four other reviews that were quite laudatory.

7. According to Jacques Derrida, "As soon as genre announces itself, one must respect a norm, one must not cross a line of demarcation, one must not risk impurity, anomaly or monstrosity" (56). By withdrawing her endorsement if not her authority from her novel—and giving up a career in writing—Bowles resigns herself to Andy's evaluation of Christina: she is a monster; she has crossed a "line of demarcation" between the bourgeois norms of American life and that other world which normal people would call criminal, monstrous. To say her book is not a novel is, however, to allow readers to dismiss it as something else, something other, something too weird to require attention. Or, to put it another way, what Bowles sought instinctively to write at such a young age (she was twenty-two when the novel was completed) was a *novel,* what Mikhail Bakhtin calls the "non-canonical genre" (7), by which he means a genre that refuses to codify itself in rules. Millicent Dillon makes explicit where this desire to write in a genre that breaks with genre comes from: Jane's childhood love of and fascination for the Elsie Dinsmore books. Dillon quotes Jane's friend Miriam Fligelman Levy: "'I even felt at the time that Jane was obsessed by her. Her favorite sport was to poke fun at Elsie's endless obedience'" (*A Little Original Sin* 12). One of the attractions for many readers of the novel series is precisely that the genre comes to accept rigid rules, rules that allow expectations to be built and routinely met. In seeking to extend and deny the generic power of the Dinsmore series, Bowles concurrently extends and denies the normative power of religious stricture, fatherly power, and conventional wisdom over her activity as a writer and a thinker. Once the novel

was written and, for her, so ill-received by critics, she pulled back from that novelistic adventure into rage, impotence, and self-doubt.

8. Millicent Dillon is right to say that although Paul's alterations of the novel have made a more aesthetically unified book, we miss something very important in the absence of two characters Bowles originally thought to include: "when Jane acted on Paul's suggestion, she was doing more than cutting a character or characters out of a book. Each of the three women who were excised from the novel is single-minded in a way that neither Miss Goering nor Mrs. Copperfield can ever be. Not for any of them is there the traction of feeling that besets Miss Goering, 'torn between an almost overwhelming desire to bolt out of the room and a sickening compulsion to remain where she was'" (*A Little Original Sin* 107). I hesitate to offer the reading that Goering's very indecisiveness—undecidability in our own jargon—allows the novel to transcend mere moralizing which we would have had if the characters had been included. Yet we can only be indecisive until some editor decides to restore the text as Bowles had completed it, before Paul's editorial work. Having said this, for me the novel's power lies precisely in its ability to see beyond the confines of its contemporary bourgeois ideology into nothing more definite than the possible alternatives named by her excursions.

WORKS CITED

Adorno, Theodor. "People Are Watching You." *Minima Moralia: Reflections from Damaged Life.* London: Verso Editions, 1974.

Bakhtin, Mikhail. *The Dialogic Imagination.* Ed. Michael Holquist. Trans. Caryl Emerson and Michael Holquist. Austin: University of Texas Press, 1981.

Belenky, Mary Field, Blythe McVicker Clinchy, Nancy Rule Goldberger, and Jill Mattuck Tarule. *Women's Ways of Knowing: The Development of Self, Voice, and Mind.* New York: Basic Books, 1986.

Bowles, Jane. "A Guatemalan Idyll." *My Sisters Hand in Mine: The Collected Works of Jane Bowles.* New York: Ecco Press, 1978.

———. *Out in the World: Selected Letters of Jane Bowles, 1935–1970.* Ed. Millicent Dillon. Santa Barbara, Calif.: Black Sparrow Press, 1985.

———. *Two Serious Ladies.* New York: Dutton, 1984.

Derrida, Jacques. "The Law of Genre." *Critical Inquiry* 7.1 (1980): 55–81.

Dillon, Millicent. *A Little Original Sin: The Life and Work of Jane Bowles.* New York: Holt, Rinehart, and Winston, 1981.

Emerson, Ralph Waldo. "Self-Reliance." *The Essays of Ralph Waldo Emerson.* Ed. Alfred R. Ferguson and Jean Ferguson Carr. Cambridge: Harvard University Press, 1987.

Foucault, Michel. *Language, Counter-Memory, Practice.* Ed. Donald Bouchard. Ithaca, N.Y.: Cornell University Press, 1977.

Rich, Adrienne. "Compulsory Heterosexuality and Lesbian Existence." *Powers of Desire: The Politics of Sexuality.* Ed. Ann Snitow, Christine Stansell, and Sharon Thompson. New York: Monthly Review Press, 1983.

Walton, Edith. Review of *Two Serious Ladies* by Jane Bowles. *New York Times Book Review,* May 9, 1943, 14.

Joan Kirkby

The Spinster and the Missing Mother in the Fiction of Elizabeth Jolley

> Spinster-Spooking is also re-calling/re-membering/re-claiming our witches' power to cast spells, to charm, . . . learning to hear and respond to the call of the wild, learning ways of encouraging and enspiriting the self and other spinsters. . . . In essence the spinster is a witch. She is derided because she is free and therefore feared.
>
> —Mary Daly, *Gyn/Ecology*

> The old maid, tolerated most easily as society's piteous victim, is in her fullest incarnation its leader, endowed with ambiguously awesome powers that intimate the destined future of the race.
>
> —Nina Auerbach, *Woman and the Demon*

> *Spinster* is a word that has kept its history as a name for women who do not marry, who are sexually self-determined and even lesbian.
>
> —Judy Grahn, *The Queen of Wands*

From her earliest work, Elizabeth Jolley has been engaged in a radical process of what Alice Jardine calls "gynesis"—"the putting into discourse of 'woman' or 'the feminine' as problematic."[1] Although Jolley herself disavows a particular concern with women, her fiction reveals a continuing interest in reworking the cultural stories women have been impelled to live. She has been a Kristevan dissident, experimenting with the limits of identity in a playful language that overturns, violates, and pluralizes the symbolic order.[2] The complex, polyphonic form of novels like *Foxybaby* and *Miss Peabody's Inheritance* evoke the potency of the pre-Oedipal, semiotic maternal space, in Julia Kristeva's words, "bearing witness to women's desire to lift the weight of what is sacrificial in the social contract from their shoulders, to nourish our societies with a more flexible and free discourse, one able to name . . . the enigmas of the body, the dreams, secret joys, shames, hatreds of the second sex."[3]

A favorite and recurring figure in Jolley's reconceptualization of woman has been the spinster. Indeed, for over twenty years Jolley has explored the lives of women without men, and her fiction is celebrated for its extraordinary spinsters—strong, capable, proud, self-directed, sexual beings assertively oriented toward the world. Laura in *Palomino*, Thorne, Hopewell, and Peabody in *Miss Peabody's Inheritance*, Weekly in *The Newspaper of Claremont Street*, Miss Hailey in *Mr. Scobie's Riddle*, Porch, Peycroft, and Paisley in *Foxybaby*, Hester in *The Well*, not to mention those in her shorter fiction, are all visionary spinsters attempting to effect innovative life-styles outside the dominant gender system. All are associated with the transfiguring and potentially redeeming power of the imagination.

What is most radical about Jolley's spinsters is their attempt to reconceptualize their sexual identity and life-style. Jolley's spinsters are erotically attached to women and participate in the figuring of woman as lesbian that Monique Wittig articulates: "Lesbian is the only concept I know of which is beyond the categories of sex (woman and man), because the designated subject (lesbian) is not a woman, either economically or politically, or ideologically."[4] The thematic dissolution of conventional social patterns in Jolley's fiction is presented in a dazzling diversity of fictional forms, supporting Alice Jardine's notion that multiplicity, polyphony, genitality, rhythm, repetition, and violence are inscribed "in another register, to an *other* degree" in women's writing.[5]

Notwithstanding their accomplishments and creativity, however, Jolley's spinsters are all crippled in ways inextricably linked to their female sexuality. They are inevitably caught up in the dominant configurations of woman. The novels contain some remnant of a damaging Oedipal scenario; her spinsters, no matter how seemingly self-directed and woman-focused, are father-identified and have rejected the maternal. A paradigm of Jolley's spinsters might go something like this. They are motherless, the mother having died at an early age. They are father-identified. In their father-identification and rejection of the maternal, they have in different ways repressed their access to the feminine, to their own sexuality and *jouissance*. ("Weekly," for instance, "forgot about her breasts almost as soon as she was aware of them. She was sent into service, and from then on hardly noticed her own body at all, being well covered with the uniform supplied by the Lady of the Big House.")[6] Their rejection of the maternal impels them at times to a violent rejection of other women, the murder or sacrifice of another who is in reality the self. The denial of the maternal, however, leads to a violent return of the repressed. There is a vengeance of the denied element.

Almost inevitably they encounter a woman who is an exaggerated representation of woman as inscribed in the symbolic order, woman bound by her corporeality. Treading their way amid the perilous shoals of an Oedipal plot, Jolley's spinsters confront two particular manifestations of woman that disturb, disquiet, and finally undermine them: a voluptuous mother-woman, the healthy primapara who is both erotically pursued and ultimately forbidden; and an aging, ailing, postmenopausal woman. Both are powerful figurations of what recent theorists refer to as the maternal blackness, "the spectral presence of a dead-undead mother, archaic, and all encompassing, a ghost signifying the problematics of femininity which the heroine must confront."[7] The novels are redolent, almost excessive, with female imagery. I would argue that it is the missing mother—the spectral presence of the dead-undead mother signifying the problematics of femininity—that haunts the fiction of Elizabeth Jolley. While the novels are concerned with the spinster's attempt to forge new life-styles, they also illustrate the cruel codes which work against this, the damaging patterns which have been internalized by women.

These motifs affirm Julia Kristeva's perception that for a woman, who does not easily repress her relationship with her mother, participation in the symbolic order—that is, the dominant patriarchal social order—is likely to be masochistic. According to Kristeva, sexual difference does not exist in the pre-Oedipal phase; the question of sexual difference becomes relevant only at the point of entry into the symbolic order. The options then are "mother-identification, which will intensify the pre-Oedipal components of the woman's psyche and render her marginal to the symbolic order, or father-identification, which will create a woman who will derive her identity from the same symbolic order."[8] The daughter is rewarded by the symbolic order when she identifies with the father, thereby gaining access to "the symbolic mastery which is necessary to wipe out all trace of dependence on the mother's body."[9] Ever afterward, she wages "a vigilant war against her pre-Oedipal dependence on her mother" (149). "Thus," Kristeva writes, "at the price of censuring herself as a woman, she will be able to triumph in her henceforth sublimated sadistic attacks on the mother whom she has repressed and with whom she will always fight, either (as a heterosexual) by identifying with her, or (as a homosexual) by pursuing her erotically" (150).

Kristeva also highlights the father-identified woman's extreme but perilous investment in the symbolic order. Whereas a man may laugh or feel liberated when he flees the symbolic paternal order, "a woman has nothing to laugh about when the symbolic order collapses": "the invasion of her speech by these unphrased, nonsensical, maternal rhythms, far from soothing her, or making her laugh, destroys her symbolic armour and makes her ecstatic, nostalgic or mad" (150). Because "she has been deprived of a successful maternal identification and has found in the symbolic paternal order her one superficial, belated and easily severed link with life," a woman can "die from this upheaval" (150). For the woman, then, "the call of the mother" can generate hallucinations, voices, and madness (156–57). The options for women within the dominant social order, as Kristeva's articulation suggests, are grim indeed. Although Kristeva has been criticized for her acceptance of the Freudian model and her sense of the inevitability of the symbolic order, she does provide an astute analysis of its tragic effect on women.

In *Powers of Horror: An Essay on Abjection,* Kristeva articulates the fear that leads to violent rejection of the mother. For the child, the mother is the first other, the one from whom s/he must differentiate to achieve autonomy. Abjection, an annihilating sense of meaninglessness and nonexistence, is first experienced when the child attempts to establish autonomy by separating itself from the mother:[10] "The abject confronts us . . . with our earliest attempts to release the hold of maternal entity even before existing outside of her, thanks to the autonomy of language. It is a violent, clumsy breaking away, with the constant risk of falling back under the sway of a power as securing as it is stifling" (13). Abjection is experienced as "what disturbs identity, system, order," "what does not respect borders, positions, rules. The in-between, the ambiguous, the composite" (4). It is related to the logic of separation, the attempt of a subject who is not yet a subject to separate itself from the mother whom it is not yet able to see as an object. The experience of abjection is a reminder of the frailty of the symbolic order, and both individuals and societies strive to repress this reminder of early dependence on the mother.

Moreover, because the mother forms the original mapping of the body into clean and unclean, she is associated with excrement and its equivalents—decay, infection, disease, blood—in short, with defilement and pollution. Paternal law—the order of language and culture—represses maternal authority and the corporeal mapping of the body (72). Kristeva argues that just as the subject fears his own identity will sink into the mother, the symbolic order has a violent need to subordinate the maternal: "the masculine, apparently victorious, confesses through its very relentlessness against the other, the feminine, that it is threatened by an asymmetrical, irrational, wily, uncontrollable power" (70). However, abjection, signified by corporeal waste—menstrual blood, excrement, decay—evokes the presymbolic maternal fusion and suggests the frailty of the symbolic order in its attempts to repress the mother (70). Abjection exerts an extraordinary fascination. "Devotees of the abject," writes Kristeva, "do not cease looking, within what flows from the other's 'innermost being,' for the desirable and terrifying, nourishing and murderous, fascinating and abject inside of the maternal body" (54).

This fascination with the maternal has characterized both philosophers and writers in the twentieth century. Alice Jardine argues in *Gynesis: Configurations of Woman and Modernity* that "what is generally referred to as modernity is precisely the acutely interior, unabashedly incestuous exploration of these new female spaces: the perhaps historically unprecedented exploration of the female, differently maternal body."[11] The paternal fiction is in decline and the M(other)—what has been excluded from the symbolic order—has become a major preoccupation. For Kristeva, the mother is the first "other." "For Lacan and psychoanalysis, the mother is constitutive of the subject; for Derrida, she is the only possible *survivante,* the 'survivor' as 'more than alive,' of any ecriture; for Deleuze, it is the rejection of the mother that is the founding fantasy of the West. For all these writers, the mother must be rediscovered, differently, if we are to move beyond the repetitive dilemmas of our Oedipal, Western culture" (116). Jardine goes on to note that "the theories and practices of modernity, *when taken up by female voices,* become strangely and irresistibly subversive" and that in France, "many of the most important women writers, like the women theorists, are participating in the conceptual reworking of 'male' and 'female'": "They too have embraced 'the feminine,' and are writing woman in what they see as an effort to radically change, from their very conceptual foundations, the male stories women—and men—have been forced to live" (258). In this context, Jolley's gynocentric fiction is particularly exciting.

Jolley's most exuberant novel, *Miss Peabody's Inheritance* (1983), is like Virginia Woolf's *Orlando,* "a rollicking consideration of profound questions about gender and love."[12] The novel within the novel focuses on the indomitable headmistress, Dr. Arabella Thorne, who treats her girls to Dionysian bra-burning ceremonies and lectures on "Chasing the Orgasm: How When and Where."[13]

Miss Thorne's aim is to initiate her sometimes too well-beloved "gels" into all that may be experienced of this manifold earth, notwithstanding age, sex, and physical comeliness. Her amorous exploits are extraordinary, from the first water fight with a colleague, Miss Snowden, in a motel shower ("'Oh Super! . . . Good strong jets of water too. . . . Mmm yes. Erotic. . . . You exquisite naughty. Oh indecently exquisite.'" [11]) to the bedding of a favorite student, Fraulein Valkyrie, for a night that was "idyllic, tender, hilarious and ludicrous. There was the laughing and the trying not to laugh . . . " (61). Within her sixty-year-old breast is an excitement and wisdom about love: "Bodies in passion need to toss themselves and to be tossed. Where could anyone stretch out or reach out in love and in passion in such a narrow room and on such a narrow bed. She does not . . . spend time wondering why hotels invest in cheap frail furniture. The idea that there is something ridiculous in a travelling Headmistress and her entourage leaving behind them a trail of broken beds does not present itself to her" (140). Nor can Miss Thorne comprehend the appeal of marriage or children—"all those years with the intellectual and musical background of Pine Heights" exchanged for "the kitchen, the ironing board and the baby bath" (76). She nevertheless realizes all three of her junior mistresses have, "for love and other mysterious reasons," gone through the arduous task of bearing and caring for their children: "It is not the first time that Miss Thorne has been confronted by this apparent paradox of human behaviour. And here she was stout and well fed, able to travel twice a year as a rule, as cheaply as possible of course but comfortably; here she was lying in bed contemplating the terminating of their employment" (58).

Reading about the exploits of Miss Thorne and corresponding with her creator, Miss Diana Hopewell, transfigure the life of another spinster, Miss Dorothy Peabody, who finds in the pages of the novel "an exotic smell"—"a sweetness as of strange pleasures to be had from smoking wild herbs and specially prepared roots" (35). Excited by reading about the water fight of Miss Thorne and Miss Snowden, Miss Peabody "wondered if it was possible to have a water fight by oneself" (12). Through the story of Miss Arabella Thorne, Miss Dorothy Peabody experiences a sensuous awakening: "She would, later, lie in bed with her window open to the summer night fragrance of the small suburban gardens. She would, in the dark, reach out to Diana and Diana would enfold her" (100).

Ultimately, Miss Peabody sheds the role of spinster as society's piteous victim. She leaves England and voyages to an Australia associated in her mind with the homoeroticism of Miss Thorne and her gels and with her vision of the novelist Diana Hopewell as a splendid horsewoman galloping across the Australian outback: "Diana, the Goddess of the Hunt, would be a tall woman graceful and shapely about the neck and breast. She would wear tall riding boots" (8). Though Diana Hopewell dies before Miss Peabody reaches Australia, she has left Miss Peabody a valuable inheritance. Indeed, Diana Hopewell has been both mother and muse to Miss Peabody, and Miss Peabody, with the "enormous possibilities" of Diana's manuscript in her handbag, takes up the mantle of creativity Diana has offered her (157). She determines to continue writing Diana Hopewell's story of Arabella Thorne. She becomes Hélène Cixous's "woman writing herself."[14] As Cixous writes,

> To write—that act will "realize" the un-censored relationship of woman to her sexuality, to her woman-being giving her back access to her own forces; that will return her goods, her pleasures, her organs, her vast bodily territories kept under seal. . . . Write yourself: your body must make itself heard. Then the huge resources of the unconscious will burst out. Finally the inexhaustible feminine Imaginary is going to be deployed. Without gold or black dollars, our naphtha will spread values over the world, un-quoted values that will change the rules of the old game. (97)

In this novel, Jolley's spinsters conjure up Mary Daly's glorious hags, crones, and spinsters weaving their cosmic tapestries and the images of the spinster Nina Auerbach unmasks in *Woman and the Demon*. Miss Peabody becomes the free, untrammeled, voyaging consciousness associated with immigration to the new world and prophetic of new social orders. In Auerbach's articulation, "The old maid, tolerated most easily as society's piteous victim, is in her fullest incarnation its leader, endowed with ambiguously awesome powers that intimate the destined future of the race."[15] Threatening to the patriarchal social order because she exists "amorphously beyond women's traditional identities as daughter, wife and mother," the spinster is "associated with the promise and terror of a new world" (153).

There is, however, a darker side to the gynesis of Jolley's novels. Even in the exuberant *Peabody*, the empowering novelist Diana Hopewell is herself a cripple; indeed, forcing her to endure a hip operation, knee-joint operations, and a deformity of the feet—"Since this last operation . . . I am practically helpless" (87)—Jolley might be said to have stacked the cards against her novelist heroine. Certainly, she is limited by her body, even as the woman artist Arachne was trapped in the body of a spider for her audacity in rivaling the creativity of the gods. This motif is interesting in the context of Nancy Miller's study of the Arachne myth. Miller argues that the representation of writing in texts by women might reveal the way female artists are shaped by their societies: "When we tear the web of women's texts we may discover in the representations of writing itself the marks of the grossly material, the sometimes brutal traces of the culture of gender; the inscriptions of its political structures."[16] That much of women's writing expresses anger and violence directed at the self is seen by Alicia Ostriker as "the bringing into literary consciousness of elements long present and long denied in our psychic and cultural netherworlds."[17] It is striking how many of Jolley's women artists are crippled. In addition to Diana Hopewell, Miss Hailey in *Mr. Scobie's Riddle* (1983) is prematurely senile as a result of her Thorne-like escapades and is confined to a nursing home, and Hester Harper, the storyteller of *The Well,* is congenitally lame.

There are other disconcerting motifs in the novel. Jolley's writer Diana Hopewell is also the author of *Love at Second Sight,* a sordid story about "two utterly abject women, both post menopausal, who have a brief and unexciting love affair": "The affair lasts from Christmas till Easter and Easter is early that year" (47). The pathos of Miss Thorne's rejected lovers also intrudes on the exuberant tone of the novel. Miss Thorne, who is not "dangerously touched or moved by the human predicament," will nevertheless "never forget the face, the red eyes and red blotched cheeks and nose" of Joan, the victim first of an incestuous relation and then of Miss Thorne, who "did not pay sufficient attention to the responsibility she had so lightly undertaken": "In the end the girl had become ill in an unheated, unventilated room in the attic and had to be taken away" (118–19). Similarly, another rejected lover, the menopausal Miss Edgely with the slow-moving bowel, is "abjected" by Miss Thorne. Miss Thorne frequently fights off "the desire to break every bone in Miss Edgely's boring body": "She only just restrains herself from instantly breaking both Miss Edgely's legs and twisting her silly head off. How much simpler life would be without her, she reflects. Probably her head would only half twist off and that would not do at all" (31). Edgely suffers recurring humiliations: "Somewhere between Vienna and Paris Miss Edgely gets left behind in a station lavatory" (100). Another time, "Miss Edgely waits unsuccessfully for Miss Thorne on the wrong street corner for twelve hours," while Miss Thorne flies back to Australia (143).

Other ruptures in the text are the passages describing the "slow-moving, massive body" of the big sixteen-year-old gel, Gwendaline Manners: "'*Sie ist,* how you say, *eine Valkyrie,*' the older woman, the mother, who keeps the Pension, unashamedly, in front of them all, caresses, with the back of her freckled hand, the full curve of Gwenda's breast. Miss Thorne, a little proud and more than a little fond, looks on with approval. There is an attractive blush spreading on Gwenda's smooth white neck . . ." (61–62). In another scene:

> Gwenda is sitting, bloodstained, on a chair. . . . The police woman smiles, "Is only," she consults a battered phrase book, "is *ihre*—her, *ihre Monatsfluss,* is her menses? *Ich,* I, fix her, how you say, fix up?" She pats her own pubic region in explanation. . . . ". . . who would have thought, there could be so much blood . . . Shakespeare." . . . Gwenda's flooding . . . is an indication of her youth and the purpose of her body to which Miss Thorne knows she has no right. . . . Gwenda's *Monatsfluss,* what a splendid name, almost poetic, monthly flow, however, sounds definitely working class. . . . For a moment Miss Thorne wishes Gwenda to be pregnant and abandoned so that she, Miss Thorne, could take her to herself and look after her. (93–97)

Blood, even in this metafictional context, has a powerful resonance. It is, in Kristeva's words, "a fascinating semantic crossroads, the propitious place for abjection where death and femininity, murder and procreation, cessation of life and vitality all come together."[18] Gwenda is indeed an emblem of the fecund, procreative mother-woman who marries the father of one of her classmates, leaving Miss Thorne with considerable heartache thinking of "the sweet curve of Gwenda's neck and of her rather thick but smooth girlish shoulders . . . [and] of her hopeful white breasts" (140).

Palomino (1980) is, however, the grand gynocentric novel in the Jolley canon, with its gynecologist protagonist, its sappho-erotic relationships, and the gravid female symbolism which suffuses the entire novel. In contrast to the spinsters of Hopewell's novel—"neither of them cares too deeply for other human beings and they are not dangerously touched or moved by the human predicament" (3)—the spinster Laura in *Palomino* is passionately involved with her work, her relationships with women, and her meditative solitude:

> I have written several worthwhile contributions on obstetrics and gynaecology. These were my subject, my life really. . . . In the old days I studied the needs of women from ectopic gestation to the normal menstrual cycle and the gravid uterus. I knew everything about women, changes in their hair and their skin and the more subtle

> things too interested me deeply. Everything I wrote was written clearly and intelligently. I loved my work and the thoughtful correspondence with my colleague Dr. Esmé Gollanberg. . . . "Let the orgasm come quickly whichever way it will." She wrote this and I made it the text of one of my more important chapters. I believed it and the chapter is about the needs of women in love and women who are not in love and are not loved.[19]

> Together we explored every aspect of woman, the physiology and the psychology of women, the lonely woman, women together from choice and those who have no choice. In your work I studied the mature woman, intellectual, deep thinking and capable of great depths in friendship and in love. . . . My subject? The tender beauty of the pregnant woman, her loveliness, sacred in its limitation, the soft rich skin of the breasts, the smooth white thighs and the tender expression in the eyes of the healthy young primapara.
>
> From your teaching, we studied everything from the normal to the abnormal in obstetrics and gynaecology, from the menstrual cycle and ovulation and the gravid uterus to ectopic gestation. In teaching I emulated your technique in every detail, from the more complicated stages of surgery down to the gentle methods you described for the use of the vaginal speculum. (175)

In her personal life, Laura is also fascinated with pregnant women. She loves her friend Eva during her pregnancies: "I let myself look upon Eva, her pregnancy is advanced, her breasts are full and heavy. The white skin of her breasts is delicately traced with fine blue veins in a strange design belonging only to Eva herself. Today I looked upon her with wonder and reverence and love" (145). Years later she loves Eva's pregnant daughter Andrea, whose breasts are full and tender and whose skin glows with "the radiance of the healthy prima para" (196).

Laura's fascination with pregnant women suggests a preoccupation with the maternal, rivaling that of French theorists of the feminine. Furthermore, *Palomino* is suffused with female imagery, as if to suggest a female variant of Freud's notion that "a multiplication of penis symbols signifies castration while mitigating its horror by replacing the dreaded absence by a plurality of presences."[20] Laura has many recollections heavy with female resonance: "When I was at boarding school often, at night, I had times of make believe when on the borders of sleep I was at the opening of a tent in a quiet clearing in a deep forest and I put out my hand to open the folds in almost a caressing way, slowly, holding back from the moment of going in to my beloved" (26). Another time she recalls, "When I was a child I thought if only I could burrow through the leaves and grasses and the undergrowth, I would emerge in some magic place where I would make some sort of fresh discovery" (36–37). She thinks of "the secret perfection" of a lark's nest with four eggs, which she and her father found in the misty hills of Scotland (85).

The land itself is imbued with sexuality. As a farmer, Laura is aware of "the secret flesh of sweet fruit whitening beneath the glow of fragrant ripening" (15) and experiences in the land a "voluptuous" solitude, which wraps around and somehow calms and comforts (19); she fingers "the tiny nipple-like fruits of the quince" (126) and sings fragments of Schiller's "Ode to Joy": "'Daughter of Elysium. We approach with hearts aflame, O Goddess your sanctuary'" (71). Much of the book sensuously details the lovemaking of Andrea and Laura. Even the palomino mare that Laura gives to Andrea is in foal. Infused throughout is a heavy female perfume, "a warm sweetness in the air" (68); there is the fragrance of little girls at Eva's house (133), and at the beach house "the room is full of women and the smell of them" (150). Laura often thinks of the girl who used to work for her, "sweet Dora," "red cheeked always like a child her plump arms folded round her breasts" (27).

It is in this context that Laura struggles to evolve a sappho-erotic life-style for herself and her lover Andrea. Acting as mother and muse to Andrea, much as Diana Hopewell acted in relation to Miss Peabody, Laura encourages Andrea not to measure herself against imagined standards. Laura argues, "'People should live without consequence, should be allowed to live their own kind of lives'" (218): "'Being mixed up depends on what you're measuring yourself against.' I tried to explain to her the things I had discovered years ago when I felt I had in some way to measure myself against the standards of the conventional married couples I know" (91). She reasons, "'Instead of wars and politics we are concerned with a friendship between two women, with the harvest from the land and with the birth of a baby'" (219). Although Laura emphasizes the solitary nature of their experiment—"'We are not making any laws. Our world together is an isolated one. We are not imposing a structure which is harmful to anyone or out of harmony with other structures'" (193)—their friendship does replace what Gayatri Spivak has called a uterine social organization with a clitoral organization, that is, one which inscribes the pleasure of woman outside of her place in the reproductive-exchange system of the dominant society. As Spivak writes, "The clitoris escapes reproductive framing. In legally defining woman as object of exchange, passage, or possession in terms of reproduction, it is not only the womb that is literally 'appropriated'; it is the clitoris as the signifier of the sexed subject that is effaced . . . [and that] at least symbolic clitoridectomy has always been the 'normal' accession to womanhood. . . ."[21]

Laura's life-style and anarchic erotic philosophies certainly imply a dissolution of the dominant order. The tragedy of Jolley's spinsters, however, is their inability to escape the crippling legacies of the symbolic order. Laura remains a father-identified woman: "My father and my uncle were surgeons, both professors of obstetrics" (15). Both Laura and Andrea ultimately experience a revulsion against female corporeality. During her pregnancy, Andrea feels smothered and is repelled by the rank female associations of the land. In the past, Laura's revulsion against female flesh led her to murder another woman; indeed, there is something of Nabokov's Humbert in Laura's disgust with aging female flesh. On the day that Laura gives up her gynecological practice, she is repulsed by the "warm oppressive smell" of pregnant women: "On the last day I found it disgusting. . . . I was struck suddenly by the passive ugly stupidity of a mass of pregnant females" (176). She murders her colleague Esmé Gollanberg when, after years of loving correspondence, they finally meet and Esmé is ugly and old, with senile vaginitus and blotched, wrinkled skin:

> I first saw you, small, thick set and stout, an animal stranded from its hole in the night. . . . Your appearance and your age startled me. . . . You peered up at me through thick-lensed spectacles. I saw your pale eyes, bulging, and the whites of your eyes yellowish and red-veined. That you might be elderly and not in good health had not occurred to me. . . . My bathroom seemed to be taken over by your soap, and you had left your teeth in plastic cups on the window ledge. . . . In the pockets of your loose jacket you had little bottles and various packets of silver foil. . . . something for the heart, for the circulation, for the bowels. . . . "Vitamin E extract . . . for senile vaginitis." . . . Your food intruded. Little dishes of chopped up liver, shreds of fried onion and breadcrumbs covered over with saucers. The bathroom, warm, inhabited by your needs, repelled. (178–81)

For Laura, the encounter with Esmé is an encounter with abjection. Esmé's grossly repellent body becomes an emblem of "the desirable and terrifying, nourishing and murderous, fascinating and abject inside of the maternal body"[22] that shows the frailty of the symbolic order to the father-identified Laura. It is a threat to her autonomy reminiscent of the child's first attempt to separate from the maternal fusion, and in a violent attempt to assert her autonomy Laura kills Esmé. Only in prison does Laura see her own deficiency: "I created for myself your perfection. I should have loved you for the pleasure you had in living. . . . What has happened to the proud friendship? All those long hours of work? And where are the dreams? Where are my dreams?" (180–81). Laura, however, is doomed to repeat this pattern.

Once out of prison and retired to the solitude of her land, Laura is troubled by the presence of Mrs. Murphy, the hostile, dying wife of the man who works Laura's farm—"'her kidneys is all shriveled up into knots'"(78). "Swollen and puffy," "with the fluid swelling all the tissue of her thin body" (110), Mrs. Murphy is constantly surrounded by her brood of urine-smelling children. ("'They've all got the squitters now. I'm afeared for the septic'" [42]). Laura is oppressed by Mrs. Murphy: "*there was something about Mrs. Murphy that made her feel dirty as if she, Mrs. Murphy, had smeared her with something*" (129, emphasis added). "As a doctor I was accustomed to a position of authority but in Mrs. Murphy's presence everything I once possessed, authority, dignity, integrity, personality, everything fades; everything I have is destroyed. This destruction starts immediately I am with her . . . " (32). These passages uncannily echo Kristeva's articulation of abjection as that which disturbs identity, system, order; that which does not respect borders, positions, rules—a reminder of the frailty of the symbolic order in its attempts to repress the maternal.

Images of abjection continue to haunt Laura. She is devastated by the change in her former lover Eva: "'Eva has had a slight stroke. . . . This time she fell on the back steps, that explains her black eye and bruised lip.' . . . Eva smiles slowly and crookedly because of her swollen face. . . . 'Laur-ah it's be-en a lo-ong ti-me!' Eva speaks slowly, with difficulty and with some emphasis, the words slurring as her voice is not clear" (211). Eva eats with a napkin under her chin, "which I notice is wet with saliva all the time" (213). Laura observes that "Eva obviously has difficulty in swallowing. She will lose weight and strength. Already she has passed from one kind of life to another. Her hair is quite changed, it is white and soft. The wisps of old age. . . . I am older than Eva. . . . Concern over her children has claimed the greater part of her life. . . . Eva was always protected, first by stupidity and now by cerebral lesion" (220–21). It is a brutal attempt to distance herself from the decay of the woman she once loved.

After this encounter with Eva, however, Laura is visibly altered: "It's an extraordinary lack of will, an ebbing of energy" (229). Laura's subsequent rejection of herself because of the potential gracelessness and indignity of her own aging flesh also impels her to reject the pregnant Andrea: "As the years go by age will add to age and make old age. . . . And what about the loveless time when the loving comes to an end and there will be only the expected bored enquiries about the qualities of separated sleep and the concern and discussion about the functioning of each other's bowels or whether the tea or the soup is hot enough" (222). A later story, "The Libation," reveals that the price of this rejection is suicide, for both women.[23]

There is in this a confirmation of Kristeva's perception that for woman "the call of the mother"—of the repressed maternal element—can be devastating, leading to hallucination and madness: "After the superego, the ego founders and sinks. It is a fragile envelope, incapable of staving off the irruption of this conflict, of this love which had bound the little girl to her mother, and which then, like black lava, had lain in wait for her all along the path of her desperate attempts to identify with the symbolic paternal order. Once the moorings of the word, the ego, the superego, begin to slip, life itself can't hang on: death quietly moves in."[24] Laura, for all her independence and forging of a radical life-style, in the end is a victim of the father-identification demanded by her culture for autonomy. Her attempt to formulate a life-style outside the dominant order fails because she has internalized the woman-hatred of her culture—its violent suppression of the female body.

Jolley's novel *Foxybaby* (1985) is entirely different from *Palomino.* In *Foxybaby,* the tragic motifs are contained and transcended. Indeed, *Foxybaby* enacts a riot of the semiotic that subverts at every turn the rigidity of the symbolic order. Kristeva maintains that within the symbolic order a trace of the maternal remains in a space she calls the semiotic. The semiotic, in Kristeva's version of Lacan's imaginary, is the pre-Oedipal space of polymorphous drives, rhythms, impulses, the disposition within the body of instinctual drives—body energy before it is ordered by the constraints of social structures.[25] It is "a maternal space, the space where the child's body and the mother's body occupy a mutual space . . . a 'threshold' where first vocalisation and later naming and language can take a hold."[26] Kristeva contends, as Toril Moi points out, that "any strengthening of the semiotic, which knows no sexual difference, must therefore lead to a weakening of traditional gender divisions."[27] The semiotic certainly overflows and erodes the symbolic order in *Foxybaby*; there are exuberant transgressions of gender, the kind of unsettled separation between masculine and feminine that threatens the symbolic order with disintegration.[28]

Foxybaby is literally the dreamworld of another of Jolley's promiscuously imaginative spinsters. Miss Porch, whose very name suggests "threshold," takes the position of writer-in-residence at the Towers School for Girls. There she meets with every sort of exuberant transgression and excess. Indeed, the days and nights at the school are all carnival-like, rigid demarcations of gender are exploded, and there is no hint of moderation in the food, revelry, bathing, sleeping, or sexual arrangements: "The mind dances from scene to scene, unites all pleasures in all combinations, and riots in delights which nature and fortune, with all their bounty cannot bestow."[29]

As soon as she is ensconced in her room, Miss Porch hears the low growlings of half-spoken endearments floating upward through the warm drowsy afternoon: "'Of course Rennett, you understand, I am not able to offer you marriage. Naturally as we are, er, of the same sex we are not in a position to marry but . . . '" (18). The headmistress, Miss Peycroft, whose courses include "Better Body through the Arts" and "Multiracial Tolerance Through Fasting," dubs herself a musical hermaphrodite and invites Miss Porch to an orgy with Miss Paisley and her. Other inmates include the bright-eyed, red-lipped widow, Jonquil Castle, who is missing her boudoir exercise ("'all my widowed friends agree, one misses the boudoir exercise'" [56]); Mrs. Viggars, with quivering chins and white body hair like a cheap but durable hearthrug; the pale, pregnant Anna Brown and her sickly, illegitimate children; and the aging actress, Miss Harrow, who has brought two young gentlemen—Anders and Xerxes—who have taken a fancy to each other and spend their time wrestling naked in "a wild entangling ecstasy into the green fleshiness of the agapanthus" (226).

Transgressive sexual energy pervades the novel. Mrs. Viggars celebrates summer schools for the very reason that they are outside the dominant gender system: "'Schools,' Mrs. Viggars said, 'don't mind if you're a person on your own. That is one of the delights. You don't need to be a couple or a triangle as you do in ordinary life'" (255). Sexual philosophies are freely exchanged: "'after all, if no man—then a woman, and if no woman—what is the harm in looking after oneself? *Alors!*'" (100). Anders envies the anarchic sexuality of woman: "'women can please themselves—with men—with women—or by themselves and no one expects from them the conventional—the performance—the expected—you know what I mean'" (66). This is all to Miss Peycroft's satisfaction, since the point of their studies is as she says, to "'take an honest, a complete look in the direction of our own sexuality, at sexual freedom and at the directions our own sexual requirements are taking. . . .' She raised an eyebrow in the direction of Miss Porch who pretended to be searching for Steadman's sexual needs in her folder" (218).

Inevitably, Miss Porch's imagination grows promiscuous imagining the sexual scenarios occurring in the school—two people caressing in a bathtub full of water, Miss Peycroft and her colleague Miss Paisley in a tartan sleeping bag, an assiduous surgeon "groping with long, strong, beautiful fingers in the secret regions of the Potter's alimentary system" (249). Almost involuntarily, she accepts Miss Harrow's invitation to an orgy with Anders and Xerxes. It transpires on the very last page of the novel that Miss Porch has not yet arrived at the Towers School for Girls, having fallen asleep and dreamed the entire novel, but this does not alter the disruptive force of the text. Dreams also release the hold of the symbolic order and allow the mind to revel in new combinations and delights. Moreover, until that very last page, the reader is also unaware that the novel is a dream.

The structure of the novel is significant because it is within this anarchic, semiotic context that Miss Porch's Oedipal novel *Foxybaby* is workshopped. Miss Porch's novel is an incest story dealing with the relationship between Sandy Steadman and her widowed father:

> Between them, the lonely father and his tiny daughter, it was the foxybaby game. . . .
>
> She climbed into his bed early in the morning. She climbed astride him as if he could be ridden. . . .
>
> Along his strong arm the light foxyfur ran and ran, alive, covering her wriggly childish laughter.
>
> "Foxybaby. No!"
>
> "Yes. Foxybaby."
>
> And still she laughed. Tormenting. And when she cried, shrill, delight and terror, he comforted her and himself.
>
> Every time Steadman knew it must end. (201)

Both father and motherless daughter are trapped in this Oedipal scenario. Once again there are the familiar motifs of abjection. Sandy Steadman as a girl is "infected" and "rotten": "Her mouth is hidden in sores, infected eruptions" (90). Her baby is ill with his mother's illness: "My baby's rotten like me. Even his mouth. He can't suck" (89). Like other daughters in the Oedipal scenario, she is eventually driven to self-mutilation. It was "a scene of horror, during which the girl had torn up her clothes and defaced the walls of the pretty nursery at home. She had smashed cups and plates and mirrors and pictures and bitten her own arms and fingers till everything was bloodstained" (141). "She is screaming. The baby is screaming. The table and the floor are littered with combs and curlers. The mirror is smashed and Sandy's hands are bleeding. . . . As Steadman looks at the child and at his daughter he seems to see Sandy as a baby, pretty and smiling on the bed in place of the little grey infected one" (199).

The motifs of abjection surrounding the tale—both within the manuscript and as it is enacted by the motley crew at the Towers School for Girls—suggest we are once more in the presence of the repressed maternal. Miss Porch is pleased with the pallid-looking girl who is to play the part of Sandy Steadman: "It was pleasing too to notice an area of roughness and a few spots about the chin. A lip sore, she thought, would have been acceptable, but she was pleased with Anna's hair. . . . a greenish colour . . . the stringlike quality of the hair of a sick person. . . . She felt there was a blossoming of the right kind of ugliness necessary for the part of Sandy" (84–85).

That Miss Porch herself is bound in a father-identified Oedipal bind is suggested by her repeated negations of her mother, the quickness with which she denies any maternal longings, and the fox fur, with its sensuous masculine associations, which she carries with her: "The fox was perhaps the only autobiographical detail in the fiction of Miss Porch" (47). "The golden eyes of the fox were bright still, frightened and cunning. They held in their glassiness a knowledge of things not found in a spinster's luggage. It was as though the ways of the fox and his one-time energy, his swift movements, his thoughts and his freedom were held forever somewhere inside a heart sewn up in the smooth bronzed silk of his lining. The fox reposed on the white cotton quilt. It was the repose of an outward lifelessness only" (47). The fox motif appears in *The Well* and the autobiographical short story "One Christmas Knitting"; in both it is associated with the sexual energies of the father. Much as in D. H. Lawrence's *The Fox,* the fox is the male demon that "knows," "possesses," and "masters" the spirit of the spellbound March preparing her for sexual mastery by the man: "He was identified with the fox. . . . She could at last lapse into the odour of the fox. . . . She was still and soft in her corner like a passive creature in a cave."[30] In Jolley's fiction, the fox motif would seem to suggest the daughter's thralldom with the sexual energies of the father to the negation of the mother.

Throughout the novel, Miss Porch consistently denies her attachment to her mother, except as an excuse against unwelcome intrusions: "Miss Porch, for the first time in twenty years, regretted the untimely death of her mother. Had her mother been alive she could have instructed her to phone with an urgent message" (73). She longs for a mother as she would for a disagreeable and forbidding cat: "An invalid mother would have been so useful; she often wished for one; not in too much pain of course, but someone who was demanding and tiresome so that people could be full of pity and understanding" (224). In spite of these denials, thoughts of her mother recur: "She did not want to visit that clean house and her mother, but up until her mother's death there had always been the possibility of re-entering the familiar. This no longer existed" (114). She thinks of her mother's varicose veins and acknowledges the now painful similarity between her mother and her: "Miss Porch sighed, remembering her mother's painful swollen legs resting on the sofa cushions. Her own legs were swollen. She longed for the sofa . . . " (173). The rejection of her mother is associated with the rejection of her own female corporeality.

Miss Porch's dream fantasy suggests a potential resolution of the unresolved Oedipal scenario. Viggars, who plays the part of the father in the dream, tells Miss Porch that she feels ennobled by the role—it has given her "the wish to cherish and to nurture"—and that in "real life" she wishes to adopt Anna Brown and her children:

> "I am not able to see into the future like the prophet, Teiresias. He, though blind, was able to make predictions about the future but was not able to change it." She paused. "I am looking," she said, "into the future and feel that I am able to make some changes. . . . I want to take that girl home with me. . . . The one who is pretending to be my daughter while I am pretending to be her father. I don't want to go on pretending, I want the real thing. You may or may not believe this, Alma, but your book has made a great difference to my life, perhaps more so because it is not finished. I want to take the young girl and her three children. . . . I know . . . there's a lot of talk about rôle-playing these days and that people, especially women, should not be cast into certain expected rôles—it goes right back into kindergarten games, I'm told. But, as a woman, I dearly long to play the rôle I might have had. . . . I want to give them a home. . . . It's your novel, I know, but I'd like to make my offer. I've thought about it a great deal. . . . I do hope that you don't think I'm vulgar." (256–57)

Miss Porch is indeed touched that her novel has brought about this transformation in the lives of Mrs. Viggars and Anna Brown, but she remains concerned about the ending of her novel. Viggars encourages her to explore "'the idea of some sort of awakening'" (259). As Miss Porch walks slowly toward her characters, she suddenly wakes up, but not without the intuition experienced earlier: "There are times, Miss Porch thought, in life when one might be walking towards oneself. Either the child towards the adult or the other way round. Either way it was a passing confrontation, not recognizable until it was over" (246). There is the suggestion that as a result of her dream of pre-Oedipal freedom and the dream figures her mind has created—in particular Mrs. Viggars and Miss Peycroft—Miss Porch may be nearer the resolution of the Oedipal conflict.

The fact that the Oedipal plot, the dominant scenario of the symbolic order, is contained within the semiotic dreamworld of the novel suggests the possibility of its dissolution and transformation. Miss Porch's bizarre dream of the abject inmates of the Towers School for Girls and their nightly excesses and transgressions, both alimentary and sexual, is a riotous expression of the semiotic space that knows no laws and no gender and threatens the symbolic order with dissolution. In its celebration of chaos, misrule, and transgression, the novel makes fluid the relations between the semiotic and the symbolic.[31]

Jolley returns to a darker reworking of the themes of *Palomino* in her 1986 novel *The Well*, the story of Hester, a crippled older woman, and Katherine, a young girl from an orphanage who comes to live with her on her remote farm in the wheat belt. Gone is the exuberance of *Miss Peabody's Inheritance* and *Foxybaby;* the novel focuses on the maternal blackness, here symbolized broodingly by the well into which the couple throw the body of a man. The motifs of the other spinster novels are once again in evidence—the father-identified and motherless spinster, the damaging Oedipal scenario, the extravagant female imagery, and the threat of abjection represented by various female characters in the novel. There is Joanna, Katherine's friend from the orphanage, whose letters have "a sweet heavy scent, something powerful which she could not define";[32] the always pregnant Mrs. Borden ("Mr. Borden gave the impression of setting about the male task of servicing frequently and thoroughly with a view to enriching his property with a number of sons" [70]); the one-armed woman whose boyfriend, "one night in a fit of pique, cut off the other arm" (35); the lonely young mother whose need Hester scorns (29); and Hester's beloved governess Hilde Herzfeld ("she noticed again, in her memories, the stains in the armpits of Hilde's dresses. . . . dark moist half-circles, fascinating and repelling, in the too warm stuff of which the dresses were made" [16]).

Hester, the father-identified woman, is crippled and motherless. As a pubescent child, she betrays the voluptuous Hilde Herzfeld whom she adores rather than share Hilde with her father:

> She realized quite soon that all the hours, after she, a little girl of twelve, thirteen, fourteen was in bed, belonged to Hilde and to someone else. . . . One night, Hester, hearing a noise . . . limped, without her special boot . . . to the bathroom which she shared with Hilde. In the soft candlelight she saw Hilde crouched on the floor, her nightdress spread like a tent, red splashed, round about her. . . . [Hilde] groaned again and seemed to fall forward to her knees under the nightdress. . . . "I have to say your fazère." . . . Hester, staring at the blood-stained woman who was her dearest friend, knowing something of the scene already—never having been banned from the sheds and out-houses—began slowly to understand something dreadful. Without really telling herself that she could not reveal to her father what it would seem she knew about him privately, she limped back to her own room. . . . (120–22)

Hester is never able to forget "that she had slipped away, had avoided Hilde's terrible pain and loneliness. . . . had done something Hilde would never have done to her" (125). Hester's dreams, like Laura's in *Palomino,* are suffused with female imagery: the idea of "crawling through a hole in a hedge into some magic place, a meadow it was called, deep with long grass, yellow flowers" (48); "the idea of secret streams and caves beneath the ordinary world of wheat paddocks, roads and towns" (131), "caverns lined with jewels and . . . the possibilities of magic practices" (144).

Until the advent of Katherine, Hester has entirely repressed her own *jouissance,* which now erupts in extravagant irresponsibilities toward the farm and carnivalistic shopping sprees: "She bought clothes, food, furniture, cassette players and transistors. They were always needing batteries, cassettes, cooking utensils, jewelry, materials and trimmings, oil paints . . . guitars . . . a new piano . . . Italian leather boots, soft and gracefully elegant, two pairs, one plum coloured and the other the colour of cream on fresh milk. . . . There was no end to their wishes and to their shopping" (23–24). They wear "slippery silky nightgowns" and spend hours preparing "piquant" sauces for "succulent" roast ducklings (39): "Between them they developed a capacity for pleasure" (38).

Their re-creation of a pre-Oedipal, semiotic space, however, is inevitably halted by an intruder, much as the female world of

Lawrence's *The Fox* ends with the coming of the young soldier, in a sense a reenactment of the intrusion of the father on the mother-child symbiosis. Indeed, Hester's father is associated with "the great red fox," and recalling his "red fox stories" Hester often finds herself on "the edge of a memory" that is suddenly closed off, even as the well is finally nailed shut (141).

The resolution of the novel is highly ambiguous. The most powerful presence in the novel remains the well itself, an emblem of the archaic, irrepressible mother. The well is a place where Hester and Katherine sit and sun themselves: "On bright hot days, where they could see a little way into it, the inside of the well seemed cool and dark and tranquil. Mysterious draughts of cold air seemed to come from somewhere deep down in the earth. . . . Hester often threw broken or badly burned dishes down the well" (31–32). Wells, of course, have long been associated with the mother goddesses: "Springs, fountains, ponds, wells were always female symbols in archaic religions, often considered water-passages to the underground womb. . . . "[33] The Celts worshipped wells as emblems of the earth mother and threw pottery, bones, coins, and pebbles into the well as offerings to the great mother. "The traditional pagan worship of mother goddesses at holy wells, the natural interpretation of the well as a secret entrance into the body of the Earth Mother or even as her womb, the belief in the life-giving or procreative powers of water—all combined to instill in people the certainty that the holy well was the source of fertility."[34]

However, the well with its dark secrets—was it a man they threw down the well? what was the thing they tried to kill?—is nailed shut by the aggressively masculine Mr. Borden, with Hester's assent. The forces represented by the well are not confronted but are once again violently suppressed. Hester finds herself a somewhat reluctant storyteller, mythologizing the experience to the Borden children. There is perhaps herein a sense of the symbolic order—the order of language and culture—resting uneasily on the warring irrepressible rhythms of the pre-Oedipal, maternal space. Long after the novel is put aside, the well resonates as a powerful figuring of maternal blackness, of female sexuality perceived as threatening fissure and wound—an emblem of "the spectral presence" of the "dead-undead mother . . . signifying the problematics of femininity" that haunts Jolley's fiction.

The dark motifs haunting Jolley's proud, innovative spinsters are a reminder of the difficulties involved in reconceptualizing feminine sexuality. Nevertheless, Jolley's "fantastic" texts share in the impulse that Rosemary Jackson ascribes to fantasy; that is, they "image the possibility of radical cultural transformation through attempting to dissolve or shatter the boundary lines between the imaginary and the symbolic."[35] They express a desire for that "which has not yet been allowed to exist, the unheard of, the unseen" (91). Yet the self-mutilation, cruelty, horror, and violence suggest the difficulties inherent in the project. If women cannot completely escape the discursive forms and practices that inform their lives, at least they can constantly challenge, subvert, and disrupt. This, indeed, is Kristeva's view of the subversive power of woman: "A woman is a perpetual dissident as regards the social and political consensus; she is an exile from power and thus always singular, divided, devilish, a witch. . . . Woman is here to shake up, to disturb, to deflate masculine values, and not to espouse them. Her role is to maintain differences by pointing to them, by giving them life, by putting them into play against one another."[36]

NOTES

1. Alice Jardine, *Gynesis: Configurations of Woman and Modernity* (Ithaca, N.Y.: Cornell University Press, 1985) 236.

2. Julia Kristeva, "A New Type of Intellectual: The Dissident," *The Kristeva Reader,* ed. Toril Moi (New York: Columbia University Press, 1986) 295.

3. Julia Kristeva, "Women's Time," *The Kristeva Reader* 207.

4. Monique Wittig, "One Is Not Born A Woman," *Feminist Issues* 1, Pt. 2 (1981): 53.

5. Alice Jardine, "Pre-Texts for the Transatlantic Feminist," *Feminist Readings: French Texts/American Contexts,* Yale French Studies 62 (New Haven: Yale University Press, 1981) 230. Jardine argues that within the classical Oedipal structure which has dominated the West, the female child has necessarily retained a special relationship to the semiotic space: "The impossibility of ever completely establishing herself as Other than the mother—even if that is what patriarchal culture has told her she must do if she wants to write—has combined with that culture's constant denial of her ability to write through its designation of her, with the mother, as The Other" (229).

6. Elizabeth Jolley, *The Newspaper of Claremont Street* (Fremantle: Fremantle Arts Centre Press, 1981) 7.

7. Claire Kahane, "The Gothic Mirror," *The (M)other Tongue: Essays in Feminist Psychoanalytic Interpretation,* ed. Shirley Nelson Garner, Claire Kahane, and Madelon Sprengnether (Ithaca: Cornell University Press, 1985) 336.

8. Toril Moi, *Sexual/Textual Politics: Feminist Literary Theory* (London: Methuen, 1985) 164–65.

9. Julia Kristeva, "About Chinese Women," *The Kristeva Reader* 149. Subsequent page numbers are incorporated into the text.

10. Julia Kristeva, *Powers of Horror: An Essay on Abjection* (New York: Columbia University Press, 1982) 2. Subsequent page numbers are incorporated into the text.

11. Jardine, *Gynesis* 33–34. Subsequent page numbers are incorporated into the text.

12. Louise Bernikow, *Among Women* (New York: Harper and Row, 1980) 160.

13. Elizabeth Jolley, *Miss Peabody's Inheritance* (St. Lucia: University of Queensland Press, 1983) 1. Subsequent page numbers are incorporated into the text.

14. Hélène Cixous and Catherine Clement, *The Newly Born Woman* (Minneapolis: University of Minnesota Press, 1986) 97.

15. Nina Auerbach, *Woman and the Demon: The Life of a Victorian Myth* (Cambridge: Harvard University Press, 1982) 148.

16. Nancy K. Miller, "Arachnologies: The Woman, the Text and the Critic," *The Poetics of Gender,* ed. Nancy K. Miller (New York: Columbia University Press, 1986) 286. Subsequent page numbers are incorporated into the text.

17. Alicia Ostriker, *Stealing the Language* (Boston: Beacon, 1986) 127.

18. Kristeva, *Powers of Horror* 96.

19. Elizabeth Jolley, *Palomino* (St. Lucia: University of Queensland Press, 1984) 15. Subsequent page numbers are incorporated into the text.

20. Charles Bernheimer, "Huysman: Writing against (Female) Nature," *Poetics Today* 6 (1985): 315.

21. Gayatri Chakravorty Spivak, "French Feminism in an International Frame," *Feminist Readings* 181.

22. Kristeva, *Powers of Horror* 54.

23. Elizabeth Jolley, "The Libation," *Woman in a Lampshade* (London: Penguin, 1983) 105–18.

24. Kristeva, "About Chinese Women" 156–57.

25. Julia Kristeva, *Desire in Language: A Semiotic Approach to Literature and Art,* ed. Leon S. Roudiez (Oxford: Blackwell, 1980) 18.

26. Liz Gross, "Women and Writing: The Work of Julia Kristeva in Perspective," *Refractory Girl* (October 1982): 31.

27. Moi 165.

28. Kristeva, *Powers of Horror* 78.

29. Elizabeth Jolley, *Foxybaby* (St. Lucia: University of Queensland Press, 1985) 8. Subsequent page numbers are incorporated into the text.

30. D. H. Lawrence, *The Complete Short Novels* (London: Penguin, 1982) 147–48.

31. Rosemary Jackson, *Fantasy: The Literature of Subversion* (London: Methuen, 1981) 89–91.

32. Elizabeth Jolley, *The Well* (Ringwood: Viking, 1986) 49. Subsequent page numbers are incorporated into the text.

33. Barbara G. Walker, ed., *The Woman's Encyclopedia of Myths and Secrets* (San Francisco: Harper and Row, 1983) 1067.

34. Janet Bord, and Colin Bord, *Earth Rites: Fertility Practices in Pre-Industrial Britain* (London: Granada, 1983) 98.

35. Jackson 178.

36. Julia Kristeva, *Polylogues,* cited by Josette Feral, "The Powers of Difference," *The Future of Difference,* ed. Hester Eisenstein and Alice Jardine (New Brunswick, N.J.: Rutgers University Press, 1985) 92–93.

SUSAN JARET MCKINSTRY

A Ghost of An/Other Chance: The Spinster-Mother in Toni Morrison's *Beloved*

> Perhaps it is an exaggeration, even of historical expectations, to say that the meaning of a woman's life lies in marriage and motherhood and that life without marriage must mean painful isolation, virtually the equivalent of death. But the underlying cultural ideology is not an exaggeration. . . . Women, regardless of their other qualities, are ideologically defined through their sexuality and its attendant roles—wife, mother, sex partner.
>
> —Joanne Frye, *Living Stories, Telling Lives*

> But our distrust of maternity is an innocuous preoccupation in contrast to our resentment of those who do not take part in it. Nothing is more reliable than the irritability of all references to prolonged virginity: behind us, and undoubtedly before us, stretch infinite tracts of abuse of *maiden ladies, old maids, schoolmarms, dried-up spinsters*, etc., etc.
>
> —Mary Ellmann, *Thinking about Women*

> But titles were absurd, definitions were absurd; she'd always known that: words used to simplify relationships between one person and another: granting one privilege, the other disadvantage.
>
> —Fay Weldon, *Praxis*

The spinster is a white, middle-class creation. The term describes relational possession: a woman with leisure and without husband, a spinster was recognized by the social roles she filled as quasi wife, child-caretaker, and family servant in a social system that needed the domestic labor of these "surplus," "redundant" women (Victorian terms for spinsters) as the price of their nonparticipation in the marriage market. The title describes an alternative economic use for the female body, not as wife or mother but as marginal, dependent, selfless, sexless spinster, still defined by (lack of) family relationships. To use the term for an African-American woman character allows a swerve that emphasizes the assumptions of ownership underlying the definition. Certainly there are some African-American characters who could be, albeit loosely, defined as spinsters—among them, Sula in Morrison's *Sula*, Pilate in her *Song of Solomon*, and Nettie in Alice Walker's *Color Purple*. *Beloved*'s Baby Suggs also fits the definition in some ways. A freed slave, a cobbler, and a holy woman, she is both independent and dutiful: "How come she always knows what to do and when? Giving advice; passing messages; healing the sick, hiding fugitives, loving, cooking, cooking, loving, preaching, singing, dancing and loving everybody like it was her job and hers alone" (*Beloved* 137). The spinster's "job"—balancing dependence and nurturance—upholds traditional marriage by buttressing the wife's role, confirming female domesticity as natural, and enabling male absence from domestic labors, all with little economic cost to the family system.

Yet the social system that presented marriage and children as the fulfillment of female destiny had little relevance to the lives of African-American slave women, historically and overtly perceived as possessions. No subtle ideology was required to validate marriage to a group for whom marriage was often not a matter of choice but of command. Certainly slave women, like other women, were defined through their sexuality, but their roles as wife, mother, or lover are distorted by the culture's refusal to give them any permanence: African-American slave women lose their husbands, their children, their lovers at the whim of the "whitepeople." The family in a slave system is reduced to its reproductive function, as are any notions of love, parenting, selfhood. Sexuality and self-definition become economic rather than romantic issues. If, as Mary Poovey claims, "the fundamental assumption of romantic love . . . is that the personal can be kept separate from the social, that one's 'self' can be fulfilled in spite of—and in isolation from—the demands of the marketplace" (172), slavery foregrounds the literal marketplace, ignores love, and makes selfhood meaningless.

The struggle for African-American slave women was not the ideological dilemma of defining a self against the prevailing relational definitions—wife, mother, lover, spinster. Rather, it was locating any self outside of these relational parameters. That situation highlights the paradox of female definition as self-effacement and illustrates the impact of defining women through their sexuality and, more precisely, through their relationships with others: with husbands, lovers, children, or owners of the female body. Slavery erases the emotional meaning of femaleness and reduces it to economically valuable bodily functions (sexual intercourse, childbearing, nursing children).

That system produces the most radical spinsters of all: women who are, like white spinsters, kept on the margins of the social system, defined by (failed) relationships, but without any alternate ideology of dutiful, spiritual selflessness as spinsters. To gain a self, African-American women must reject the cultural ideology that defines them as objects, possessions, spiritless bodies with economic value. The price tag is not a tolerable measure of self-worth for anyone, as Paul D in *Beloved* realizes: "He has always known, or believed he did, his value—as a hand, a laborer who could make a profit on a farm—but now he discovers his worth, which is to say he learns his price. The dollar value of his weight, his strength, his heart, his brain, his penis, and his future" (226). For women, for Sethe, the property value is even higher: "When he thought about it now, [Sethe's] price was greater than his; property that reproduced itself without cost" (228). That measure of self-worth is revolted against (and revolting). Yet it mirrors the market value given to women who can—or cannot—marry, who also reproduce "without cost" to the system, but often at great personal cost. Most appropriately, then, I have chosen Morrison's *Beloved* as a text that explores the economics of ownership underlying female relations and definitions: sexuality, marriage, maternity, domesticity, labor.

"Spinster" is, after all, a social term, a label for a precise sort of woman and for worlds in which the "erotic text" of relationship prevails. In *Living Stories, Telling Lives,* Joanne Frye argues (using Nancy K. Miller's terms) that in fiction women are trapped in the erotic text of community and unable to experience the ambitious text of autonomy. Womanhood and adulthood are oppositional definitions: "Women's plots are nearly always 'familial' or 'erotic' because our cultural notions of womanhood require a personal context. Female characters lack autonomy because an autonomous woman is an apparent contradiction in cultural terms" (Frye 5). Frye posits the fantastic plot as one escape from traditional emplotments of femininity and sees the first-person narrative as a means of retelling female lives in ways that empower female self-definition and identity through dichotomies: "Women need individual self-definition; women need a sense of shared reality. Selfhood is a function of systems; selfhood is a claim to responsible individuality" (11).

In *Beloved,* Morrison confronts those dichotomies by disrupting the systems that normally define the female self. The novel is culturally restricted to a specific time and place (late nineteenth-century Ohio) and yet is fantastic (a ghost comes to life). Together the unnatural system of slavery and the supernatural world make the erotic text and the ambitious text untenable plots of self-definition. Subverting relational terms to expose the definitions of selfhood that merely camouflage an economics of ownership, the novel breaks the dichotomy between wife or mother and spinster and explores the possessive extremes inherent in these familial roles. The choices here are not between marriage and spinsterhood but between slavery and self-possession.

The novel begins shortly after the Civil War, but the oppressive lessons of slavery haunt the characters. "Responsible individuality" is dangerous; African-Americans asserting a right to self-definition are hanged. The characters are defined as property, not persons; without independence of movement or desire, their emotional and physical lives are determined by the lustful or economic desires of their masters. Although Baby Suggs and her daughter-in-law Sethe are married women in a "manner of speaking" (142), their "marriages" are merely labels they give to relationships sanctioned by their owners for breeding, not emotion. Family names are not recognized signs of identity or community. When Baby Suggs is freed, she keeps that name, "all she had left of the 'husband' she claimed" (142), so her husband, whom she has not seen in years, might be able to locate her, but her identity papers list her as "Jenny Whitlow"—a name she has never heard. Seven of Baby Suggs's eight children, all with different fathers, are sold. Her daughter-in-law Sethe "had the amazing luck of six whole years of marriage to [Baby's] 'somebody' son who fathered every one of her children" (23), but Sethe flees slavery and, in the process, loses her husband, kills one child, and scares off her two sons. The slave system undermines community and erases the female self by denying the emotional validity of terms like "marriage," "wife," "husband," "mother."

The novel illustrates the agonizing process of reclaiming the past to create new self-definition, indeed self-possession, since the system defines African-Americans as property. Instead of Frye's "responsible individuality," the novel focuses on the self caught in systems of domination and possession that eliminate both selfhood and rebellion. The result is painful, as Collette Guillaumin notes: "'When one is appropriated, or dominated, thinking means going against the vision of (and against) the social relationships imposed by the dominators. It does not mean ceasing to know what the relationships of appropriation harshly teach you'" (quoted in Meese 122). Since that vision of social relationships identifies selfhood as impossible for slaves and for all women, Myra Jehlen claims that women "have to confront the assumptions that render them a kind of fiction in themselves in that they are defined by others, as components of the language and thought of others" (582). The lesson of appropriation is painfully learned in the novel. *Beloved* illustrates what Jehlen calls "not actual independence but action despite dependence—and not a self-defined female culture either, but a subculture born out of oppression and either stunted or victorious only at often-fatal cost" (581–82).

Jehlen's comment might function as a definition of traditional spinsterhood: the unmarried woman's economic dependence demands domestic "action despite dependence" as a sort of camouflage for rage at the system that allows her no meaning in herself but only in relation to those she dutifully nurtures. That "subculture" is "stunted" or "victorious" only within the bounds of the cultural definitions of womanhood as relational and controlled by males. The oppressive world of *Beloved* further destroys self-identity by taking away family, destroying the bonds that define selfhood, and leaving only questions like those Baby Suggs asks about her lost mother and her own seven lost children: "Did Patty lose her lisp? What color did Famous' skin finally take? Was that a cleft in Johnny's chin or just a dimple that would disappear soon's his jawbone changed? . . . All seven were gone or dead" (139). Without husband or children to define her, Baby Suggs has no self-identity. She has only "the desolated center where the self that was no self made its home" because she "never had the map to discover what she was like. Could she sing? (Was it nice to hear when she did?) Was she pretty? Was she a good friend? Could she have been a loving mother? A faithful wife? Have I got a sister and would she favor me? If my mother knew me would she like me?" (140). The shift from third- to first-person narrative in the passage reflects the difficulty of self-definition outside relationships. The third-person, multiple-selective, omniscient narrative voice only occasionally gets close enough to speak for a character directly, and then it is often, as in this case, a matter of questioning rather than asserting identity. The process of telling the stories requires working toward a personal voice that can speak, locating and possessing a self to articulate.

Asking these questions, attempting to identify herself through her family, Baby Suggs proves the system cannot fully sever the bonds of community and love that in more traditional worlds define the female self as wife, mother, lover. At the same time, she emphasizes the fragility of a self-definition dictated by relationships with others: "in all of Baby's life, as well as Sethe's own, men and women were moved around like checkers. Anybody Baby Suggs knew, let alone loved, who hadn't run off or been hanged, got *rented* out, *loaned* out, *bought* up, brought back, *stored* up, *mortgaged, won, stolen* or *seized*. So Baby's eight children had six fathers. What she called the nastiness of life was the shock she received upon learning that nobody stopped playing checkers just because the pieces included her children" (23, emphasis added). The economics of exchange highlighted by Morrison's language of property denies these characters any agency or desire. African-American women are doubly bound, as females—sexual, maternal, relational objects—and slaves—property of whites and valued only for their bodies (labor, strength, reproduction). They can sell their bodies—Halle "buys" his mother by working during his "free time," and Sethe "buys" Beloved's tombstone with her body. But such trading can be revoked at the whim of the owners; Halle's time is reclaimed by his new masters, and Sethe is abused as an object of reproduction and possession by others.

The novel creates a world that emphasizes the dangers of ownership, the violence of possession. As property, African-American women cannot attain Frye's "responsible individuality" in a system that does not recognize them as individuals; they cannot live the traditional female text of erotic community because they do not own their bodies, even to give them to husbands or children. The women attempt to assert ownership of the products of their bodies, however. In a harrowing reversal of "female nature," the maternal instinct becomes murderous. Sethe's mother, whom Sethe only meets once, had many children but "'she threw them all away but you. The one from the crew she threw away on the island. The others from more whites she also threw away. Without names, she threw them. You she gave the name of the black man'" (62). The power to create life becomes the right to own it, to name or refuse to name it, to legitimize or destroy it.

That relational ownership is at the center of the novel's tension. If the traditional role of the spinster, as a "failed wife," was to deny desire, to nurture others' children, to be dependent on the kindness of others, and to experience family life only from the margins, *Beloved* reveals the economics underneath that ideology: as a slave, the African-American woman was unable to be a wife, unable to care for her own children or forced to care for others', and ultimately dependent. The definitive spinster in some ways, the slave lived for others. Yet in fleeing the system, Sethe reclaims herself and her children:

> "I did it. I got us all out. Without Halle [her husband] too. Up till then it was the only thing I ever did on my own. Decided. And it came off right, like it was supposed to. We was here. Each and every one of my babies and me too. I birthed them and I got em out and it wasn't no accident. I did that. I had help, of course, lots of that, but still it was me doing it; me saying, *Go on*, and *Now*. Me having to look out. Me using my own head. But it was more than that. It was a kind of selfishness I never knew nothing about before. . . . But when I got here, when I jumped down off that wagon—there wasn't nobody in the world I couldn't love if I wanted to." (162)

Without her husband, Sethe directs the family and constructs a new life for them all, with emotional, physical, and economic freedom. Such "selfishness" is a first step toward self-possession. Paul D agrees: "to get to a place where you could love anything you chose—not to need permission for desire—well now, *that* was freedom" (162).

Sethe's self-created freedom is an attempted escape from relational ownership, but she still accepts that possessive system. When the slave catchers come to reclaim the family, she says her children are "her best things," and she attempts to kill them to protect them from repossession as slaves. Without her husband, without her owners, she must act for and by herself. Her act—the murder of one child and the attempted murder of the other three—reasserts the violent ownership of children exercised by Sethe's own mother. One of the white slave catchers describes the event: "Two boys bled in the sawdust and dirt at the feet of a nigger woman holding a blood-soaked child to her chest with one hand and an infant by the heels in the other. She did not look at them; she simply swung the baby toward the wall planks, missed, and tried to connect a second time . . . " (149). By that "simpl[e]" act, she makes the entire family unsalable and thus becomes owner of them herself (149).

The act of killing a child to save it defines Sethe as a radical spinster, a woman living outside social codes. That horrifying act forces us to reconsider the system that grants husbands (or owners) such power over women's bodies and judges women's value through relationship, self-denial, effacement, and duty. The novel asks us to reevaluate our assumptions about the most basic rights (and wrongs) of self-definition. By presenting the act through the words of a terrified white witness, Morrison demands a suspension of simple judgment. The tale reverses our belief in maternal instinctive protection, for this is murder as a political act; the scene tells much about a system that could necessitate such violence in the name of safety.

Joanna Russ comments on the need for recognizing multiple values that reflect differing identities: "In everybody's present historical situation, there can be, I believe, no single center of value and hence no absolute standards. That does not mean that assignment of values must be arbitrary or self-serving. . . . It does mean that for the linear hierarchy of good and bad it becomes necessary to substitute a multitude of centers of value, each with its own periphery, some closer to each other, some farther apart. The centers have been constructed by the historical facts of what it is to be female or black or working class or what-have-you" (120). We may reconstruct the historical facts of Sethe's life at Sweet Home through the narrative; we may recognize the anguish caused by her losses. The violence of Sethe's act demands more than empathetic reading, however. The novel presents the murder scene through multiple narrative stances to demand the optional values that Russ recommends by presenting alternative views and (mis)understandings of Sethe's motives. Baby Suggs and Stamp Paid cannot condone her act; the townspeople reject Sethe; her daughter fears her; her sons leave her; the characters discuss other, more reasonable options she might have tried to protect her children from slavery. The characters' need to judge Sethe's act illuminates the community's assumptions about definitions of femaleness and powers of relationship and its rejection of the violence of Sethe's self-definition and self-assertion.

The murder ends Sethe's participation in a community that defines the self through relations with others: "The twenty-eight days of having women friends, a mother-in-law, and all her children together; of being part of a neighborhood; of, in fact, having neighbors at all to call her own—all that was long gone and would never come back" (173). Ironically, the twenty-eight days of Sethe's community, the same length of time as the menstrual cycle, ends with a sort of birth: Sethe embraces her self-identity as mother, with absolute rights of ownership over her children. The result of Sethe's dramatic assertion of ownership is not freedom from definition through relationships but instead is an even more restrictive system of ownership, a fragile family system that Sethe, her surviving daughter

Denver, and the baby ghost construct out of the extremes of relational possessiveness. Sethe demands the right to define herself through her children: "I'll protect her [Beloved] when I'm live and I'll protect her when I ain't. . . . If I have to choose—well, it's not even a choice" (45). Sethe's assumption that she has the right to define Beloved's life and confine Denver's life to a haunted house presumes unnatural (indeed, supernatural) ownership of her children and puts her outside social rules.

Paul D's arrival reawakens memory, revives old stories, and thus endangers Sethe's spinster-like autonomy that rejects community. "Alone with her daughter in a haunted house she managed every damn thing. Why now, with Paul D instead of the ghost, was she breaking up? getting scared?" (97). Alone, the women can survive; with Paul D, Sethe's precarious independence is threatened, the ghost is banished, and Sethe collapses. The danger of love—of losing the self into another and then losing both—is overt in this world. The danger of men is that they encourage dependence; "they encouraged you to put some of your weight in their hands and soon as you felt how light and lovely that was, they studied your scars and tribulations, after which they did what [Paul D] had done: ran her children out and tore up the house" (22). There is no choice: for Sethe, loving Paul D means losing her emotional and relational independence, her autonomy as protective owner of her children's lives. She is unwilling to make that change.

The novel is more complicated than that, however. Sethe's desire to be self-defined as mother-owner of her children is a form of obsessive possession. Her desire to protect them includes power over them and subjection to them; she is their creator and their destroyer, and they have the same dichotomous relationship with her. Sethe understands this: "When I tell you you mine, I also mean I'm yours. I wouldn't draw breath without my children. I told Baby Suggs that and she got down on her knees to beg God's pardon for me. Still, it's so" (203). Sethe defines herself as mother, Denver as daughter, and Beloved as baby ghost. Their relational definitions become a construction of the self through language, through telling stories about the unspeakable past, a process of balancing the autonomy of isolation and the community of suffering that binds Denver, Sethe, and Beloved together in a system as dangerously restrictive, as linguistically confining, as the social systems traditionally entrapping women.

The murder of her child Beloved exiled Sethe from the community of relationships and redefined her as a radical spinster forced—

and able—to do anything necessary to protect her "property," her children. She posits a right to Beloved's life: "if I hadn't killed her she would have died and that is something I could not bear to happen to her" (200). Such an exaggeration of self-effacing duty is inevitably judged and misjudged by others who accept the system that defines women through their relationships. Paul D mistakenly assumes that Sethe lives "in helpless, apologetic resignation because she had no choice; that minus husband, sons, mother-in-law, she and her slow-witted daughter had to live there all alone making things do" (164). Instead, he discovers that Sethe lives by a different system: "This here Sethe talked about love like any other woman; talked about baby clothes like any other woman, but what she meant could cleave the bone. This here Sethe talked about safety with a handsaw. This here new Sethe didn't know where the world stopped and she began" (164).

Such amorphous identity is dangerous to others and dangerous even to Sethe. Unwilling to live in the world's system, Sethe creates one in which the boundaries between self and other, mother and child are dissolved. But this semiotic self-perception, this maternal body, has its own terrifying laws. Paul D runs from her, as did Sethe's sons, and Denver fears her: "I love my mother but I know she killed one of her own daughters, and tender as she is with me, I'm scared of her because of it. She missed killing my brothers and they knew it" (205). Sethe's maternal protection becomes unlawful possession that terrifies Denver: "I have to warn [Beloved] about that. Don't love her too much. Don't. Maybe it's still in her the thing that makes it all right to kill her children" (206).

The town rejects Sethe; her daughter fears her; her lover leaves her. Yet Beloved, the baby ghost, returns. Indeed, ironically, Beloved (made eighteen-year-old flesh, "the age it would have been had it lived" [255]) becomes the erotic object of the text, the character who defines the others through their relationship with her. She herself remains single, isolated; she becomes the powerfully independent woman even as she is the ultimately dependent child. She pushes the definitions of the female self to fantastic extremes. As a baby ghost, she is not mother, lover, or wife but is always other. She is always outside the terms of relational possession used for woman, yet she also is fully female in her elusive, indefinable existence as object of desire.

The ghost seemingly embodies the fulfillment of the erotic text, re-creating community and defining relationships in a supernatural, shared reality. Yet that community is divisive. Beloved inspires not autonomy but more possessive eroticism. Sethe favors Beloved over Paul D and Denver, and Paul D, despite his love for Sethe, is helpless against Beloved's sexual advances. Denver, abandoned by her brothers and then by the baby ghost, resentful of Paul D's power over her mother, and afraid of her mother's murderous love, defines Beloved as her erotic goal: "Nothing was out there that this sister-girl did not provide in abundance: a racing heart, dreaminess, society, danger, beauty" (76). In retelling the tale of the past, Denver tries "to construct out of the strings she had heard all her life a net to hold Beloved" (76). But hunter and prey become indistinguishable; as Denver recounts the story of her birth, "the monologue became, in fact, a duet, Denver nursing Beloved's interest like a lover whose pleasure was to overfeed the loved" (78).

Beloved becomes the lover, the other, whom Denver needs for self-definition, which ironically mirrors the violence of the mother-child bond asserted by Sethe. "Nursing" Beloved to "overfeed" her, Denver repeats the excesses of Sethe's maternal model. "To go back to the original hunger was impossible" because Denver has already severed the primary mother-child bond with Sethe; the "hunger" of the erotic text replaces that bond and results in a narrative of eating disorders symptomatic of the violent self-definitions in the text. Beloved is the relational other who feeds Denver's hunger: "looking was food enough to last. But to be looked at in turn was beyond appetite; it was breaking through her own skin to a place where hunger hadn't been discovered. . . . It was lovely. Not to be stared at, not seen, but being pulled into view by the interested, uncritical eyes of the other" (118). Seeking the nurturance of the semiotic bond, Denver goes "beyond appetite" to the gaze that defines her, the place without boundaries between self and other.

Denver discovers a self, but it is as fragile as any culturally defined female selfhood because it is dependent on the other's gaze, on Beloved's gaze. The "original hunger" is replaced with a gaze that can be broken. This image of food, of nurturant feeding, becomes distorted so that love-as-food veers between gluttony and starvation. When she fears Beloved has left, Denver despairs: "This is worse than when Paul D came to 124 and she cried helplessly into the stove. This is worse. Then it was for herself. Now she is crying because she has no self. Death is a skipped meal compared to this. She can feel her thickness thinning, dissolving into nothing" (123).

Beloved threatens Denver and Sethe; their emotional self-definitions and physical bodies are at risk. As Ella notes, "Nobody needed a grown-up evil sitting at the table with a grudge. . . . She didn't mind a little communication between the two worlds, but this was an invasion" (257). With Beloved's presence, Sethe and Denver define themselves as mother and as sister, without forming a community that nurtures, food that satisfies. The novel presents a nightmare vision of the mother-child bond as unnatural, as a mother-other (sister-other) bond that destroys. Sethe rejects the outside world for the isolated, claustrophobic life in the house: "Paul D convinced me there was a world out there and that I could live in it. Should have known better. *Did* know better. Whatever is going on outside my door ain't for me. The world is in this room. This here's all there is and all there needs to be" (183). Interestingly, the next line is "They ate like men. . . ." Such self-isolation, self-containment is anticommunity and thus antifemale; again, the text veers between overfeeding and anorexia.

The novel uses *l'ecriture feminine* to explain the excessive, oppressive, possessive female community created by Sethe, Denver, and Beloved inside the house. The house is surrounded by female voices, as Stamp Paid hears when he tries to visit:

> He thought he heard a conflagration of hasty voices—loud, urgent, all speaking at once so he could not make out what they were talking about or to whom. The speech wasn't nonsensical, exactly, nor was it tongues. But something was wrong with the order of the words and he couldn't describe or cipher it to save his life. All he could make out was the word *mine*. . . . When he got to the steps, the voices drained suddenly to less than a whisper. . . . They had become an occasional mutter—like the interior sounds a woman makes when she believes she is alone and unobserved at her work. . . . Nothing fierce or startling. Just that eternal, private conversation that takes place between women and their tasks. (172)

The sound moves from voices, community, and language to single, "interior," "eternal" sounds of women in isolation as he approaches the house. He is unable to enter. "When Sethe locked the door, the women inside were free at last to be what they liked, see whatever they saw and say whatever was on their minds" (199). But language is not all speakable, and much of the novel deals with the undefinable, the unknowable; Beloved is, after all, a ghost-made-flesh, an unnatural embodiment of a relationship. Leaving the social definitions of female life behind, the women confront the unknown, the other: "Mixed in with the voices surrounding the house, recognizable but indecipherable to Stamp Paid, were the thoughts of the women of 124, unspeakable thoughts, unspoken" (199).

The novel produces those "unspeakable thoughts" in three monologues from Sethe, Denver, and Beloved that assert relationship as ownership: "Beloved, she my daughter. She mine" (200); "Beloved is my sister. . . . She's mine, Beloved. She's mine" (205, 209); "I am Beloved and she is mine. . . . how can I say things that are pictures I am not separate from her there is no place where I stop her face is my own and I want to be there in the place where her face is and to be looking at it too" (210). These definitions conflate self and other, defining self(possession) through possession of the other, and the dialogues continue that linguistic identification: "Will we smile at me?" Beloved asks Sethe (215).

The final section of these three monologues illustrates a complete breakdown of individual identity as the three voices interweave:

> Beloved
> You are my sister
> You are my daughter
> You are my face; you are me . . .
>
> You are my face; I am you. Why did you leave me who am you? . . .
> I drank your blood
> I brought your milk
>
> You forgot to smile . . .
>
> You are mine
> You are mine
> You are mine (216–17)

The pronouns mix as the three voices speak in disorder. "You" refers to Beloved as Denver speaks, then Sethe; then "you" is Sethe as Beloved speaks, and so on; continuing the images of feeding, Denver "drank your [Beloved's] blood," Sethe "brought your [Beloved's] milk." "Why did you leave me who am you?" asks Beloved. Such linguistic and bodily exchanges confuse differences among the three characters but also assert them: "You are mine" claims a competitive owning, a desire to possess the other completely.

Such possession is destructive, for the self is absorbed into the other and disappears. These characters have not freed themselves from relational definitions but have translated them into female terms with a vengeance. The struggle for possession becomes deadly, and Denver alone recognizes the necessity for escape: Sethe and Beloved "were too busy rationing their strength to fight each other. So it was she who had to step off the edge of the world and die because if she didn't, they all would" (239). To die—as in

Sethe's murder of Beloved—becomes a movement into safety. To die is, here, to escape from the mother-child bond that devours the self, that allows possessive ownership.

Denver fears Sethe "would kill again. But it was Beloved who made demands. Anything she wanted she got, and when Sethe ran out of things to give her, Beloved invented desire" (240). The freedom to love is perverted into an invention of desire, a test of possession. Love becomes starvation rather than nurturance. They were all "limp and starving but locked in a love that wore everybody out" (243). Their desire to love the other thus becomes desire that devours the other. Having refused the social definitions that distinguish female roles, having transcended the traditional limits of self, the women lose identity; the mother does not feed the child, but the child feeds on the mother: "Then it seemed to Denver the thing was done: Beloved bending over Sethe looked the mother, Sethe the teething child. . . . The bigger Beloved got, the smaller Sethe became. . . . Beloved ate up her life, took it, swelled up with it, grew taller on it. And the older woman yielded it up without a murmur" (251).

The novel returns, finally, to a world of social roles, a world of speakable selves. Denver steps out into that world and reasserts community by seeking help: "Somebody had to be saved, but unless Denver got to work, there would be no one to save, no one to come home to, and no Denver either. It was a new thought, having a self to look out for and preserve" (252). Self can be defined, but not confined, by community; self-preservation can also be nurturance of the other, feeding without devouring. Like the radical spinster, female marginality can become a way to produce new fictions of selfhood.

Recounting the excesses of the past becomes a means of forming the community rather than re-creating the isolation of the "original hunger." The neighbors must hear the story—"Nobody was going to help her unless she told it, told all of it" (253)—and define the characters: "Sethe's dead daughter, the one whose throat she cut, had come back to fix her," and Sethe, who "had lost her wits" in "trying to do it all alone with her nose in the air" (254), was "worn down, speckled, dying, spinning, changing shapes and generally bedeviled" (255). Finding terms to explain the relationships in the house, the community of women march to 124 to confront the ghost. Like the "conflagration of voices" that Stamp Paid heard, they surround the house with voices—first prayer, then sound: "They stopped praying and took a step back to the beginning. In the beginning there were no words. In the beginning was the sound" (259). Together, in chorus, "the voices of women searched for the right combination, the key, the code, the sound that broke the back of words" (261).

That sound returns them to a world of revised relationships. Beloved disappears, exploded perhaps, and Paul D reappears to love Sethe: "He wants to put his story next to hers" (273). When Sethe mourns her "best thing" Beloved, Paul D corrects her: "You your best thing, Sethe" (273). Redefining her, he gives her back herself. She can be mother, she can be lover, but she can also be Sethe, defined outside relationships that presume ownership. Beloved disappears from memory, from that story of the past, for she has no definition, no place in the social world: "Everybody knew what she was called, but nobody anywhere knew her name. Disremembered and unaccounted for, she cannot be lost because no one is looking for her, and even if they were how can they call her if they don't know her name? . . . It was not a story to pass on" (274). Yet the novel ends with the word "Beloved," the name that is not a name but a relationship, to remind us of the excesses of relational possessiveness the novel depicts.

By passing on this story, Morrison explores the relational definitions of women in a world where slavery erases the right of self-definition or self-possession. She reasserts the value of definition through relationships that are bounded by rules and are self-expressive rather than other-possessive. Without limits, ownership of others is always destructive—even when it is love of mother for child, child for mother, sister for sister. To live as autonomously as Sethe did, to live without others, is as dangerous as living only through and for others. By living both extremes, Sethe illustrates the dangers of excessive female roles—nurturing woman whose life is defined by others' needs, possessive mother whose children belong to her. The subversive power Sethe takes on when she takes her baby's life and the submissive self-effacement she uses to pay for it are both disastrous to female self-definition.

In an interview, Toni Morrison claims that African-American writers are united in "the clear identification of what the enemy forces are, not this person or that person and so on, but the acknowledgement of a way of life dreamed up for us by some other people who are at the moment in power, and knowing the ways it can be subverted" (Davis 146). By forgetting Beloved and by returning to the community as Denver's mother, Paul D's lover, and "her own best thing," Sethe subverts the "way of life" required for the traditional definition of woman as relational possession, so exaggerated in the experience of African-American slave women. Relationship cannot presume possession. Relationship cannot disguise emotional or physical slavery. Undermining the traditional dichotomies, Sethe shows that women can be both strong and weak, independent and dependent. They can have the spinster's freedom, mother's nurturance, lover's love, and other's difference as parts of a self that can, finally, hold together.

WORKS CITED

Davis, Christina. "Interview with Toni Morrison." *Presence Africaine* 145 (1988): 141–50.

Ellmann, Mary. *Thinking about Women.* New York: Harcourt Brace, 1968.

Frye, Joanne S. *Living Stories, Telling Lives: Women and the Novel in Contemporary Experience.* Ann Arbor: University of Michigan Press, 1986.

Jehlen, Myra. "Archimedes and the Paradox of Feminist Criticism." *Signs* 6 (1981): 575–601.

Meese, Elizabeth A. *Crossing the Double-Cross: The Practice of Feminist Criticism.* Chapel Hill: University of North Carolina Press, 1986.

Morrison, Toni. *Beloved.* New York: Knopf, 1987.

Poovey, Mary. *The Proper Lady and the Woman Writer.* Chicago: University of Chicago Press, 1984.

Russ, Joanna. *How to Suppress Women's Writing.* Austin: University of Texas Press, 1983.

Weldon, Fay. *Praxis.* London: Hodder and Stoughton, 1978.

Notes on Contributors

NINA AUERBACH is Morton Kornreich Professor of English at the University of Pennsylvania. She is the author of *Communities of Women; Woman and the Demon; Romantic Imprisonment;* and *Ellen Terry, Player in Her Time.* Her most recent book is *Private Theatricals: The Lives of the Victorians.*

DALE M. BAUER is associate professor of English and women's studies at the University of Wisconsin, Madison. Her work includes *Feminist Dialogics* (1988) and articles on Edith Wharton, Henry James, Kate Chopin, and feminist theory. Her current research focuses on Wharton, reproductive rights, and the politics of fascism.

BARBARA BROTHERS, professor and chairperson of the English department at Youngstown State University, is the 1989–90 president of the College English Association and co-editor of the *CEA Critic* and *CEA Forum.* She has served on the Ohio Humanities Council (the state-based NEH program) and the executive committee of the Association of Departments of English. *Reading and Writing Women's Lives: A Study of the Novel of Manners,* a book she co-edited and for which she contributed an essay on Barbara Pym, has just been published. In addition, her essays on Sylvia Townsend Warner have appeared in *Women's Writing in Exile; Rewriting the Good Fight; Women in History, Literature and the Arts;* and the *Dictionary of Literary Biography.* She has also published essays on Henry Green, Margaret Kennedy, Elizabeth Bowen, William Butler Yeats, and the profession.

LAURA L. DOAN is an associate professor of English at the State University of New York at Geneseo, where she teaches contemporary British literature and culture. Her current project, "War Time as Women's Time," focuses on women's writing and World War II.

GAYLE GREENE has published articles on Shakespeare, contemporary women writers, and feminist literary theory. A professor at Scripps College, Claremont, California, she co-edited *The Woman's Part: Feminist Criticism of Shakespeare* (1980) and *Making a Difference: Feminist Literary Criticism* (1985). She is at work on a book, "Re-Visions: Contemporary Women Writers and the Tradition."

SUSAN KATZ has a Ph.D. in English and comparative literature from Columbia University and an M.A. from Brown University. Her essay for this volume grew out of her dissertation, " 'Singleness of Heart': Spinsterhood in Victorian Culture." She has taught courses in literature and women's studies at Columbia and Bard College. She is now living, writing, and raising a son in New York City.

CATHERINE KENNEY, a writer and critic, holds a Ph.D. in English from Loyola University of Chicago. She is a member of Mystery Writers of America and the author of numerous scholarly and general works of nonfiction, including *The Remarkable Case of Dorothy L. Sayers* (1990) and *Thurber's Anatomy of Confusion* (1984). Her literary criticism has focused on fiction as a genre and the comic tradition. Her work on Dorothy L. Sayers has been supported by research grants from the American Association of University Women and the Wade Center of Wheaton College, Wheaton, Illinois. Currently on leave from her position as associate professor of English at Chicago's Mundelein College, where she was chair of the department for many years, she is writing a novel.

JOAN KIRKBY, professor of American and Australian literature and head of the English discipline at Macquarie University, Sydney, Australia, received her B.A. and M.A. at the University of Oregon in 1964 and 1965, respectively, and her Ph.D. from Macquarie University in 1968. Her current research focuses on women's writing and feminist theory, in particular French psychoanalytic theory. Her books include *The American Model: Influence and Independence in Australian Poetry* (1982) and *Emily Dickinson* (1990). She currently is writing a book, "The Lure of Abjection," on attitudes toward authority and gender in Australian literature.

ANDREW M. LAKRITZ, assistant professor of English at Miami University, received his B.A., M.F.A. (in poetry), and Ph.D. at the University of California, Irvine, in 1978, 1980, and 1985, respectively. He writes on modernist figures in poetry and fiction and has published on Henry James, Kate Chopin, and contemporary literary theory and criticism. He currently is completing a study of lyric poetry as social praxis in the work of Robert Frost, Wallace Stevens, and Marianne Moore.

JUDY LITTLE is a professor of English at Southern Illinois University, Carbondale, where she teaches courses in modern literature and women's studies. Along with several essays on women's comedy, her publications include two books, *Keats as a Narrative Poet* (1975) and *Comedy and the Woman Writer: Woolf, Spark and Feminism* (1983).

SUSAN JARET MCKINSTRY is an associate professor of English at Carleton College, Northfield, Minnesota. Her research interests include narrative theory, film theory, and contemporary fiction. She has published articles on Margaret Atwood, T. S. Eliot, Ann Beattie, Emily Brontë, Jane Austen, and Emily Dickinson; she has completed a book on literary theory and is editing a collection of articles on Mikhail Bakhtin and feminist theory with Dale M. Bauer.

VALERIE MINER'S fiction includes the novels, *All Good Women; Winter's Edge; Blood Sisters; Movement;* and *Murder in the English Department*, as well as a collection of short stories, *Trespassing*. Her stories, essays, and reviews have appeared in *TLS, Village Voice, Conditions, New York Times, The Nation, Sinis-*

ter Wisdom, and many other journals. She is the co-author of *Tales I Tell My Mother; More Tales;* and *Her Own Woman* and co-editor of *Competition: A Feminist Taboo?*. She is a member of the creative writing faculty at Arizona State University. She also travels widely, giving readings and lectures.

SYBIL OLDFIELD is a lecturer in English at the University of Sussex, Brighton, U. K. She is the author of *Spinsters of This Parish* (1984), the life and times of the political activist Mary Sheepshanks (1872–1954) and the novelist Flora Macdonald Mayor (1872–1932), and *Women against the Iron Fist: Alternatives to Militarism, 1900–1989* (1989), which includes a chapter on the pacifism of Virginia Woolf.

MARLON B. ROSS is an associate professor of English language and literature at the University of Michigan, Ann Arbor. He is the author of *The Contours of Masculine Desire: Romanticism and the Rise of Women's Poetry* (1989), in addition to various essays on nineteenth-century literature and culture. He currently is writing a cultural history of verse romance during the eighteenth and nineteenth centuries in Britain.

Index